Legal Research: Step by Step

THIRD EDITION

Margaret Kerr • JoAnn Kurtz • Arlene Blatt

2010
Emond Montgomery Publications Limited
Toronto, Canada

Emond Montgomery Publications Limited
60 Shaftesbury Avenue
Toronto ON M4T 1A3
http://www.emp.ca/college

Printed in Canada.

We acknowledge the financial support of the Government of Canada through the Book Publishing Industry Development Program (BPIDP) for our publishing activities.

Page and screen reproductions from the *Canadian Encyclopedic Digest*, *Canadian Abridgment*, and Westlaw Canada's LawSource are reprinted by permission of Carswell, a division of Thomson Reuters Canada Limited.

Screen reproductions from Ontario e-Laws (http://www.e-laws.gov.on.ca) are reprinted by permission. © Queen's Printer for Ontario, 2009.

Screen reproductions from Justice Canada (http://canada.justice.gc.ca) are reproduced with the permission of the Minister of Public Works and Government Services Canada, 2009.

Acquisitions and development editor: Peggy Buchan
Marketing manager: Christine Davidson
Sales manager, higher education: Dave Stokaluk
Supervising editor: Jim Lyons
Copy editor: David Handelsman
Typesetter: Shani Sohn
Production editor: Nancy Ennis
Assistant production editor: Jamie Bush
Proofreader and indexer: Paula Pike
Cover designer: John Vegter

Library and Archives Canada Cataloguing in Publication

Kerr, Margaret Helen, 1954-
    Legal research : step by step / Margaret Kerr, JoAnn Kurtz, Arlene Blatt. — 3rd ed.

Includes index.
ISBN 978-1-55239-352-9

    1. Legal research—Canada—Textbooks. I. Kurtz, JoAnn, 1951-
II. Blatt, Arlene III. Title.

KE250.K477 2009   340.072'071   C2009-903559-6

To Sarah and Gael.
To Ely, Max, Jacob, and Danny.
To Jeffrey, Jordan, and Matthew.

Contents

PART I

Introduction to Legal Research

Don't let anyone tell you that legal research is easy. But, if you enjoy problem solving, legal research can be interesting—even fun.

Legal research often is taught as a series of exercises in using resources—for example, the *Canadian Abridgment* or Quicklaw. However, there's not much point in working with resources if you don't know how to read and understand the basic sources to which the Abridgment or Quicklaw direct you—statutes, regulations, and cases. Nor is there any point in working with resources if you don't know how to identify the issues you have to research.

The purpose of this book is to take you through the research process step by step so that you can

- identify an issue after hearing the story of a client's problem;

- identify and use the right research tools, in both paper and computerized format, to find information about that issue;

- read and understand the basic sources to which the research tools point you; and

- apply the law you find so that you can solve the client's problem.

CHAPTER 1

The Basics of Legal Research

Research is something that lawyers, paralegals, and law clerks are always doing, whether it's strictly "legal" research—that is, finding out the law from statutes and cases—or various other kinds of research, such as

- finding out the name of a person or company your law firm wants to sue;

- finding out whether there are executions against the vendor of real property that your client is purchasing;

- finding out whether there's a security lien under the *Personal Property Security Act* on a chattel your client is purchasing;

- finding out the legal description of real property;

- finding out in what municipality a town or city is located;

- finding an expert witness;

- finding an ordinary witness to an accident or incident; or

- finding out exactly what happened to a client so you know what you have to do to get a remedy for that client.

As a result, the ability to find things out—in other words, to research—is an essential skill for a lawyer, paralegal, or law clerk.

We live in an information age. Information is all around us—in books, magazines, and newspapers and on television and the Internet. The information containing the answers to a lawyer's questions is available somewhere, but you have to know where and how to find it and be able to understand, evaluate, and apply it.

In this chapter, we look at the basics of legal research:

- the purpose and basic steps of legal research;

- categories of law;

- sources of law;

- primary sources versus secondary sources;

- paper sources versus computerized (electronic) sources; and

- what it takes to be a good legal researcher.

THE PURPOSE AND BASIC STEPS OF LEGAL RESEARCH

All research, legal or otherwise, has the same purpose—either to find out something that you don't already know, or to confirm the accuracy of something you know, but about which you are unsure. All research, legal or otherwise, involves the same basic steps whether you are using traditional paper sources or electronic sources:

- identifying the issue to be researched in order to solve a specific problem;

- identifying and using the right research tools to find information about that issue;

- reading and understanding the sources to which the research tools point you; and

- applying the information you find to solve the problem.

In legal research, the something you don't know is the law; therefore, the research steps are a bit more complicated because

- you must be able to identify a *legal issue* after hearing the story of a *client's* problem;

- you must be familiar with and be able to work with specialized *legal research tools and sources*; and

- you must be able to apply the *law* you find so that you can solve the *client's* problem.

A lawyer, paralegal, or law clerk will engage in legal research to learn about the law in order to take action or advise a client how to proceed in a given situation. For example:

- A commercial lawyer researches case law to advise a client whether a contract she entered into is valid and the other party can be forced to carry it out.

- A family lawyer researches statute law to advise a client whether the divorce he got in Mexico is valid so that he can marry again without accidentally committing bigamy.

- A tax lawyer researches statute law and regulations to find out if a client's business expense is deductible for tax purposes.

- A litigation lawyer researches case law to prepare for legal argument in a motion, trial, or appeal.

- A paralegal researches statute law to advise a landlord client whether she has grounds to evict her residential tenant.

CATEGORIES OF LAW

No lawyer knows all the law all the time. Instead, lawyers know enough law to fit a client's problem into the proper category of law, so that they know where to look to find the answers to their clients' problems. In order to navigate your way through the vast amount of legal information out there, it is important to have some understanding of the categories of law.

Law is categorized among substantive law, procedural law, and the law of evidence. **Substantive law** defines legal rights and obligations. Legal rights may be enforced by way of legal proceedings; substantive law also sets out the defences to such proceedings. **Procedural law** sets out the procedure that a party must follow to enforce his or her rights in a court proceeding or to defend a proceeding. The **law of evidence** sets out the manner in which facts are proved in a trial or a proceeding.

Substantive law may be divided between public law and private law. **Public law** governs the relationship between persons (individuals and corporations) and the state, and includes such areas of law as

- municipal law,

- immigration and refugee law,

- environmental law,

- constitutional law,

- criminal law, and

- tax law.

Private law governs the relationship between persons, and includes such areas as

- contracts,

- family law,

- property law,

- real estate,

- torts, and

- wills and estates.

SOURCES OF LAW

Canadian law is made up of a combination of

- statutes passed by either the federal Parliament or provincial legislatures;

- regulations made by the federal or a provincial government pursuant to statutes; and

- decisions made by judges in court proceedings (case law).

The law in all the categories in the previous section is derived from these sources.

substantive law
defines legal rights and obligations; legal rights may be enforced by way of legal proceedings, to which substantive law sets out the defences

procedural law
sets out the procedure that a party must follow to enforce his or her rights in a court proceeding or to defend a proceeding

law of evidence
sets out the manner in which facts are proved in a trial or a proceeding

public law
governs the relationship between persons (individuals and corporations) and the state, and includes such areas of law as municipal law, immigration and refugee law, environmental law, constitutional law, criminal law, and tax law

private law
governs the relationship between persons, and includes such areas as contracts, family law, property law, real estate, torts, and wills and estates

PRIMARY VERSUS SECONDARY SOURCES

In legal research we make a distinction between primary sources and secondary sources. **Primary sources** are the actual statutes, regulations, and case decisions that create the law. **Secondary sources** are sources that summarize, discuss, or explain primary sources and include

- legal encyclopedias,
- digests of cases,
- indexes to statutes,
- textbooks, and
- articles.

When you perform legal research, you cannot rely on secondary sources alone. Secondary sources are tools that help you gain an understanding of the law and that, as finding tools, direct you to the primary sources that actually create the law. You must then examine the primary sources you have been referred to—that is, read them and understand what they say.

primary sources
the actual statutes, regulations, and case decisions that create the law

secondary sources
sources that summarize, discuss, or explain primary sources, and include legal encyclopedias, digests of cases, indexes to statutes, textbooks, and articles

PAPER VERSUS COMPUTERIZED SOURCES

Until recently, all primary and secondary legal sources came in paper format only. Over the last few years, more and more legal information has become available in computerized format as well. It is now possible to do everything with computerized sources that was previously done using only paper sources.

Computerized legal sources take a variety of forms:

- CD-ROM and online versions of secondary sources such as legal encyclopedias, digests of cases, and indexes to statutes;
- online versions of primary sources—statutes, regulations, and cases— available on free Internet sites or through subscription services; and
- online services such as Quicklaw and Westlaw Canada that combine the finding features of a secondary source with access to the primary source, such as the text of statutes and case reports.

Paper legal research sources are discussed in part IV of this book; computerized legal research sources are discussed in part V.

WHAT IT TAKES TO BE A GOOD LEGAL RESEARCHER

The legal research you perform will be relied on to take legal action or to give legal advice to a client. Your legal research must therefore be:

- Accurate: You must find *all* the relevant statutes, regulations, and case decisions; you must understand the meaning of the statutes, regulations, and cases that you find; and you must summarize or copy them accurately.

- Reliable: Your information must come from the most reliable sources—in other words, primary sources.

- Current: You must make sure that the statutes and regulations you find have not been amended or repealed; that the cases you find have not been overturned on appeal; and that the legal principles in statutes, regulations, or cases have not been changed by subsequent statutes, regulations, or cases.

KEY TERMS

law of evidence	public law
primary sources	secondary sources
private law	substantive law
procedural law	

Research Exercise

This exercise will introduce you to the basic steps of research and allow you to develop some basic research skills using both paper and electronic sources.

Read the following fact situation. Answer the questions that follow, *twice.* The first time, use only a local telephone book. The second time, use the Internet. Use your creativity and powers of deduction. You are not being asked to consider questions of legal jurisdiction, procedure, or substantive law.

Fact Situation

Angelina Jolly was visiting Niagara Falls, Ontario. While she was driving near the falls, her car was struck by a car driven by Jennifer Annistone. Brad Pitts, a driver in another car, witnessed the incident; he gave his name and telephone number to Angelina before Angelina was taken by air ambulance to Toronto Slicendice Hospital. While Angelina was recuperating at the hospital, a nurse entered her room in the middle of the night and stole her watch, a gift she received from her brother, valued at $3,000.

After her release from the hospital, Angelina approaches your firm to represent her in two separate actions: a Superior Court action against Jennifer Annistone for damages for her injuries and the damage to her car, and a Small Claims Court action against the Slicendice Hospital for the theft of her watch.

After meeting with Angelina, the firm asks you to find the answers to some preliminary inquiries:

1. What is the filing fee for a claim in the local Small Claims Court? How can you find that out?

2. Angelina has already filed a statement of claim relating to the car accident at the local Superior Court office. You have to contact the court office to find out whether a statement of defence has been filed. How can you find the location and telephone number of the court to contact?

3. You need to contact the witness, Brad Pitts. Unfortunately, Angelina lost his telephone number, but remembers that he lives in Los Angeles, California. How can you find Brad's telephone number?

4. You're going to telephone Mr. Pitts long distance. You want to know the cost of the telephone call so that the firm can bill Angelina for all disbursements at the end of this month. The telephone bill won't come in until after the billing date. How can you find out the cost of the call right away?

5. Angelina is claiming that she suffered neurological injuries in the accident. If the action goes to trial, your firm will need an expert witness in the field of neurology to testify about the effects of Angelina's injuries on her ability to work. Where can you find an up-to-date list of all neurologists registered in your province?

6. It turns out that Angelina's watch was bought in the United States and Angelina has an insurance certificate valuing it at U.S.$3,000. Because the legal proceedings will be brought in Canada, you need to know the Canadian dollar equivalent of the U.S. dollar amount at today's exchange rate. Where can you find this information?

7. Another lawyer who used to practise in the city represented a client in a similar car accident case (the well-known case of *Holmes v. Kidman*). This lawyer is no longer listed in the city telephone book, but someone mentioned that she had moved to a small town, either to the north or the east, to set up a new practice. How can you find the lawyer's address and/or telephone number?

8. A Small Claims Court summons has to be served on Angelina's roommate, who was in the next bed at Slicendice when the nurse made off with Angelina's watch. Angelina happens to know the roommate's home telephone number, but not her street address. It doesn't seem like a good idea to alert the roommate to the summons by calling her. How can you use the roommate's telephone number to find out her address so that she can be personally served?

9. In an unrelated commercial matter, you need to send a package to the Banff Springs Hotel in Banff, Alberta, but the courier service won't accept the package without a postal code. You don't want to call the hotel directly because then you'll have to pay long distance charges. How can you find the postal code?

10. In another unrelated matter, you need to write to a member of Parliament on behalf of a client. How can you find out the name and address of your client's MP, the member for the Trinity-Spadina riding in Toronto?

PART II

Sources of Canadian Law

The basic sources of legal research are statutes, regulations, and case law. Statutes are created by Parliament and the provincial legislatures, regulations are created by government departments, and case law is created by judges to explain their reasons for making a decision after hearing a case. A client who needs legal advice may be affected by one, two, or all three of these kinds of law. The purpose of legal research is to solve a client's problem. When you know what law governs the problem, you know what can be done and you can give the client choices on how to proceed.

CHAPTER 2

Statutes

Statutes are one of the three primary sources of law in Canada mentioned in Chapter 1. Lawyers, paralegals, and law clerks need to know how to read and understand a statute. This chapter discusses

- why we read statutes,
- how to read a statute, and
- how to read a statutory provision.

WHY READ A STATUTE?

Statutes lay down the law. They set out approved methods of doing things that are required or permitted. They may require people to do things in certain circumstances; they may require people *not* to do things in other circumstances; or they may permit people to do things. Statutes create penalties for not doing what is required, or for doing what is prohibited. A client who seeks legal advice needs to know what statutes apply to him or her and how he or she is affected.

statute
law created by Parliament or a provincial legislature

HOW TO READ A STATUTE

Most statutes are organized as follows:

1. Statutes are headed by the *chapter number* of the statute, and, when first enacted, by the statute's **long title** (the full name of the statute, beginning with "An Act respecting" or a similar phrasing). Either at the end or at the beginning of the statute there may be a section that sets out the **short title** of the statute (beginning with "This Act may be cited as"). If a statute has a short title, use this in citing it. When statutes are subsequently amended they use the short title only. An amended statute will also list the amendments that have been made. Lengthy statutes may include a table of contents setting out all the parts and sections of the statute.

    long title
    full, unabbreviated title of a statute

    short title
    abbreviated title of a statute

2. Statutes may begin with a **preamble**, which sets out the purpose and main principles of the statute. The preamble usually begins with "Whereas."

    preamble
    part of a statute that outlines its purpose and main principles

3. Statutes are usually subdivided as follows:

> I Part
>> 1. Section
>>> (1) Subsection
>>>> (a) Subsection
>>>>> (i) Subsection

Brief notes in the margins may indicate what the sections (and sometimes subsections) are about.

4. Statutes have introductory sections that set out

    a. the *scope* of the statute (what the statute applies to),

    b. the definitions of words used in the statute,

    c. the officials who are to administer the statute, and

    d. other details about how the statute is to be administered.

5. The law itself is contained in the *body* of the statute. In some statutes, the body concludes with sections that create offences for disobeying the law and penalties.

housekeeping provisions
sections that cover the details of statutes, such as the date of coming into force

6. Statutes end with **housekeeping provisions**, which can include the date when the statute will come into force and the right of officials who administer the statute to make regulations under the statute.

The organization of a statute is illustrated in figure 2.1, which reproduces some provisions from the *Family Law Act* (as first enacted). Note the following:

- The long title of the original statute is *An Act to revise the Family Law Reform Act.*

- The Act is quite lengthy—77 sections—and is divided into six parts.

- Definitions are found in s. 1.

- A housekeeping provision—the power to make regulations—is found in s. 69.

- The short title of the Act is set out in s. 77.

In later versions of the statute, only the short title is used. Figure 2.2 shows the first page of the 1990 version of the same statute. Note that the statute is now entitled the *Family Law Act.*

FIGURE 2.1   Selections from the Family Law Act, 1986

CHAPTER 4

**An Act to revise the
Family Law
Reform Act**

Assented to January 17th, 1986

TABLE OF CONTENTS

FIGURE 2.1   Continued

Chap. 4   FAMILY LAW   1986

Section   **Section**

PART V   PART VI
DEPENDANTS' CLAIM FOR   AMENDMENTS TO THE
DAMAGES   COMMON LAW

61. Right to sue in tort   64. Legal capacity of spouses
62. Offer of global sum   65. Actions between parent and
63. Assessment of damages   child
                                               66. Recovery for prenatal injuries
                                               67. Domicile of minor
                                               68. Onus of proof

                                               GENERAL

                                               69. Regulations
                                               70. Transition
                                               71.-75. Complementary amendments
                                                   and repeals
                                               76. Commencement
                                               77. Short title

Preamble

Whereas it is desirable to encourage and strengthen the role of the family; and whereas for that purpose it is necessary to recognize the equal position of spouses as individuals within marriage and to recognize marriage as a form of partnership; and whereas in support of such recognition it is necessary to provide in law for the orderly and equitable settlement of the affairs of the spouses upon the breakdown of the partnership, and to provide for other mutual obligations in family relationships, including the equitable sharing by parents of responsibility for their children;

Therefore, Her Majesty, by and with the advice and consent of the Legislative Assembly of the Province of Ontario, enacts as follows:

Definitions

1.——(1) In this Act,

"enfant"

"child" includes a person whom a parent has demonstrated a settled intention to treat as a child of his or her family, except under an arrangement where the child is placed for valuable consideration in a foster home by a person having lawful custody;

"cohabiter"

"cohabit" means to live together in a conjugal relationship, whether within or outside marriage;

"tribunal"

"court" means the Provincial Court (Family Division), the Unified Family Court, the District Court or the Supreme Court;

"contrat familial"

"domestic contract" means a domestic contract as defined in Part IV (Domestic Contracts);

FIGURE 2.1 Continued

Chap. 4   FAMILY LAW   1986

"père ou mère"   "parent" includes a person who has demonstrated a settled intention to treat a child as a child of his or her family, except under an arrangement where the child is placed for valuable consideration in a foster home by a person having lawful custody;

"accord de paternité"   "paternity agreement" means a paternity agreement as defined in Part IV (Domestic Contracts);

"conjoint"   "spouse" means either of a man and woman who,

    (a) are married to each other, or

    (b) have together entered into a marriage that is voidable or void, in good faith on the part of the person asserting a right under this Act.

Polygamous marriages   (2) In the definition of "spouse", a reference to marriage includes a marriage that is actually or potentially polygamous, if it was celebrated in a jurisdiction whose system of law recognizes it as valid.

Staying application   **2.**—(1) If, in an application under this Act, it appears to the court that for the appropriate determination of the spouses' affairs it is necessary or desirable to have other matters determined first or simultaneously, the court may stay the application until another proceeding is brought or determined as the court considers appropriate.

All proceedings in one court   (2) Except as this Act provides otherwise, no person who is a party to an application under this Act shall make another application under this Act to another court, but the court may order that the proceeding be transferred to a court having other jurisdiction where, in the first court's opinion, the other court is more appropriate to determine the matters in issue that should be determined at the same time.

Applications in Supreme or District Court   (3) In the Supreme or District Court, an application under this Act may be made by action or application.

Statement re removal of barriers to remarriage   (4) A party to an application under section 7 (net family property), 10 (questions of title between spouses), 33 (support), 34 (powers of court) or 37 (variation) may serve on the other party and file with the court a statement, verified by oath or statutory declaration, indicating that,

    (a) the author of the statement has removed all barriers that are within his or her control and that would prevent the other spouse's remarriage within that spouse's faith; and

FIGURE 2.1   Continued

Chap. 4   FAMILY LAW   1986

GENERAL

Regulations   **69.** The Lieutenant Governor in Council may make regulations respecting any matter referred to as prescribed by the regulations.

Application
of ss. 5-8   **70.**—(1) Sections 5 to 8 apply unless,

R.S.O. 1980,
c. 152

   (a)   an application under section 4 of the *Family Law Reform Act* was adjudicated or settled before the 4th day of June, 1985; or

   (b)   the first spouse's death occurs before the day this Act comes into force.

Extension of
limitation
period   (2) The limitation period set out in clause 7 (3) (b) does not expire until six months after this Act comes into force.

Application
of Part II   (3) Part II (Matrimonial Home) applies unless a proceeding under Part III of the *Family Law Reform Act* to determine the rights between spouses in respect of the property concerned was adjudicated or settled before the 4th day of June, 1985.

Interpretation
of existing
contracts   (4) A separation agreement or marriage contract that is validly made before the day this Act comes into force and that excludes a spouse's property from the application of sections 4 and 8 of the *Family Law Reform Act*,

   (a)   shall be deemed to exclude that property from the application of section 5 of this Act; and

   (b)   shall be read with necessary modifications.

   71.—(1) The *Family Law Reform Act*, being chapter 152 of the Revised Statutes of Ontario, 1980, except the title, subsection 27 (1) and sections 69, 70 and 71, is repealed.

   (2) Subsection 27 (1) of the *Family Law Reform Act* is repealed.

   (3) Section 3 of the *Children's Law Reform Amendment Act, 1982*, being chapter 20, section 179 of the *Courts of Justice Act, 1984*, being chapter 11, section 10 of the *Courts of Justice Amendment Act, 1984*, being chapter 64 and section 18 of the *Land Registration Reform Act, 1984*, being chapter 32, are repealed.

FIGURE 2.1 Concluded

Chap. 4 FAMILY LAW 1986

(4) The title to the *Family Law Reform Act* is repealed and the following substituted therefor:

DOWER AND MISCELLANEOUS ABOLITION ACT

72. Subsection 12 (2) of the *Ontario Municipal Employees Retirement System Act*, being chapter 348 of the Revised Statutes of Ontario, 1980, is repealed and the following substituted therefor:

Application of subs. (1)

(2) Notwithstanding subsection (1), payment to a person out of the Fund is subject to execution, seizure or attachment in satisfaction of an order for support or maintenance enforceable in Ontario.

73. Subsection 27 (3) of the *Pension Benefits Act*, being chapter 373 of the Revised Statutes of Ontario, 1980, as enacted by the Statutes of Ontario, 1983, chapter 2, section 5, is repealed.

74. Subsection 34 (4) of the *Public Service Superannuation Act*, being chapter 419 of the Revised Statutes of Ontario, 1980, as enacted by the Statutes of Ontario, 1984, chapter 22, section 15, is repealed.

75. Subsection 43 (3) of the *Teachers' Superannuation Act, 1983*, being chapter 84, is repealed.

Commencement

76. This Act comes into force on a day to be named by proclamation of the Lieutenant Governor.

Short title

77. The short title of this Act is the *Family Law Act, 1986.*

FIGURE 2.2   First Page of the 1990 Family Law Act

CHAPTER F.3

Family Law Act

CONTENTS

1. Definitions
2. General
3. Mediation

PART I

FAMILY PROPERTY

4. Definitions
5. Equalization of net family properties
6. Estates
7. Applications to court
8. Statement of property
9. Powers of court
10. Questions of title
11. Business or farm
12. Preservation orders
13. Security
14. Presumptions
15. Conflict of laws
16. Application of Part

PART II

MATRIMONIAL HOME

17. Definitions
18. Matrimonial home
19. Spouse's right of possession
20. Designation of matrimonial home
21. Alienation of matrimonial home
22. Right of redemption and to notice
23. Powers of court
24. Orders for possession
25. Variation of order
26. Title to matrimonial home
27. Registration
28. Application of Part

PART III

SUPPORT OBLIGATIONS

29. Definitions
30. Obligation of spouses for support
31. Obligation of parent to support child
32. Obligation of child to support parent
33. Order for support
34. Powers of court
35. Filing of domestic contracts
36. Effect of divorce proceeding
37. Variation
38. Indexation of existing order
39. Existing orders
40. Restraining orders
41. Financial statement
42. Access to information
43. Arrest of absconding debtor
44. Provisional orders
45. Credit for necessities of life

CHAPITRE F.3

Loi sur le droit de la famille

TABLE DES MATIÈRES

1. Définitions
2. Dispositions générales
3. Médiateur

PARTIE I

BIENS FAMILIAUX

4. Définitions
5. Égalisation des biens familiaux nets
6. Successions
7. Requêtes
8. Déclaration des biens
9. Pouvoirs du tribunal
10. Questions relatives à la propriété
11. Commerce ou ferme
12. Ordonnance pour conserver les biens
13. Sûreté
14. Présomptions
15. Conflit des lois
16. Champ d'application

PARTIE II

FOYER CONJUGAL

17. Définitions
18. Foyer conjugal
19. Droit de possession du conjoint
20. Désignation du foyer conjugal
21. Aliénation du foyer conjugal
22. Droit de rachat et de recevoir des avis
23. Pouvoirs du tribunal
24. Ordonnances relatives à la possession
25. Modification de l'ordonnance
26. Titre du foyer conjugal
27. Enregistrement
28. Champ d'application

PARTIE III

OBLIGATIONS ALIMENTAIRES

29. Définitions
30. Obligation alimentaire des conjoints
31. Obligation alimentaire du père et de la mère
32. Obligation alimentaire de l'enfant
33. Ordonnance alimentaire
34. Pouvoirs du tribunal
35. Dépôt du contrat familial
36. Effet de l'action en divorce
37. Modification
38. Indexation
39. Ordonnances existantes
40. Ordonnances de ne pas faire
41. État financier
42. Accès aux renseignements
43. Arrestation du débiteur en fuite
44. Ordonnances conditionnelles
45. Crédit pour les objets de première nécessité

HOW TO READ A STATUTORY PROVISION

You are more likely to read a **provision** (a section or subsection) in a statute than to read a whole statute.

provision
section or subsection

When you quote a statute for research, never paraphrase. Quote the statute exactly, or you'll change its meaning. For example, "any individual may apply" does not mean the same as a researcher's own words "any person may apply" ("individual" excludes corporations, but "person" usually includes corporations).

In order to understand a statutory provision, begin by asking the following questions:

1. With what matters in general does the statute deal?

2. With what matters does this particular provision of the statute deal?

3. To whom is the particular section directed—for example, the general public, a corporation, a real estate agent, or a spouse?

4. Does the provision

   a. order,

   b. prohibit, or

   c. permit

   something to be done? What? In what circumstances?

5. If there is an order or prohibition, how is it enforced?

These questions give you a general idea about the provision.

In order to understand a provision more particularly, break it down into its elements. Once you understand these, you will be able to identify all the important information in the provision.

Example

Section 265(1)(b) of the *Criminal Code*, R.S.C. 1985, c. C-46 defines a particular form of assault. As written in the statute, it looks like this:

265(1) A person commits an assault when . . .
    (b) he attempts or threatens, by an act or gesture, to apply force to another person, if he has, or causes that other person to believe upon reasonable grounds that he has, present ability to effect his purpose.

Broken down into its separate elements, it looks like this:

A person
commits an assault when

(ONE OF THE FOLLOWING)

1. he attempts	2. he threatens
by an act	by an act
or a gesture	or a gesture
to apply force	to apply force
to another person	to another person

(PLUS ONE OF THE FOLLOWING)

1.	if he has	2.	if he causes
	present ability		that other person
	to effect his purpose		to believe on reasonable grounds
			that he has
			present ability
			to effect his purpose

If you break down a provision into its elements, you can use the breakdown as a checklist to compare with your client's fact situation. Each element must be accounted for in the facts of your client's situation if the statutory provision is to be applicable. For example, if your client (who has been charged with assault under s. 265(1)(b)) yelled at and raised his fist to a ticket seller who was safely inside a locked Plexiglas booth, then he threatened by a gesture to apply force to the ticket seller. But he had no present ability to effect his purpose, and the ticket seller had no reasonable grounds to believe that he had present ability. Therefore, your client has not committed assault as defined by s. 265(1)(b).

Sometimes you will have to research further to find out what each element of a statutory provision means. For example, what exactly is "present ability"? Would your client have present ability to apply force to the ticket seller if your client were standing outside the locked booth with a tire iron in his hand? Or what are "reasonable grounds" for believing that the accused has present ability? Would the ticket seller have reasonable grounds to believe that your client could get into the booth using only his bare hands? To answer these, you might have to look at another section of the statute for a definition, or you might have to look for cases that discuss these issues.

As well as breaking down a statutory provision into its elements, you may have to build up the elements by referring to other provisions. You may have to look in the definition section of the statute in order to understand the legal meaning of a word. For example, the *Change of Name Act*, R.S.O. 1990, c. C.7, s. 4(3) says:

> 4(3) An application by a child requires the written consent of every person who has lawful custody of the child.

In order to know exactly who is a "child," you must look at s. 1 of the Act, which contains definitions. There, "child" is defined as "a person under the age of eighteen years."

Building up a statutory provision can be more complex than that, however. Instead of adding the definition of a word, you may have to add other entire provisions. For example, s. 108(1) of the *Canada Business Corporations Act*, R.S.C. 1985, c. C-44 reads:

> 108(1) A director of a corporation ceases to hold office when,
> (a) he dies or resigns;
> (b) he is removed in accordance with section 109; or
> (c) he becomes disqualified under subsection 105(1).

So, in order to find out what s. 108(1) *really* means, you have to refer to these other sections. Section 109(1) says:

109(1) Subject to paragraph 107(g), the shareholders of a corporation may by ordinary resolution at a special meeting remove any director or directors from office.

Section 105(1) says:

105(1) The following persons are disqualified from being a director of a corporation:
    (a) anyone who is less than eighteen years of age;
    (b) anyone who is of unsound mind and has been so found by a court in Canada or elsewhere;
    (c) a person who is not an individual; or
    (d) a person who has the status of bankrupt.

The sections referred to have to be incorporated into s. 108 to understand it. For example, s. 108(1)(c) would have to be read like this:

108(1) A director of a corporation ceases to hold office when, . . .
    (c) he becomes disqualified under subsection 105(1).

    105(1) The following persons are disqualified from being a director of a corporation: . . .
        (b) anyone who is of unsound mind and has been so found by a court in Canada or elsewhere; . . .
        (d) a person who has the status of bankrupt.

Once you have built up a statutory provision by adding all the references, you have to break down your new creation into its elements in order to understand it properly. A built-up, broken-down s. 108(1)(c) will look like this:

108(1)   A director of a corporation
ceases to hold office
when . . .

(c)   he becomes disqualified
under subsection 105(1).

105(1)   The following persons
are disqualified from being
a director of a corporation: . . .

(b)   anyone who is of unsound mind
and has been so found by a court
in Canada or elsewhere; . . .

(d)   a person who has the status of bankrupt.

KEY TERMS

housekeeping provisions   provision

long title   short title

preamble   statute

Exercises

1. Break down the following statutory provisions into their separate elements.

   a. The *Criminal Code*, R.S.C. 1985, c. C-46, s. 265 provides, in part, as follows:

      265(1) Any person commits an assault when . . .
      (c) while openly wearing or carrying a weapon or an imitation thereof, he accosts or impedes another person or begs.

   b. The *Criminal Code*, R.S.C. 1985, c. C-46, s. 265 provides, in part, as follows:

      265(1) Any person commits an assault when
      (a) without the consent of another person he applies force intentionally to that other person directly or indirectly; . . .

      265(3) For the purposes of this section, no consent is obtained where the complainant submits or does not resist by reason of
      (a) the application of force to the complainant or to a person other than the complainant;
      (b) threats or fear of the application of force to the complainant or to a person other than the complainant;
      (c) fraud; or
      (d) the exercise of authority.

   c. The *Land Titles Act*, R.S.O. 1990, c. L.5, s. 93, prior to its amendment in 1998, provided, in part, as follows:

      93(2) A charge that secures payment of money shall contain the amount of the principal sum that the charge secures, the rate of interest, and the periods of payment including the due date.

d. The *Canada Evidence Act*, R.S.C. 1985, c. C-5, s. 4 provides, in part, as follows:

> 4(3) No husband is compellable to disclose any communication made to him by his wife during their marriage, and no wife is compellable to disclose any communication made to her by her husband during their marriage.

2. Read the following fact situations and answer the questions, using the applicable statutory provision from question 1.

a. A mortgage (charge) made in Ontario in 1997 contains the following payment clauses. Does it meet the statutory requirements then in effect?

> The amount of principal secured by this Charge/Mortgage of Land is Thirty Thousand ($30,000) dollars and the rate of interest chargeable thereon is Ten (10%) per cent per annum calculated quarter-yearly not in advance.
>
> Provided this Charge/Mortgage to be void on payment of Thirty Thousand ($30,000) dollars of lawful money of Canada with interest at Ten (10%) per cent per annum as follows:
>
> Five hundred ($500) dollars on account of the principal sum shall be payable on the 8th days of each of the months of May, August, and November in the year 1998 and the 8th days of each of the months of February, May, August, and November in the year 1999. The first payment of interest is to be computed from the 8th day of February 1998 upon the whole amount of principal hereby secured, to become payable on the 8th day of May 1998.

b. Richie and Maya lived together for years. During that time, he robbed several banks and told her the details of each robbery. Eventually, Richie and Maya decided to get married and had the ceremony performed at the city hall. Unfortunately, as they were leaving the building, a police officer who had been called to the scene of one of the robberies bumped into them and recognized Richie. Two days later, Richie was in jail, charged with armed robbery. Should he worry that Maya will be forced to testify against him at his trial?

c. Is it assault?

    i. Lisa and her husband, David, were having an argument. To emphasize a point, David threw a vase at the wall. He expected it to shatter, but the vase bounced off the wall and hit Lisa.

    ii. When their next-door neighbour dropped by to show off the karate moves she had just learned, Lisa's husband told the neighbour that she had his permission to demonstrate on Lisa. The neighbour whacked Lisa across the arm.

    iii. Lisa went to her doctor to set her broken arm. It was excruciatingly painful, far worse than she expected. The only reason she went through with it and didn't run screaming from the doctor's office was that she was afraid of ending up with a deformed arm.

    iv. Lisa later found out that the doctor who had set her arm was not licensed to practise medicine.

CHAPTER 3
Regulations

Regulations are the second primary source of law in Canada, and lawyers, paralegals, and law clerks must know how to read and understand a regulation. This chapter discusses

- why we read regulations, and
- how to read a regulation.

WHY READ A REGULATION?

Regulations, also called subordinate legislation, are rules made under the authority of a statute. They are not created by Parliament or a legislature, but by department or ministry officials to whom the statute gives the power to make regulations.

Regulations are as important as statutes. In the case of **framework legislation**—legislation that creates a general framework and leaves the details to be worked out in the regulations—the regulations may be more important than the statute. Regulations are also important to those working in civil or criminal litigation because the rules of court are regulations made under the authority of the statute that creates the court system.

As with statutes, regulations require, prohibit, or permit certain actions and set out a method of doing what is required or permitted. They also create penalties for not doing what is required, or for doing what is prohibited.

regulations
rules made under the authority of a statute

framework legislation
legislation for which the details are worked out in the regulations

HOW TO READ A REGULATION

The text of a regulation is much like the text of a statute, except that it may be more detailed. You read a regulatory provision the same way that you read a statutory provision. In order to understand the law fully, it may be necessary to read a regulation together with one or more provisions of the statute under which it was made.

KEY TERMS

framework legislation

regulations

Exercises

Read the following regulations and answer the questions below.

A provision from SOR/93-392, made under the *Canada Student Loans Act*, states:

17. Subject to section 9, the Minister may grant a special interest-free period to a borrower if

(a) the borrower resides in Canada;

(b) the borrower has signed, in respect of

(i) full-time guaranteed loans, a consolidated guaranteed student loan agreement in accordance with subsection 7(1) or (2), and

(ii) part-time guaranteed loans, a part-time guaranteed loan agreement;

(c) all of the risk-shared loan agreements and guaranteed student loan agreements referred to in paragraph (b) are held by a lender, or, in the case where an event referred to in any of paragraphs 9(1)(c) to (g) has occurred, by the Minister or a lender;

(d) the borrower submits a duly completed application, in the prescribed form, for a special interest-free period in respect of all of that borrower's loans referred to in paragraph (b); and

(e) the borrower's monthly family income is equal to or less than the applicable amount indicated in Schedule 1 to the *Canada Student Financial Assistance Regulations*, taking into consideration

(i) the number of persons comprising the borrower, the borrower's spouse or common-law partner and their dependants, and

(ii) the total amount of all monthly instalments required from the borrower and, if applicable, the borrower's spouse or common-law partner, in accordance with their outstanding guaranteed loan agreements and loan agreements.

Liquor Licence Act, R.S.O. 1990, c. L.19, ss. 30(1), (13)(a), and 31(1) and (2) state:

30.(1) No person shall knowingly sell or supply liquor to a person under nineteen years of age. . . .

(13) This section does not apply,

(a) to the supplying of liquor to a person under nineteen years of age in a residence as defined in section 31 or in a private place as defined in the regulations by a parent of the person or a person having lawful custody of the person. . . .

31.(1) In this section, "residence" means a place that is actually occupied and used as a dwelling, whether or not in common with other persons, including all premises used in conjunction with the place to which the general public is not invited or permitted access, and, if the place occupied and used as a dwelling is a tent, includes the land immediately adjacent to and used in conjunction with the tent.

(2) No person shall have or consume liquor in any place other than,

(a) a residence;

(b) premises in respect of which a licence or permit is issued; or

(c) a private place as defined in the regulations.

Revised Regulations of Ontario, Reg. 718, ss. 3(1), (2), and (3), made under the *Liquor Licence Act*, state:

3.(1) For the purposes of clauses 30(13)(a) and 31(2)(c) of the Act, "private place" means a place, vehicle or boat described in this section.

(2) An indoor place to which the public is not ordinarily invited or permitted is considered to be a private place except at the times when the public is invited or permitted access to it.

(3) Despite subsection (2), an indoor place that is available for rental by members of the public for occasional use is not a private place.

Criminal Appeal Rules (Ontario), SI/93-169, rules 14(1)(a-k), made under the authority of the *Criminal Code*, state:

APPEAL BOOKS

Contents of Appeal Book

14.(1) Except in an inmate appeal, the appeal book shall contain, in consecutively numbered pages arranged in the following order, a copy of,

(a) a table of contents describing each document, including each exhibit, by its nature and date, and, in the case of an exhibit, identified by exhibit number or letter;

(b) the notice of appeal and any supplementary notice of appeal;

(c) the order granting the leave to appeal, if any, and any order or direction made with reference to the appeal;

(d) the information or indictment, including all endorsements;

(e) the formal order or decision appealed from, if any, as signed and entered;

(f) the reasons for judgment, if not included in the transcript of the trial or hearing, together with a further typed or printed copy if the reasons are handwritten;

(g) any order for release from custody pending appeal and any other order suspending the operation of the sentence;

(h) all documentary exhibits filed at the trial arranged in order by date, or, where there are documents having common characteristics, arranged in separate groups in order by date;

(i) all maps, plans, photographs, drawings and charts that were before the trial judge and are capable of reproduction;

(j) the agreed statement of facts, if any;

(k) where there is an appeal as to sentence, the pre-sentence report, the criminal record of the convicted person and any exhibits filed on the sentencing proceedings.

Questions

1. Your client, Sam Johnston, has received a student loan from a Canadian university and wants to know whether he is entitled to a special interest-free period.

    a. Make a list of the terms in the regulation you need to define (by looking at the definition section at the beginning of the regulation) before you go any further.

    b. Make a list of other sources that you need to see before you can answer the client's question.

2. You have been put in charge of preparing the appeal book for client Ava Bump's appeal. She is appealing the sentence imposed on her after her conviction for criminal negligence causing death (she is not appealing the conviction). She is at present free, pending the outcome of the appeal.

    a. Make a list of the documents that must be created by your law firm.

    b. Make a list of court documents that may have to be included in the appeal book.

    c. Make a list of documents from the trial that may have to be included in the appeal book.

    d. Make a list of any legal terms you do not understand but need to understand in order to prepare the appeal book.

3. Your client J.W. Hart, president and CEO of Hart Industries Inc., is having a party to which both adults and children will be invited. The client intends to serve champagne and would like to serve the older children (the 17- and 18-year-olds) as well, with their parents' permission. The legal drinking age in Ontario is 19. The client wouldn't ask if the party were being held in his own home, but he's concerned because the party is being held in a big tent on the grounds of a well-known public garden. A large area around the tent will be roped off to keep out uninvited people.

Can the client legally serve wine to anyone under 19 at the party? Explain, quoting the relevant statute and regulation.

CHAPTER 4

Cases

Cases are the third primary source of Canadian law. Just as with statutes and regulations, lawyers, paralegals, and law clerks have to know how to read and understand a case. This chapter discusses

- what a case is,

- why we read a case, and

- how to read a case.

WHAT IS A CASE?

A case is the written record of a judge's reasons for deciding a legal dispute. Before a case gets into a report series or a legal database, it is known as the **reasons for decision** in a legal action.

reasons for decision
term for a case before it is included in a report series or legal database

WHY READ A CASE?

Case law research can tell you many things—for example, whether a client has a cause of action, how much a client could expect to be awarded in damages, and what evidence has to be presented at trial for the client's action to succeed.

All cases contain law, but that law is only useful to your particular client if

- the issues in the case and in the client's situation are similar,

- the facts in the case and in the client's situation are similar, and

- the case is binding or at least persuasive in your jurisdiction (see Chapter 6 under the headings "What Is Binding Law?" and "Case Law: What Decisions Bind Which Courts?").

If the issues and the facts are similar, and the case is at least a persuasive authority, the law in the case can be applied to your client's situation.

HOW TO READ A CASE

If you haven't read many cases, any case looks like just a mass of words; but all cases, however long or short, share the same structure. Once you learn how to identify the different parts of a case that make up its structure, you will be able to use the case in research. Cases or reasons for decision contain these structural elements: purpose, facts, issues, law, *ratio decidendi* (Latin for "reason for deciding"), decision, and disposition. If there are several decision makers, such as in a Court of Appeal, the Supreme Court of Canada, or the House of Lords in England, there may be several separate reasons for decision in the same case—sometimes very different from each other.

If the reasons for decision have been edited for a report series or database, a short **headnote** at the beginning will explain the case. For example, a headnote might read "Children—Custody and access—Factors governing award of custody—Best interest of child." A brief summary of the facts, *ratio decidendi*, and decision usually follow. The headnote and summary are useful in several ways. They let you know before you read the case whether the subject matter is relevant to your problem. They usually identify the issues and this helps to understand the case. Finally, if you do use the case, they will remind you what the case is about, so that you don't have to reread it too often as you prepare a memo of law. A word of warning about headnotes and summaries, however: they are not always correct, and they rarely quote the judge word for word. Never rely on the headnote and summary alone. Read the case yourself, and quote that rather than the headnote or summary.

headnote
editor's explanation of the case before the body

Purpose

purpose
the nature of the proceedings

Before the judge's reasons, there usually will be a short reference to the **purpose**, or nature of the proceedings, which has been provided by the editor of the report series—for example, "Action for damages for negligence," "Motion for summary judgment," and "Appeal from a decision of the General Division." If no such reference appears to give you a hint, you'll find that judges usually begin their reasons with a brief mention of why the case is before them.

Facts

Although most judges set out the facts at the beginning of their reasons, they often do not include *all* the facts in that section and instead scatter them throughout their reasons, usually putting facts in with the issue to which they are relevant.

The facts can fall into these categories:

1. The events leading up to the moment when the cause of action comes into existence. Note that important facts may exist before the plaintiff even comes into the picture.

2. The theory of the plaintiff and the theory of the defendant. A party's theory (or **theory of the case**) consists of the cause of action or the defence, plus the evidence that supports that cause of action or defence.

theory of the case
the cause of action or the defence, and the evidence that supports that cause of action or defence—also known as "the theory"

3. The decision at trial and the grounds of appeal (if the case is a decision on appeal).

Look for the facts that are relevant to the issues decided. You will have to examine the issues and the law before you can decide which facts are relevant. Many written decisions—especially at the trial level—are long and contain much information that is not necessarily essential in understanding the issues. With practice, you can learn to identify the facts that were used to reach the actual decision on an issue.

Issues

The **issues** are the specific problems that the judge must solve in order to reach a decision. Often, they are set out in question form or introduced by the word "whether."

Once the judge has identified an issue, he or she must consider all the elements that make up that issue. The judge does this by

- looking at the law concerning the issue to find out what the elements involved are, and then

- looking at the relevant facts in that particular situation to see whether the legal test set out by the law has been met.

For example, if the issue is "whether the defendant committed battery on the plaintiff," the judge has to examine the law to see what the legal test for battery is (what elements make up the tort of battery). Then the judge has to examine the facts to see whether the defendant's actions meet that test.

Students often find that identifying issues is the hardest part of legal research. It takes practice to identify issues either in a case or your own client's fact situation. For help, see Chapter 5 under the heading "Identify the Issues on a Preliminary Basis."

issues
specific problems that the judge must solve to reach a decision

Law

After the judge sets out the issues, there is usually a discussion of the existing law on each issue. Statutes, other cases, and texts may be quoted, cited, and relied on as authorities. Sometimes the judge simply will make a general statement of the law without referring to any authority, if the law is well known—for example, "A plaintiff must prove his or her case on the balance of probabilities." At other times, a judge will not set out a statement of law for every issue addressed.

Because the two sides in a case usually cite different **lines of authority** to persuade the judge to decide the case in each side's favour, the judge may cite two or more cases, statutes, or texts that give very different views of the law on a single issue. The judge must choose which line of authority to follow before applying the law to the facts of the case and reaching a decision. If the judge has examined more than one line of authority on a single issue, note which one he or she has chosen to follow before proceeding to the *ratio* for that issue.

lines of authority
statement of existing law found in statutes, cases, and texts

The law that the judge chooses to follow is law for which you can cite the case for research. Again, do not paraphrase because that will change its meaning. Quote it exactly from the case.

Ratio Decidendi and Decision

The **ratio decidendi** is the pre-existing principle of law on which the judge based the decision on an issue, applied to the facts of the particular case. The *ratio* is frequently introduced by words such as "here," "in this case," or "in my view," and is often short—a sentence or a brief paragraph. The *ratio decidendi* of a case is law for which you can cite the case when you are using it for research. Do not paraphrase because that will change its meaning. Quote it exactly from the case.

ratio decidendi
Latin for "reasons for deciding"

A decision is made on each issue that the judge addresses. The decision itself—for example, "The action in negligence must fail," or "The plaintiff has made out a good case in battery"—usually appears either at the beginning or the end of the *ratio*.

If there is more than one issue, there probably will be more than one *ratio* and more than one decision.

Disposition

disposition
judge's orders set out at
the end of a case

At the end of the case, the judge's **disposition** or orders about the entire case are set out—for example, "Judgment for the Plaintiff," "Judgment for the Plaintiff in the amount of $30,000," "Motion for summary judgment granted," or "Appeal dismissed." The disposition usually includes an award of costs to one party and also may include administrative directions to the parties, such as an order that documents be filed by a certain date or a referral of the matter to another judicial official for an accounting or an assessment of damages.

KEY TERMS

disposition	purpose
headnote	*ratio decidendi*
issues	reasons for decision
lines of authority	theory of the case

Exercises

1. Read the following cases. In each one, identify the purpose, facts, issues, law, *ratio decidendi*, decision, and disposition.

Cyrenne v. Moar
(1986), 2 R.F.L. (3d) 414
Manitoba Court of Appeal,
Monnin C.J.M., Huband, and Twaddle JJ.A.

M.J. Bennett, for appellant.

C.N. Guberman, for respondent.

(No. 193/86)

16th June 1986. The judgment of the court was delivered by

MONNIN C.J.M. (orally):—This is an appeal from a decision of Helper J. who dismissed the mother's application to strike out the access privileges granted to Mr. Cyrenne by a prior order of Simonsen J.

We are of the view that it is not in the best interest of the child, Sonya Rose Moar, that access be given to Mr. Cyrenne. The original order most probably would not have been made if all the facts had been disclosed.

We strike out the access rights granted to Mr. Cyrenne and will give more detailed reasons in due course.

The matter of costs is reserved and will be dealt with in our extended reasons.

20th June 1986. Written reasons for judgment. The judgment of the court was delivered by

HUBAND J.A.:—This court has decided that the visiting privileges accorded to John Cyrenne should end. What follows are my reasons for allowing the appeal of Annette Moar on 16th June 1986.

John Cyrenne is not the father of the child, Sonya, in whom he has taken such keen interest. John Cyrenne met Annette Moar in 1979 and had some form of relationship with her extending through to 1982. During part of 1981 and 1982 they maintained adjoining suites in the same dwelling house, and during that period of time the relationship seemed to have been at its closest.

Annette Moar was already the mother of a son who was born in 1974. The daughter, Sonya, was born on 19th June 1981. Initially John Cyrenne believed that he had fathered the child, but subsequent blood tests have confirmed that he is not the father of the child.

Believing the child to be his, John Cyrenne participated to some degree in the care of the baby, although he made no significant financial contribution. No doubt he developed a genuine fondness for the child.

In June 1982 John Cyrenne was sentenced to jail for six months, and the somewhat tenuous relationship between himself and Annette Moar began to crumble. When he was released from prison two months later, Annette Moar had moved to different accommodation. She began a new relationship with another man in the fall of 1982—a relationship which has persisted through to the present date. In October 1982 she told John Cyrenne that he was not the father of the child, Sonya, but John Cyrenne did not accept her statement at that time.

During 1983 John Cyrenne continued to visit the child from time to time, but with growing reluctance on the part of the mother and her new companion.

By the beginning of 1984 Annette Moar made it clear that she wanted John Cyrenne's visits with her daughter to end. His response was to seek custody or access by way of proceedings in court. On 22nd February 1984 he applied in the Provincial Court, Family Division, for custody of, or access to, the child. Annette Moar caused an answer to be filed asserting that John Cyrenne was not the father of the child, and on 27th February his application for custody or access was withdrawn.

A fresh application seeking custody or access was filed in the same court on 21st March 1984. This application also sought a declaration of parentage. The parties submitted to blood tests, and the results of those tests demonstrated that John Cyrenne was not the father of the child. Ultimately, this second application was discontinued on 6th December 1984.

But once again, a fresh action was commenced a few weeks later. This time a petition was filed in the Court of Queen's Bench on 17th December

1984, seeking access only, and relying upon s. 1.5 of the *Child Welfare Act* of Manitoba.

Annette Moar did not contest this petition. Later on she was to explain that she wilted under the bombardment of continuing applications and the constant harassment of John Cyrenne to gain access to the child. In any event, on 18th February 1985 John Cyrenne obtained an order from Simonsen J. in the Court of Queen's Bench granting him access to the child each Sunday from 10:00 a.m. to 7:00 p.m. While the order was made without opposition from Annette Moar, it would appear that given the unusual nature of the order allowing access in favour of a person who is not a blood relation, Simonsen J. insisted upon some evidence before making the order. John Cyrenne testified and, since the petition was not opposed, the order was made.

Problems with respect to the access arose almost immediately. About one month after the order was made, Annette Moar was seeking legal aid in order to move to set aside the access order, and within a further month John Cyrenne had instituted criminal contempt proceedings against Annette Moar for her disobedience of the access order. Attendances at Annette Moar's residence to exercise rights became confrontations. In June 1985 Annette Moar brought a motion in the Court of Queen's Bench seeking an order to vary the order of Simonsen J. by deleting the access privileges. John Cyrenne countered with a motion for an order of contempt against Annette Moar, and an order to vary the terms of the access order of Simonsen J. by "increasing the times of access." These two motions came before Schwartz J. of the Court of Queen's Bench in July 1985. In order to defuse the confrontations between the protagonists, Schwartz J. ordered an immediate variation to provide that some third party, other than John Cyrenne, attend to pick up the child. As to the merits of the motion and counter-motion, Schwartz J. ordered that they be dealt with by way of a trial in the fall of 1985.

The trial commenced before Helper J. in November 1985. After two days of testimony the learned trial judge decided to order an assessment report from a family conciliation counsellor, and the testimony of the author of that report was heard on 26th April 1986. Helper J. delivered judgment on that same date. Helper J. did not vary the access as ordered by Simonsen J. approximately a year earlier.

The learned trial judge seemed to believe that there must be proof of changed circumstances to justify a variation in the previous order of Simonsen J. She asked the rhetorical question, "What circumstances have changed since the pronouncement of the order to warrant any change in the existing order?" The learned trial judge went on to observe that animosity between John Cyrenne and Annette Moar both preceded and followed the order of Simonsen J. Helper J. found no significant change in circumstances to justify a variation.

With respect, I do not think that proof of changed circumstances is essential. The order of Simonsen J. was made pursuant to s. 1.5 of the *Child Welfare Act*, S.M. 1974, c. C80. Section 1.5 was added by way of an amendment to the Act in 1983, and the provision reads as follows:

1.5. In exceptional circumstances, a court may make an order granting any person who has had or ought to have the opportunity to visit a child, the right to visit the child at such times and on such conditions as the court considers appropriate.

The basis for varying an access order made under the *Child Welfare Act* is to be found in s. 21 of the *Family Maintenance Act*, C.C.S.M. c. F20, which reads as follows:

21. An order made under this Act or under [t]he *Wives' and Children's Maintenance Act* or under the *Family Maintenance Act*, being chapter 47 of the *Statutes of Manitoba*, 1977, or an order made under [t]he *Child Welfare Act* granting custody of, access to or maintenance for a child, may upon an application therefor be varied from time to time or discharged by the court making the order, if the court thinks it fit and just to do so, but no variation or discharge granted under this section shall be effective before the date on which the application therefor is made.

The test for a variation or discharge would seem to be what is "fit and just" and unlike a variation to an order made under the *Divorce Act* of Canada, the variation or discharge does not hinge upon proof of changed circumstances.

However, there is no need to dwell upon this difference between provincial and federal legislation, because using either test the appeal must be allowed. There were in fact changed circumstances between the granting of the access order by Simonsen J. and the trial before Helper J. The conflict between Annette Moar and John Cyrenne had escalated in intensity. Of greater significance, the passive toleration of access on the part of the mother had become firm and resolute opposition.

This was not a case where Annette Moar had consented to access on a basis approaching an agreement. Non-opposition is not the same thing as active consent. As mother and guardian of the child, Annette Moar is entitled to say that she has changed her mind, and that John Cyrenne's visits with her child are no longer welcome. In a case of this kind, where the statute requires exceptional circumstances before the court may make an order of access, the opposition of the mother is enormously significant. She has the responsibility of rearing the child, and the child has the right to be reared by her. Her opinion as to who should visit with the child and under what circumstances deserves very great consideration. When non-opposition turns to defiant hostility, the circumstances have clearly altered.

Further, I think it is "fit and just" that access be denied. The case of *Lapp v. Dupuis* (1985), 45 R.F.L. (2d) 28, 31 Man. R. (2d) 261, was a decision by this court dealing with similar circumstances. The petitioner had a brief romantic interest in the mother of the child, which was not reciprocated. The petitioner became good friends with the mother, however, and from that relationship he developed an interest in her 5-month-old child. That interest continued over a period of a few years, and for approximately a year and one half the petitioner served as principal babysitter for the child. As time went by, the mother entered into a relationship with another man.

There was animosity between the petitioner and the mother's new friend. When the mother insisted that the petitioner's visits cease, the petitioner applied for access, and the application was firmly opposed by the mother of the child. This court decided that an association emerging out of a babysitting arrangement, albeit over a lengthy period of time, was insufficient to establish the "exceptional circumstances" required under s. 1.5 of the *Child Welfare Act*. In that case, as in the present case, the petitioner had a genuine interest in the child, and his visits were not disagreeable from the standpoint of the child. But the court concluded that an access order in favour of someone who is not a blood relation should be set aside in face of the opposition of the mother who wished to exercise responsible control over the destiny of her child and herself. As in the *Lapp v. Dupuis* case, a fit and just disposition is to cancel the access privileges.

In my opinion, it was appropriate for the learned trial judge to vary the order of Simonsen J. and, given the evidence presented before her, she should have done so by deleting access.

I am mindful of the argument on behalf of John Cyrenne that the paramount consideration is the best interests of the child. The very wording of s. 1.5 of the *Child Welfare Act*, however, suggests that it will only be under rare circumstances that court-ordered visits of a non-relative will be considered to be in the child's best interests, at least where there is opposition by the parent or parents. As noted in the case of *Lapp v. Dupuis*, the parents' attitude is not to be relegated to a parity with all other surrounding circumstances in determining what is best for the child. While not determinative, the parents' position is of prime importance in making the determination of best interests. I have no hesitation in this case in concluding that the access awarded to John Cyrenne is not in the child's best interests.

For some period of time leading up to the date of the appeal hearing, Annette Moar was defiant of the order for access in favour of John Cyrenne. Under the circumstances, while her appeal is allowed, it is allowed without costs.

Appeal allowed;
access terminated.

In *Cyrenne v. Moar*, identify the

- purpose,

- facts,

- issues,

- law,

- *ratio decidendi,*

- decision, and

- disposition.

Bell v. St. Thomas University
(1992), 97 D.L.R. (4th) 370
New Brunswick Court of Queen's Bench, Russell J.

Grant M. Ogilvie, for plaintiff.

J. William Cabel, for defendant.

RUSSELL J.:—In 1987, the plaintiff was in the final year of a four-year program at the defendant institution leading to a Bachelor of Social Work (hereafter called a B.S.W.) degree. One of the requirements to complete that degree was the successful completion of a field practice course entitled Social Work 410. The plaintiff took that course from May to July, 1987. He failed the course and has not yet received a B.S.W.

That failing grade and the defendant's following actions have led to this litigation.

The action is framed in negligent misrepresentation and breach of contract. Paragraphs 21 and 22 of the statement of claim as amended say:

> 21. As a result of the plaintiff's protracted efforts to either change his final grade mark or be accepted to repeat SW 410 which have not been successful, the plaintiff asserts that the defendant is in breach of a contract between the plaintiff and the defendant and more particularly that the defendant:
>
> > (i) contracted to provide a course of studies leading to a BSW degree when completed and has failed to allow the plaintiff to complete the BSW program . . .
>
> 22. The plaintiff asserts that the defendant has negligently misrepresented to him the failing grade the plaintiff was to receive upon completion of SW 410 and that during the course of the field placement the defendant through its employees:
>
> > (i) neglected to properly warn the plaintiff that he was going to fail . . .

The university calendar (ex. P-1) describes Social Work 410 as follows:

> **410. Field Instruction II**
> This course is a continuation of Field Instruction 1(b), and also provides practical experience in the field, in an approved setting, under faculty supervision. Students are expected to develop knowledge and skills in the field sufficient for initial professional practice with various client constituencies. Two days per week. Two semesters. Prerequisite: Field Instruction I. Available to B.S.W. students only.

Field placements were normally made at various institutions and sites around the Fredericton area such as the Dr. Everett Chalmers Hospital and the Mental Health Clinic. These are only representative examples of the institutions that accepted placements.

The plaintiff was accepted by the Fredericton Police Department and carried out his field practicum at the so-called Devon storefront which I infer is a form of community policing service established by the Fredericton Police Department. Mr. Bell was under the direct supervision of Constable Peggy Blackmore of the Fredericton Police Department and his academic supervisors were Sandra DeVink and Gaynell Cloney both of the Faculty of Social Work.

His assignments at the Devon storefront are described in ex. P-10 as follows:

> This group experience was to involve consultation and shared leadership with Ms. Gaynell Cloney.
>
> Mike had joint responsibility with another student to design and implement a needs assessment questionnaire in order to determine the perception of and needs of a segment of the community with respect to the Storefront. Although the adolescent and young adult population was the largest group for Mike's work, he also had involvement with the adult population, primarily single-parent mothers, who attend the Storefront on a daily basis. Mike became very involved in a few cases where he took on the various roles of client advocate, educator and counsellor. He had opportunities to liaise with other agencies and consult with resource people on behalf of his clients. Finally Mike participated in some of the on-going activities at the Storefront, community meetings and attended two of the women's support group meetings, as well as a Self-Help Conference resource fair.

His supervisors were not satisfied with his performance. His mid-term assessment (ex. P-9) completed on July 2, 1987, and completed by Sandra DeVink contains the following paragraphs:

> In order to pass this field placement, Mike needs to demonstrate that he has satisfactory assessment and intervention skills and satisfactory skills in the areas requiring improvement.
>
> In the event that Mike has not been able to learn these skills to a satisfactory degree, we will consider extending this field placement and or selecting another field placement which may be more appropriate in teaching the skills required.

They were particularly concerned about several aspects of his performance. One example will suffice to indicate the nature of the supervisors' concerns.

At one point during the plaintiff's placement the Fredericton police decided to enforce a 10 p.m. curfew for children under 17 years of age who lived in the neighbourhood of the storefront operation. The plaintiff had considerable contact with the adolescents of the affected age group and his response to this effort on the police's part was somewhat outlandish. His journal (ex. P-8) kept for assessment purposes contains the following:

> Mike: The curfew law is an abuse of power and a form of state control. You cannot tell a 14 or 15 year old to be in at 10.00 p.m. It represents age discrimination, it's unconstitutional.
>
> • • •
>
> Mike: What do—think this is the Soviet Union, a totalitarian state, this is in a free country and that law restricts freedom. That's bizzare [sic] to keep a kid in the house when it's 90° outside.

The above statements were made by the plaintiff at a meeting of neighbourhood residents to discuss the curfew issue.

Naturally his sponsor—the Fredericton Police Department—was concerned about this attitude and his on-site supervisor, Constable Blackmore wrote (ex. P-12) in her final assessment:

> Mike has a tendency to want to buck the system. For instance when the children on Doone St. started to get out of hand, the police and New Brunswick Housing decided to enforce the curfew by-law. This caused an uproar amongst the children and Mike got on the band wagon and advised the kids to fight the laws of the land and start protesting what the establishment stood for. He told them laws like this were made for Russia and that it was against their charter of rights to be told when they should be in the house etc. This caused a great deal of concern amongst the parents who were already having disciplinary problems with their children. On [the] one hand they were telling their children to be in by 10 p.m. and on the other here is this professional telling them to fight the law that states they must be in by 10 p.m. My other concern was that I was hired as a police officer to uphold the laws that are written and here I am employing a guy who is telling everyone not to follow these laws.
>
> Mike and I as well as several of the mothers of the community had a long discussion about the consequences of this action he was planning, and I think after he thought about it he realized that if he had followed through with his plan of action he may have started an all out war amongst the children, their parents and the police department.

In the end Professor DeVink, in a reasoned and responsible fashion gave the plaintiff a failing grade in Social Work 410. Although not strictly necessary for me to say so in order to reach a decision on the issues it is evident that the plaintiff at the best displayed considerable immaturity and lack of judgment during the practicum and at the worst the practicum demonstrated that he had made an unfortunate career choice. These qualities were further emphasized by his behaviour toward Professor DeVink during the appeal process and his conduct during a November, 1987 Provincial Court matter as described by Laurel Lewey, at the time an employee of the Fredericton Police Department. It is not necessary to detail these incidents except to say I accept Professor DeVink's and Ms. Lewey's testimony as being factual.

The final assessment (ex. P-11) of Professor DeVink says in part:

> After careful consideration of all the facts as I know them and after having consulted with both Cst. Peggy Blackmore and Gaynell Cloney, I am recommending that Mike Bell fail this field placement.
>
> As Coordinator of Field Instruction it is my decision that any future training plans will be discussed with Mike after I have consulted with the faculty on available options.
>
> For your information, the first level of appeal of this decision is with the Chairperson of the Department of Social Work and the second level of appeal is with the Student Academic Grievance Committee.

The plaintiff then followed two approaches to alleviate the situation. He appealed the failing grade and he tried to retake the course.

He followed the appeal approach through various levels finally reaching the university senate. At each level his appeal was rejected. The university senate said in a letter to the plaintiff of February 1, 1989 (ex. P-45):

The University senate met on January 19, 1989 and considered the report from the senate committee on your appeal of your final grade in SW 410. Senate accepted the recommendation of the committee, viz. "That there be no change in the final grade in SW 410 awarded Mr. Michael Bell."

During the time the appeal was wending its way through the university bureaucracy the faculty decided to re-admit the plaintiff to S.W. 410 on certain terms. On September 28, 1987, Ms. Marilyn McKay wrote the plaintiff (ex. P-20) in part as follows:

At this point I want to formally let you know that in consultation with the faculty of the Department of Social Work I have decided to allow you to repeat SW 410, if you chose [sic] to do so, and if you are able to demonstrate that you are ready and willing to fully involve yourself in the learning process.

What I mean by "involving yourself in the learning process" is that you must be willing to:

(1) reflect on and evaluate your own professional behaviour in light of its impact on the practice situation,
(2) identify your own strengths and weaknesses and to set goals for development,
(3) take initiative in identifying and seeking out opportunities for learning and development,
(4) seek out and make use of feedback as a guide in your learning and practice,
(5) work at clearly articulating what you are learning from your practice experience. . . .

In order to demonstrate your readiness to re-enter SW 410, you must submit the following documentation:

1. A detailed account of your learnings from the placement which you did in May, June and July, 1987.
2. An evaluation of your strengths and weakness by filling out the skills evaluation sheet (attached) and drawing up a written report summarizing the results.
3. A detailed outline of your needs in relation to the learning process (i.e. the conditions under which you learn best, the kind of assistance you need from others, etc.).
4. A detailed account of how you see your responsibility in the learning process.
5. A list of learning objectives for the placement.

Pending your response to these five questions and depending on the quality of your response, plans will then be made with you to repeat SW 410.

The plaintiff made three attempts to comply with the department's demands.

The first submission which was undated, unsigned and handwritten on paper torn from a notebook met with the following response (ex. P-25) from Professor McKay:

3. Your statement regarding how you see your role and responsibility as a learner is unacceptable in the sense that being "subservient" does not suggest a willingness to take responsibility for your learning. In fact I felt your response was flippant and reflective of a lack of respect for yourself and for the social work faculty.

In summary, then, your submission is not convincing of your readiness to engage in the learning process or to undertake another fourth year field placement. We will consider another submission from you but would suggest that you take the time you need to reflect carefully on what is being asked of you in this submission and to be sure in your own mind that you are ready to do a field placement. I will expect to hear something from you by the end of the academic year (April 29, 1988) regarding your plans (i.e. either another request to redo the course or some indication of when you would be ready to do so).

Please be advised that your status in this program is in jeopardy and I would advise you to think carefully before making another inappropriate and inadequate submission or request.

The plaintiff tried again on two further occasions and each time his submissions were rejected. The university rejected his last submission as follows:

The Department has reviewed your recent application to repeat SW 410 Field Instruction II and is in unanimous agreement not to accept you for enrollment in this course.

Your written submission, once again, was not convincing that the problems which persisted in your previous field placement have been satisfactorily resolved by you—particularly in terms of your ability to accept responsibility for your own actions, and to work in collaboration with field supervisors.

This action was started in April, 1989.

The plaintiff as already mentioned has pleaded negligent misrepresentation and breach of contract.

The plaintiff's counsel in argument said the defendant negligently misrepresented in the mid-term assessment that the plaintiff could retake the course or that a different field placement would be considered (see: ex. P-9) and the plaintiff relied on this statement.

Although not specifically mentioned in the pre-trial brief or in argument I conclude the plaintiff's counsel is referring to tort liability on the basis of the *Hedley Byrne* principle when he mentioned negligent misrepresentation.

For tort liability to attach on the basis of the judgment in *Hedley Byrne & Co. v. Heller & Partners, Ltd.*, [1963] 2 All E.R. 575 (H.L.), it is generally considered there must be, inter alia, a false statement negligently made, reasonable reliance on the statement by the recipient and a loss resulting from that reliance: see *V.K. Mason Construction Ltd. v. Bank of Nova Scotia* (1985), 16 D.L.R. (4th) 598, [1987] 1 S.C.R. 271, 35 R.P.R. 118.

At the time the mid-term evaluation was written the plaintiff had not yet failed the course. He was cautioned by his faculty advisor that he stood in danger of failing the course but that, of course, was somewhat conjectural at that time and the result was largely in the plaintiff's hands.

The following statement was made on the mid-term evaluation:

> In the event that Mike has not been able to learn these skills to a satisfactory degree, we will consider extending this field placement and or selecting another field placement which may be more appropriate in teaching the skills required.

I cannot see how it can be said that it was a false statement or that the plaintiff relied on it. Perhaps after the plaintiff failed the course the faculty did "consider" extending the field placement or selecting another placement and rejected both in favour of the action they did select. Further, when the statement was written the plaintiff had not yet failed the course. He could not at that time and there is not evidence that he did rely on the statement to his detriment.

The plaintiff's action on the basis of negligent misrepresentation fails.

I turn now to the plaintiff's claim that the defendant breached the contract between them by not allowing him to retake Social Work 410.

There is no dispute that there was a contractual relationship between the plaintiff and defendant. The calendar formed an essential part of that contract in setting out the terms of the relationship: see *Acadia University v. Sutcliffe* (1978), 30 N.S.R. (2d) 423 (C.A.), and *Doane v. Mount Saint Vincent University* (1977), 74 D.L.R. (3d) 297, 24 N.S.R. (2d) 298 (T.D.).

The calendar (ex. P-1) says with reference to retaking a course:

> **Repeating Courses**
> Students may, without special permission, register for a course already taken in order to meet a prerequisite or other degree requirement or in order to improve their grade in the course. Students should note that the final grades of repeated courses will be counted in the annual gps's but the course credit will be counted only once towards the minimum number of credits required for a degree.

In his pre-trial brief counsel for the defendant argues that the "peculiarities of the situation make it reasonable to infer other terms of the relationship, specifically the right to impose reasonable conditions on the repeat of the SW 410 course."

Counsel was unable to direct me to any material which would indicate a modification or variation of the clear wording contained in the calendar.

Professors McKay and DeVink testified conditions were imposed on the plaintiff because of S.W. 410's peculiar nature. Students, while taking the practicum, come face to face with individuals who might have severe personal and social problems and there is substantial potential for damage to individuals other than the student. Such is not the case with the normal academic university course. Accordingly, the faculty imposed conditions on the plaintiff's re-entry to the course.

The faculty may well have had ample reason for imposing conditions on the plaintiff; however, those conditions, in my view, violated the terms of the contract between the plaintiff and the university. The contract should have allowed him to re-enter the course without condition or, in the words of the calendar "without special permission," and the defendant is in breach of its contractual obligations in not permitting the plaintiff to do so.

[The university goes on to say, however, that the plaintiff by attempting to answer or respond to the conditions imposed on him is now estopped from saying he is not bound by those conditions. In his pre-trial brief, counsel for the defendant cited *Hughes v. Metro Railway Co.*, [1877] 2 A.C. 439 and in argument at the conclusion of the trial, he cited *Central London Property Trust Ltd. v. High Trees House Ltd.*, [1956] 1 All E.R. 256 in support of this proposition.

In both these cases, the promise emanating from one party had the effect of loosening or improving the original contractual conditions for the other contracting party. It was then said that the party improving the contract could not go back on his word if the other party had altered his position in reliance on the changed conditions. That is not the case here. The altered conditions imposed by the defendant did not have the effect on Mr. Bell of improving the contractual relations between the parties. Promissory estoppel does not assist the defendant.]

Mr. Bell seeks damages in the following terms:

As a result of the breach of contract and negligent misrepresentation asserted above the plaintiff has been damaged in that he is unable to work as a Social Worker, his reputation has been impugned, he has suffered mental anguish and he has suffered a loss of income and the plaintiff claims damages from the defendant as follows:

i. Special damages:
   (a) Costs of registering and attending St. Thomas University; $11,550.00
   (b) Loss of income of $8,750.00 per year over 20 years; $175,000.00.

ii. General damages;
iii. Exemplary damages;
iv. Costs of this action;
v. Any other remedy this Honourable Court deems just.

[At the commencement of the trial, the plaintiff's counsel moved that the statement of claim be amended to reflect a claim for "specific performance." By using the words "specific performance," the plaintiff's counsel was asking that the court order the defendant to allow the plaintiff to retake the course. That motion was opposed by counsel for the university because of the lateness of the request and because he had not directed his mind to this type of relief in any of the pre-trial procedures.

Following the objection by defence counsel, the following exchange took place:

THE COURT: I can now do one of two things. I can allow the amendment and adjourn the matter so that the defendant can come to grips with this new issue, or I can reject your application to add a further head of claim and continue with the trial.

Do you want a few minutes to consider that course of action?

MR. OGILVIE: Well, if I could—I have discussed this with my client, My Lord, but I wonder if I could have one more minute to discuss it? Thank you.

THE COURT: Do you want to take a few minutes?

MR. OGILVIE: Just two or three minutes.

Court recessed.

THE COURT: Yes, Mr. Ogilvie?

MR. OGILVIE: Yes, My Lord, we are going to proceed.

THE COURT: Alright, the amendment is not allowed then.

The trial of the action then proceeded as originally pleaded.]

There was no evidence adduced with respect to either exemplary or general damages. Exemplary damages are of a preventative character and I do not see how the defendant's conduct warrants such damages inasmuch as its actions were, in my view, taken in good faith. General damages are not available in an action of this type: see *McBeth v. Governors of Dalhousie College & University* (1986), 26 D.L.R. (4th) 321, 10 C.P.C. (2d) 69, 72 N.S.R. (2d) 224 (C.A.).

The object of awarding damages for breach of contract is to place the aggrieved party in the same situation as if the contract had been carried through. It may be the breach has, in exceptional cases, not caused a loss. Here the breach has simply prevented the plaintiff from retaking the course.

He had already incurred substantial expenses in attending university to that point and has claimed the cost of registering and attending the defendant institution amounting to $11,500. Has he lost these expenses as a result of the defendant's actions? There was evidence the plaintiff has returned to St. Thomas and taken courses which, when coupled with the courses taken before the practicum have given him sufficient credits to obtain a Bachelor of Arts degree. In my view, the plaintiff has not established [that] the value of the money expended by him at St. Thomas has been diminished by the defendant's action.

The plaintiff further claims a loss of income of $8,750 per year over 20 years amounting to $175,000. The plaintiff's pre-trial brief says:

> Had the Plaintiff been able to fufill [*sic*] the requirements for the bachelor of Social Work degree, which he was entitled to do, he would probably have obtained gainfull [*sic*] employment as a Social Worker. The program boasts a 90 per cent employment placement rate. It is reasonable to expect that the Plaintiff would have been employed. There is, therefore, serious claim for loss of income. This would commence in the fall of 1987, when he should have received his bachelor of Social Work degree, or at least as of January, 1988 at which time he would have had all the necessary degree requirements for his degree. This would amount to loss of more than four and a half years.

The only evidence about social workers' salaries and their employment placement rate came from the plaintiff. Such evidence at the best can only be called anecdotal and not conclusive.

As well, should the plaintiff retake the course he may well fail it again. It is too remote to say that he has lost income as a social worker at this juncture.

It has been said the plaintiff has the burden of proving both the fact and the amount of damage before he can recover substantial damages: see *McGregor on Damages*, 15th ed. (London: Sweet and Maxwell, 1988), p. 1134, para. 1779, cited with approval in *Mason v. Royal Insurance Canada*; Court of Appeal of New Brunswick, June 9, 1992 [summarized 33 A.C.W.S. (3d) 1181].

I am not satisfied the plaintiff has established an entitlement to damages under this head.

The plaintiff has not established that any damages have flowed from the defendant's breach of contract. The plaintiff's action therefore fails. As I have mentioned, the question of the plaintiff's entitlement to an order compelling the defendant to re-admit him to the course is not before me. Had it been, the result might well have been different.

The plaintiff has established the defendant has breached the contract but he has not established any damages. Accordingly, each party will bear their own costs.

Action dismissed.

In *Bell v. St. Thomas University*, identify the

- purpose,

- facts,

- issues,

- law,

- *ratio decidendi*,

- decision, and

- disposition.

Banyasz v. K-Mart Canada Ltd.
(1986), 33 D.L.R. (4th) 474
Ontario High Court of Justice, Divisional Court,
Callaghan A.C.J.H.C.

S. Pasternak, for appellant.

G. Will, for respondent.

CALLAGHAN A.C.J.H.C. (orally):—This is an appeal by the plaintiff from the judgment of the Provincial Court (Civil Division) of North York, Ontario, dated February 12, 1985, wherein the plaintiff's claim for damages for false imprisonment was dismissed.

The plaintiff was suspected of shoplifting and was taken into custody by the security personnel employed by the defendant store. It was suspected that the plaintiff had stolen a battery for a walkie-talkie and had left the store without paying for the same. Upon investigation it became immediately apparent that the cashier had made a mistake in ringing up the amount chargeable to the plaintiff. Notwithstanding the admitted mistake, the security personnel continued to hold the plaintiff for a short period of time thereafter.

The learned trial judge considered the pertinent elements of the cause of action and concluded on the evidence that the plaintiff in fact was detained by the security personnel and that there was a constructive imprisonment (transcript, p. 24, line 2). As there was evidence to support such a finding this court will not interfere therewith on this appeal. The trial judge further concluded that while the plaintiff left the store with a battery he had not paid for there was no evidence of any intent on the plaintiff's part to commit theft or fraud (*ibid.* p. 76, line 15). The aforesaid conclusion was consistent with the finding that the mistake was that of the cashier in failing to charge the plaintiff the cost of the battery which was not included in the walkie-talkie. The effect of the trial judge's finding was that a criminal offence in the circumstances of this case had not been committed.

In considering a disposition of the matter, the trial judge stated the applicable test as follows:

> If there is reasonable and probable grounds. If the defendant objectively had reasonable and probable grounds for believing that fraud had been committed, then the actions of the defendant were justified.

(*Ibid.* p. 75, line 29).

The trial judge concluded that in the circumstances the security personnel had reasonable and probable grounds for believing that theft had been committed and accordingly dismissed the plaintiff's action. In so doing he erred.

At the outset it must be noted that "security personnel" employed to guard against theft of merchandise have no higher rights of arrest than those conferred on citizens generally: *Dendekker v. F.W. Woolworth Co.*, [1975] 3 W.W.R. 429. The appropriate rule is that established in the case of *Williams v. Laing* (1923), 55 O.L.R. 26 at p. 28, wherein Mr. Justice Hodgins stated:

> The law is quite clear that in order to succeed in establishing this defence the appellants must prove first that the crime they suspected had actually been committed, not necessarily by the person detained, but by some one, and that they had reasonable ground for suspecting the person detained.

Mere suspicion that an offence has been committed is not sufficient when arrest is effected by a citizen. The person alleging justification for arrest must be prepared to establish that the crime was in fact committed: see also *McKenzie v. Gibson* (1852), 8 U.C.Q.B. 100 at p. 101-2, *per* Sir John Robinson C.J.

Under s. 449 of the *Criminal Code* a citizen can make an arrest where he or she finds another committing an indictable offence. Where the defendant is unable to prove that the person arrested has committed an indictable offence, the defendant cannot arrest merely on reasonable and probable grounds: see *Hayward v. F.W. Woolworth Co. Ltd. et al.* (1979), 98 D.L.R. (3d) 345, 23 Nfld. & P.E.I.R. 17, 8 C.C.L.T. 157; *Kendall et al. v. Gambles Canada Ltd. et al.*, [1981] 4 W.W.R. 718, 11 Sask. R. 361.

The defendant/respondent herein relied on the judgment in *Karogiannis v. Poulus et al.* (1976), 72 D.L.R. (3d) 253, [1976] 6 W.W.R. 197. In that case it was held that it was not necessary that the defendant show that the plaintiff had actually committed theft but only that he had reasonable grounds for believing and did believe that a theft had been committed. The court therein held that s. 449(1)(a) of the *Criminal Code* is to be read as if it included the word "apparently" so that it would read "whom he finds (apparently) committing an indictable offence" and thereby affords justification for a defendant who arrested a person who in fact did not commit an offence. With respect, I cannot agree with that decision. I am in agreement with the reasoning of Mr. Justice Goodridge in *Hayward v. F.W. Woolworth Co. Ltd.*, *supra*, and Mr. Justice Cameron in *Kendall et al. v. Gambles Canada Ltd.*, *supra*, wherein that interpretation of s. 449 is rejected.

The problem of shoplifting is a serious one for storekeepers notwithstanding that the law of tort favours the interest in individual freedom over that of protection of property. While there may be a developing privilege of temporary detention for investigation in favour of a property owner (see Prosser, *Handbook of the Law of Torts*, 4th ed. (1971), p. 121), this is not a case where such a privilege should prevail. The continued detention after the cashier admitted her mistake negatives any consideration of such a privilege in this case.

In result, therefore, the appeal must be allowed, a verdict entered for the plaintiff, and the matter referred back to the trial judge for an assessment of damages. The plaintiff will have its costs of this appeal and the costs of the first trial in the court below. The costs of this assessment will be reserved to the trial judge.

Appeal allowed.

Note that a case may interpret or explain a statutory provision. In *Banyasz*, the court had to interpret s. 449 (now s. 494) of the *Criminal Code*.

> 449.(1) Any one may arrest without warrant
> (a) a person whom he finds committing an indictable offence; or
> (b) a person who, on reasonable grounds, he believes
> (i) has committed a criminal offence, and
> (ii) is escaping from and freshly pursued by persons who have lawful authority to arrest that person.

Section 449 should be read together with s. 450. Section 449 establishes the right of a citizen to make an arrest, while s. 450 establishes the right of a peace (police) officer to make an arrest.

> 450. [now s. 495] (1) A peace officer may arrest without warrant
> (a) a person who has committed an indictable offence or who, on reasonable grounds, he believes has committed or is about to commit an indictable offence,
> (b) a person whom he finds committing a criminal offence.

In *Banyasz v. K-Mart Canada Ltd.*, identify the

- purpose,
- facts,

- issues,
- law,
- *ratio decidendi*,
- decision, and
- disposition.

2. Read the following fact situations. Using the case law you examined in question 1, answer the question following each fact situation.

a. A babysitter in Manitoba became very fond of the little girl she looked after, and the child adored the babysitter. The parents decided to hire a live-in nanny and let the babysitter go, but the babysitter still came each afternoon to visit the child. After a while it became clear that these visits were making it difficult for the nanny to establish a good relationship with the child. The parents told the babysitter that she could no longer visit the child. The babysitter has come to you for advice. She would like to apply to the court for access.

Would the babysitter's application for access be likely to succeed? Explain, quoting the relevant law.

b. Natalie Davies is a student in the law clerk program at Maple Leaf College in your province. When she enrolled, she was given a copy of the student calendar, which stated in part:

> Withdrawal before the third scheduled class of a subject with seven or more scheduled classes will delete any reference in the student academic record. Full tuition fees less an administrative charge will be refunded.

Natalie registered in four courses, one of which was corporate law. It had 28 scheduled classes over a 14-week period. At the end of the second scheduled class, Natalie went to the registrar's office to withdraw from the course. There, she was told that no reference to corporate law would appear in her academic record, but that she would not receive a refund because too many people were registering in courses and then dropping them after one or two classes, and the college wanted to discourage students from doing that. Natalie has come to your law firm for advice.

i. What legal action can Natalie take?

ii. What is your authority for saying so? (Be specific; quote the relevant law.)

iii. In your province, does the *Bell* case have binding authority or persuasive authority? Explain. (In order to answer this question, you'll first have to read Chapter 6, pages 63-65 on binding law.)

c. In each of the following fact situations, can Mrs. McGillicuddy win an action for false imprisonment? Explain, quoting the relevant law. (In order to answer this question, you will first have to read Chapter 6, pages 63-65 on binding law.)

i. Mrs. Lucy McGillicuddy was shopping in Zellers for children's clothing. When she shops, she always carries a large straw bag for her purchases. She picked up a dress and examined it closely and then put it back on the rack. When she was leaving the store, a sales clerk followed her and said, "Excuse me, ma'am, just a minute." The clerk then signalled to a police officer who was walking past the entrance. The officer came in and the clerk said to her, "Please arrest this woman, she shoplifted something and it's in her bag." The officer took Mrs. McGillicuddy by the arm and asked her to come with her to a back room. She would not allow Mrs. McGillicuddy to leave while she searched her bag. The officer found nothing and told Mrs. McGillicuddy she was free to go. Mrs. McGillicuddy then left.

ii. Mrs. Lucy McGillicuddy was shopping in Zellers for children's clothing. When she found a little dress she liked, she dropped it into the large straw bag she always carries when she shops. After looking at various other items in the store, she went to the exit. A sales clerk stopped her just outside the store and said, "Will you please come with me. I was watching you on the security monitor and you have stolen something." The sales clerk then asked her to come with him to a back room, where he and a store manager searched her bag and found the dress. Mrs. McGillicuddy was locked in the small, windowless room for half an hour until a police officer came to arrest her and took her to the police station.

PART III

Thinking About Legal Research

Many of the exercises in this book can be done in the classroom. However, eventually you will have to go to a law library or have access to a computer to find and use the legal research resources. The exercises relating to working in a law library and working with computerized sources are necessarily general in this book. Your instructor should have exercises that will require you to find out what the law actually is during the time that you are doing the exercises, because one of the purposes of this research is to update the law as much as possible.

Sometimes legal research merely means having to find and photocopy a particular statute, regulation, or case. Analysis may not be necessary.

Other times, however, you must perform legal research involving a stated fact situation. When this happens, going to the library or turning on the computer to look for cases and statutes is *not* the first thing to do. The first thing is to analyze the given facts in order to identify which relevant issues and tools you'll need to do the research.

CHAPTER 5

How To Analyze a Fact Situation

When researching a given fact situation, you will

- identify the issues on a preliminary basis,

- formulate the issues, and

- identify the need for further information.

IDENTIFY THE ISSUES ON A PRELIMINARY BASIS

Identifying issues is not easy. Issues are the specific problems that must be solved in order to provide a solution to the entire fact situation. The following questions may help you to decide what issues arise out of a given set of facts.

What Is the Question Being Asked?

The question may be direct—for example, "Please find a case that says that an unborn child has no legal status in Canadian courts."

The question may be indirect—that is, in the form of a statement of what the client wants. The client may want to be financially compensated for an injury, to avoid having to pay damages for breach of contract in an action that has been brought against him or her, or to protect an interest in real or personal property.

What Is the Area of Law?

First,

- Identify the problem by general area—for example, criminal law, tort, contracts, family law, or real property. (If you are unsure, try this: identify key words in the fact situation and find them in the key word index of the *Canadian Encyclopedic Digest* (CED), discussed in Chapter 8. For example, in a fact situation involving a loan at a high rate of interest, the key word "interest" will lead you to the CED's "Debtor and Creditor" title.)

Then,

- Identify the problem by specific area: if the general area is contract law, is the specific area breach of contract or assignment of a contract? If the general area is family law, is the specific area divorce or custody?

Narrow the area of law further. If the specific area is custody, is the narrower area the child's best interests or the jurisdiction of a court to hear the matter? The more specific the area of law that you investigate, the more quickly and easily you will find answers.

What Is Needed?
Develop a Theory of the Case

A theory of the case is a strategy for winning. What is needed to win may be different from what is being asked for. Clients may *want* things that are not legally possible or that do not provide the best solution to the problem. The issue—the problem to be solved—may not be the one that the client has identified.

You may have to identify possible causes of action for a plaintiff or defences for a defendant, or, to be more general, the best legal means by which the client can reach the best solution. Once you have identified a cause of action or defence, examine it element by element to make sure that the requirements of that action or defence can be made out. To do this, you must review the evidence that is available in support of the action or defence. You are now developing a theory of the case.

Are There Any Hidden Issues?

The obvious issues can be hard enough to find, but you have to keep in mind that some issues, such as the following, are hidden:

- Are there any special procedural requirements—for example, is there a limitation period that may expire shortly? Are there any statutes or regulations governing procedure in the court or tribunal? Is the correct jurisdiction federal or provincial?

- Who, in law, are the parties involved? Issues may arise out of the parties' legal status. For example, are they natural persons, corporations, adults, minors, spouses, mentally incompetent persons, the Crown, or agents?

FORMULATE THE ISSUES

Write down the issues you have identified, starting with the word "whether."

Examples

- whether a person who is not a parent of a child may apply for custody of that child;
- whether the limitation period for medical malpractice begins to run from the date of the medical procedure;
- whether a defence of consent may exist in an action for assault.

IDENTIFY THE NEED FOR FURTHER INFORMATION

After you have made a preliminary identification of the issues as set out above under the heading "Identify the Issues on a Preliminary Basis," you may realize that you need more information before you can do your research. For example, you may need more facts to decide whether a cause of action has arisen, or you may need to know the legal status of all parties involved in the problem.

Exercises

Analyze the following fact situations. You need a basic understanding of tort and contract law to do this exercise; you also need to refer to statute law, covered in Chapter 2.

1. The client is an imposing man. He is 2 metres tall, weighs 100 kilograms, has a beard and several tattoos, dresses in biker clothing, and wears a small knife dangling from one ear as an earring. Two days ago, the client attended a business meeting downtown. He parked his motorcycle at a meter and inserted money. The meeting took longer than he expected and he excused himself to put more money in the meter. When he reached his motorcycle, he found that he only had a loonie and pennies, and the meter would take only quarters, nickels, and dimes. He noticed a meter officer issuing tickets four vehicles away from his. He then spoke to a woman who was passing by with a child in a stroller. He said, "Excuse me, madam, do you have any change?" The woman screamed, said "Please don't hurt my baby," and ran. The client then spoke to a man and asked him if he had change for a dollar. The man said that he did not, but that he had a quarter and the client could have it. The client accepted the quarter with thanks and was about to put it into the meter when a police officer approached him. The officer asked to see the client's identification and wrote down his name and address. The client has come into the law office on another matter, but mentioned this incident because of his concern about being charged with a crime.

    a. What is the question being asked?

    b. What is the area of law?

        i. General area

        ii. Specific area

iii. What key words helped you identify the area?

c. What is needed? Develop a theory of the case (for a defence).

d. Formulate the issues

Whether . . .

e. Are there any hidden issues?

f. Do you need any further information?

2. Your client, a Canadian charity called the World United Fund, has come to you with a problem. It recently ran a $1 million campaign to get donations to build a school in a poor country. Mrs. Euphemia Welsher promised to give $25,000; when the Fund had the entire $1 million in hand except for Mrs. Welsher's donation, it publicly declared the campaign successfully ended. Mrs. Welsher then told the Fund that she was going to give the money to a home for cats in New York City, where she lives (except for the two months in the summer when she comes to Canada). Your client wants to know if it can sue Mrs. Welsher and get the money she promised to pay.

a. What is the question being asked?

b. What is the area of law?

i. General area

ii. Specific area

iii. What key words helped you identify the area?

c. What is needed? Develop a theory of the case.

d. Formulate the issues

Whether . . .

e. Are there any hidden issues?

f. Do you need any further information?

3. A client has instructed your firm to bring an action for malicious prosecution against the local police. One night last week, he was celebrating his 21st birthday with friends at a suburban strip club. The friends didn't have a lot to drink, but when they became quite lively in the club they were asked to leave. In the parking lot, they talked to each other for a while and then left in their own cars. The client was the last to leave.

   As he was getting into his car, a man suddenly appeared and told him to step away from the car. The client asked the man who he was. The man, who was wearing jeans and a T-shirt, told him that he was a police officer, showed him a police badge, and asked him to accompany him to his car—not a marked police car—which was close by. The man told the client to sit in the back seat while he checked out the client's driver's licence and vehicle licence. He did so using a cell phone.

   The client says that at one point the man said something such as, "A bunch of us are just out here having a good time with Stan. Yeah, he's retiring, and we have to deal with some gang." At another point, the man said, "It's my day off, can't you hurry it up?" The client says he and his friends have never been in trouble with the law, and that he was just getting picked on because he's young, not because he was doing anything wrong. The client was forced to sit in the man's car for about 10 minutes before he was told he could go.

   a. What is the question being asked?

    b. What is the area of law identified by the client?

        i. General area

        ii. Specific area

        iii. What key words helped you identify the area?

    c. Why would you discourage the client from bringing this action?

    d. What different (and more promising) cause of action have you identified?

    e. Formulate the issues

        Whether . . .

    f. Are there any hidden issues?

    g. Do you need any further information?

    h. From a practical point of view, would you advise the client to go ahead with the action you have identified? Why or why not?

CHAPTER 6

How To Research a Subject

After you have analyzed the given fact situation, you will be ready to proceed with your research to find out the law that applies to your client's fact situation.

This chapter discusses the following topics:

- binding law and persuasive law,

- which secondary and primary sources may be useful, and

- performing the research.

BINDING LAW AND PERSUASIVE LAW

When you research, you are looking first for **binding law** in favour of your client, and next for **persuasive law** in favour of your client. You also want to know about binding law and persuasive law that go against your client, so that you understand what opposition you face. Unfavourable case law may be "distinguished" in argument—that is, a lawyer may persuade a judge that the facts in *this* case are so different from those in existing case law that the case law is not applicable.

What Is Binding Law?

Binding law is law that must be followed by a court and includes statute law, regulatory law, and case law.

1. Federally enacted statute law and regulations bind the courts in all provinces; provincially enacted statute law and regulations bind the courts in the province of enactment. Both federal and provincial legislation must meet the requirements of the Canadian constitution (the *British North America Act, 1867*, and the *Constitution Act, 1982*, including the *Charter of Rights and Freedoms*).

2. A **binding decision** is an existing decision in a case that a judge must follow if the facts in that case and in the case before the court are sufficiently similar. The principle that similar cases should be decided in a similar fashion is known as *stare decisis* (Latin for "to stand by those things that have been decided"). Note that the only part of a binding decision that is actually binding is the *ratio decidendi*.

binding law
law that must be followed by a court

persuasive law
law that a court is not required to follow, but may follow if it wishes (usually case law)

binding decision
existing decision that a judge must follow if the facts in that case and in the case before the court are sufficiently similar

stare decisis
Latin for "to stand by those things that have been decided"

obiter dicta
Latin for "words by the way"

3. ***Obiter dicta*** (Latin for "words by the way"—in the singular, *obiter dictum*; whether singular or plural, often referred to simply as "*obiter*") are opinions expressed by a judge in his or her reasons for a decision that did not directly concern the legal issue(s) that had to be decided in the case. *Obiter* is not binding. Note, though, that *obiter* of the Supreme Court of Canada is often treated with great respect and, according to at least one case, may be binding on lower courts.

dissent
different decision by a minority of appeal judges

4. In a case on appeal where there is a majority opinion and a **dissent** (a different decision by a minority of the appeal judges), only the majority *ratio* is binding. (If there is more than one majority opinion, of course there will be more than one *ratio*.) Dissenting opinions have no judicial value, although they sometimes have persuasive value and lead the way for a change in the law, especially when expressed by judges on the Supreme Court of Canada.

Case Law: What Decisions Bind Which Courts?

The theory underlying *stare decisis* is that it is pointless for a judge not to follow a decision of a higher court, because if the judge's decision is appealed, it will be reversed on appeal in accordance with the higher court's existing decision. Obviously, this theory does not apply unless the courts are in the same chain of appeal.

A decision of the *Supreme Court of Canada* binds every court in Canada, but it does not bind the Supreme Court itself. However, the court will not depart from its previous decisions without strong reasons.

Until 1949, a decision of the Supreme Court of Canada could be appealed to the *Privy Council* (P.C.) in Britain. The Privy Council was the House of Lords hearing an appeal from a British colony or former colony, and its decisions bound the Supreme Court of Canada and all Canadian courts below.

A decision of a *provincial Court of Appeal* binds every court and tribunal in that province, but does not bind the Court of Appeal itself, although the Court of Appeal will follow it unless there are good reasons not to. Where there are conflicting Court of Appeal decisions on an issue, lower courts should follow the most recent decision. A Court of Appeal decision is only persuasive outside the court's province.

A decision of the Federal Court of Appeal is binding on the *Federal Court* and the *Tax Court of Canada*, but is limited to the same persuasive value on courts of the provinces as a Court of Appeal decision made by a court outside the province.

A decision of the Federal Court may be persuasive to the *Tax Court of Canada* and to other judges of the Federal Court and of the provinces.

A decision of the *superior court of a province* may be considered binding on the inferior courts (the provincial courts and the small claims courts) of the province. It is not binding on other judges of the superior court but ought to be followed by them in the absence of a compelling reason to the contrary. A superior court decision may be persuasive to judges in other provinces. These are the superior courts of the provinces:

Alberta . . . . Court of Queen's Bench

British Columbia . . . . Supreme Court of British Columbia

Manitoba . . . . Court of Queen's Bench

New Brunswick . . . . Court of Queen's Bench

Newfoundland . . . . Supreme Court (Trial Division)

Nova Scotia . . . . Supreme Court

Ontario . . . . Ontario Superior Court of Justice

In Ontario, until 1984, the superior court was called the Supreme Court of Ontario and its trial division was called the High Court of Justice. From 1984 until 1999, the superior court was called the Ontario Court of Justice (General Division). Cases from the High Court or the Ontario Court of Justice (General Division) have the same binding or persuasive effect as cases from the Ontario Superior Court of Justice.

Saskatchewan . . . . Court of Queen's Bench

Northwest Territories . . . . . Supreme Court for the Northwest Territories

Nunavut . . . . Nunavut Court of Justice

Yukon . . . . Supreme Court

Until recently, there was another court level in many provinces, below the superior court, called the *County Court* or the *District Court*. County or District Court decisions may be considered persuasive in a province's superior court.

Masters are judge-like officers who decide certain procedural matters in the superior court of some provinces. A decision of a master is not binding on judges of any court but is persuasive to other masters.

master
judge-like officer who decides certain procedural matters in the superior court of some provinces

A decision of the *Provincial Court of a province* is not binding on, but is persuasive to, other judges of the Provincial Court.

Decisions from jurisdictions outside Canada, such as the United Kingdom and the United States, are not binding on Canadian courts. Whether they are persuasive depends on the similarity of the law of the foreign jurisdiction to the law in the particular Canadian jurisdiction. Be careful about using modern English cases: some of what is still "common law" in Canada is now statute law in England, and English case law in those areas will not be useful in Canadian courts.

WHICH SECONDARY AND PRIMARY SOURCES MAY BE USEFUL?

Whether you are looking for statute law or case law, it is usually wise to begin your research with a secondary source (either in paper or computerized form). Specific primary and secondary sources are discussed in detail in the chapters that follow.

To begin, look at the following secondary sources:

■ a legal encyclopedia;

■ a text;

- a loose-leaf service (a text that is updated on a continuing basis);

- articles, including conference and seminar materials;

- a digest of cases; or

- an index to statutes or cases;

or speak to a person who is knowledgeable about the particular area of law. Two reasons for taking this approach are: (1) a good legal researcher always lets someone else do the work if possible—you may find that the author of a text has considered the issue and lined up the answer for you already, together with citations of statutes and cases (all you will need to do is update); and (2) a good legal researcher does not focus on the pre-identified issue as quickly as possible, but scans the law in the area generally to check whether the issue has in fact been correctly identified, or if there is another way of looking at the problem to be solved.

PERFORMING THE RESEARCH

Performing the research can be time-consuming and require a lot of concentration. You don't want to do the research more than once if you can avoid it. Follow these guidelines:

Take Notes

As you look through primary and secondary sources, take notes. You should have notes on the following:

1. *Information that seems relevant or interesting*—for example, the citation of a case and a short description of what is useful about the case.

    A sense of *déjà vu* as you look for new information indicates that you have exhausted the topic. Then you must *update* the information. Check for

    a. amendments to a statute or regulation,

    b. interpretation of a statute or regulation in case law,

    c. whether a case was appealed, and

    d. whether a case has been considered by judges in more recent cases and, if so, whether it has been followed or ignored.

2. *The sources you have looked through*—take careful note of the edition or latest date of publication.

    After you have spent an hour or two on a particular text, statute, statute citator, or website, you may think you never will forget that you looked at that source, when you looked at it, or how much of it you looked at. But you will. If you return to research on a subject after two or three weeks, you will not remember exactly which sources you already have covered thoroughly. Noting carefully what you have done and on what date will help you to avoid doing the same research twice.

Review Your Analysis of the Fact Situation

Once you have looked at the law, you may find that the issues you identified on a preliminary basis are not right; you may also find that you need more information from the client or that you have discovered unexpected procedural problems.

If Necessary, Research the Subject Again

If your preliminary identification of the issues was faulty or if you receive new information to add to the fact situation, you may need to re-research the subject.

KEY TERMS

binding decision

binding law

dissent

master

obiter dicta

persuasive law

stare decisis

PART IV

Paper Legal Research Resources

The first question you are likely to have about the part of the book that follows is why is there so much of it? Why do you have to know so many different ways of finding one thing?

It's certainly true that there are usually several ways to find the same answer when you are doing legal research. However, unless you're in a well-equipped law library, such as a library at a big law school or a courthouse library in a large city, you won't have to worry about choosing one among many resources. Law books are expensive, and in many law libraries—in a community college, law firm, or a small courthouse—there is only one tool for finding statutes, one for regulations, and one for cases. That one tool could be any of the possibilities discussed below. So you don't need to know about all of them—just about the ones that are in the law library you use. But since you won't know what resources a law library has until you get there, you need to have an idea about when and how to use all the resources.

CHAPTER 7

An Overview of Paper Sources

The purpose of legal research is to find binding law that is relevant to a legal problem you need to solve. The law that you are looking for will be found in the form of statutes, regulations, and/or cases. These primary sources are not at all user-friendly, and, as we said in Chapter 6, it is usually wise to start your research with secondary sources, using them to gain an understanding of the law and as "finding tools" to direct you to the primary sources that actually create the law.

This chapter begins to examine the process of finding law that is binding, using paper primary and secondary sources. We will start to look at the various legal research sources, according to the purpose they serve or the job that they do, and will discuss the following topics:

- finding tools,

- primary sources,

- updating tools, and

- working with paper sources.

The various sources are discussed more fully in Chapters 8, 9, 10, and 11.

FINDING TOOLS

Generally speaking, you will start your legal research using secondary sources that we call *finding tools*. These tools can be used to help you find

- a general statement of the law,

- specific statutes,

- specific regulations, and

- specific cases.

General Statement of the Law

It is best to start your research by finding a general statement of the law as it applies to the problem to be solved. Secondary sources that provide a general statement of the law include

- legal encyclopedias such as the *Canadian Encyclopedic Digest*,

- textbooks on a particular subject, and

- journal articles on a particular subject.

These sources not only will provide you with a summary of the law, but will refer you to the relevant statutes, regulations, and cases from which the principles of law are derived.

Finding a general statement of the law is discussed in more detail in Chapter 8.

Specific Statutes

There are more specialized sources that are designed specifically to help you find statutes on a particular subject or area of law. These finding tools include a table of statutes or table of public statutes.

Finding statutes is discussed in more detail in Chapter 9.

Specific Regulations

There are also more specialized sources that are designed specifically to help you find regulations on a particular subject or area of law. These finding tools include

- Carswell's *Canada Regulations Index*, and

- Carswell's *Ontario Regulation Service*.

Finding regulations is discussed in more detail in Chapter 10.

Specific Cases

Legal encyclopedias, textbooks, and articles will refer you to only the leading cases on a particular subject. If you want to find additional cases, there are specialized sources designed specifically to help you do so. These finding tools include

- *Canadian Abridgment Case Digests* for cases dealing with specific subjects;

- *Canadian Statute Citations* (*Canadian Abridgment*) or statute citators for cases that interpret sections of statutes;

- *Words and Phrases Judicially Defined in Canadian Courts and Tribunals* (also part of the *Canadian Abridgment*) for cases considering a word or phrase;

- *Consolidated Table of Cases* or the *Canadian Case Citations* (also part of the *Canadian Abridgment*) if you are treasure hunting (in other words, trying to find a case using a partial or incorrect citation); and

- digest services and legal newspapers for unreported cases.

Finding cases is discussed in more detail in Chapter 11.

PRIMARY SOURCES

The finding tools will give you the names of the relevant statutes, regulations, and cases, and sometimes a summary of their provisions. As mentioned in Chapter 1, you cannot rely on secondary sources alone. You may use them to gain an understanding of the law and as finding tools to direct you to the primary sources that actually create the law. You must then look at the primary sources they refer you to, read them, and understand what they say.

Finding the text of statutes is discussed in Chapter 9; finding the text of regulations is discussed in Chapter 10; and finding the text of cases is discussed in Chapter 11.

UPDATING TOOLS

Once you find relevant statutes, regulations, and/or cases, you must make sure that the statutes and regulations you have found have not been amended or repealed and that the cases you have found have not been overturned on appeal or the legal principles in them changed by subsequent cases. You do this using secondary sources that we call *updating tools*.

The following sources will help you update statutes:

- statute citators;
- *Canadian Current Law: Legislation* (part of Carswell's *Canadian Abridgment*); and
- table of public statutes.

These updating tools are discussed more fully in Chapter 9.

The following sources will help you update regulations:

- Ontario Regulation Service or *Canadian Current Law: Legislation* under "Regulations" (Ontario) for Ontario regulations; and
- Canada Regulations Index or *Canadian Current Law: Legislation* under "Regulations" for federal regulations.

These updating tools are discussed more fully in Chapter 10.

The following sources will help you update cases:

- *Consolidated Table of Cases* (part of the *Canadian Abridgment*); and
- *Canadian Case Citations* (part of the *Canadian Abridgment*).

These updating tools are discussed more fully in Chapter 11.

WORKING WITH PAPER SOURCES

As you can see, there are many paper legal research sources available. Before you begin to work with a particular source, you should take some time to become familiar with it. Every source takes a little time to understand. Useful tools for understanding include

- user's guide,
- table of contents, and
- index.

User's Guide

user's guide
information in a research source about how to use that source

Most research sources include a **user's guide** or at least some information about how to use the source. In a single-volume source, the user's guide is usually found at the beginning of the volume. In a multiple-volume source, the user's guide may be found in the first volume of the source or in a separate volume. If you have not used a particular source before, it's a good idea to read the user's guide before you start.

Table of Contents

table of contents
listing of chapters or article titles in a source together with the page numbers where each chapter or article starts

Most research sources contain a **table of contents**, which is a listing of the chapters or article titles in the source in the order in which they appear in the source, along with the page numbers where each chapter or article starts. The table of contents of a single-volume source is usually found at the beginning of the volume, after the title page. Each volume of a multi-volume source, such as an encyclopedia, usually contains a table of contents. In addition, there may be a table of contents for the entire multi-volume source.

A table of contents provides a quick overview of the content and organization of the source. Some tables of contents are quite detailed and provide not only chapter names, but a breakdown of the subjects covered in each chapter, in the order in which they are covered. Reading a detailed table of contents will therefore give you a sense of the major areas of importance in a particular subject and how they fit together.

Index

index
alphabetical, detailed list of names, places, and subjects discussed in a source and the pages on which each entry appears

Most research sources also contain an **index**, which is a detailed list of the names, places, and subjects discussed in the source and the pages on which each entry appears, in alphabetical order. The index of a single-volume source is usually found at the end of the volume. Each volume of a multi-volume source, such as an encyclopedia, usually contains an index. In addition, there may be an index for the entire multi-volume source.

An index provides more detailed information about the contents of the source than the table of contents does. It is designed to help the reader quickly find information about a specific topic or concept in all of its locations throughout the source, not to give the reader an overview of what the source contains.

Table of Contents or Index?

If you are looking for information on a particular subject, start by looking at the table of contents. If there is a chapter dealing with your subject, turn to it. If the subject you are looking for is not listed in the table of contents, then look for the subject in the index. Even if the subject you are looking for is in the table of contents, you should also use the index if you are looking for specific, detailed information on a subject.

Working with Multi-volume Sources

If you are working with a multi-volume source, such as an encyclopedia, take some time to see how the volumes are organized. Generally, topics will be dealt with alphabetically across the entire source, with each volume dealing with topics starting with a particular letter (or letters) of the alphabet.

KEY TERMS

index

table of contents

user's guide

CHAPTER 8

Finding a General Statement of the Law: The Canadian Encyclopedic Digest

It is usually wise to start your research with secondary sources, using them to gain an understanding of the law and as finding tools to direct you to the primary sources that actually create the law. It is best to start your research by finding a general statement of the law as it applies to the legal problem you need to solve. Secondary sources that provide a general statement of the law include

- legal encyclopedias,

- textbooks on a particular subject, and

- journal articles on a particular subject.

These sources not only will provide you with a summary of the law, but will refer you to the relevant statutes, regulations, and cases from which the principles of law are derived.

This chapter deals with the only Canadian legal encyclopedia—the *Canadian Encyclopedic Digest* or CED. The CED is available in both print and computerized versions. This chapter focuses on the print version only. The computerized version of the CED is discussed in Chapter 14.

WHAT IS THE CED?

The CED is one of the most comprehensive secondary sources dealing with Canadian law. It is a loose-leaf multi-volume legal encyclopedia that provides a very general overview of most areas of law. The CED is an excellent place to begin when you know very little about the area of law that you are researching. In the print version, there are two editions of the CED. The Ontario edition focuses on Ontario and federal laws. The western edition focuses on the law in the four western provinces—Manitoba, Saskatchewan, Alberta, and British Columbia.

THE CED VOLUMES

The CED is made up of over 150 subject titles contained in approximately 40 loose-leaf binders. The subject titles are broad topics of information or general areas of law, such as animals, contracts, evidence, or income tax. The spine of each CED volume sets out the volume number and the alphabetical range of subject titles contained in that volume. Each binder is given a volume number and is organized alphabetically by subject title.

Each subject title contains parts, sections, subsections, and sub-subsections, breaking the title down into increasingly more topic-specific areas of information. By narrowing down your research problem within the relevant subject title, you can find the general statement of law dealing with your particular topic.

At the beginning of each subject title there is a table of contents to help you find the specific topic within that subject that you would like to research. There is also a subject index at the end of each title that refers you to relevant paragraph numbers within that subject title.

Each subject title is given a name and a title number. Each subject title is then divided into parts that are given both a number (in uppercase roman numerals) and a name. Each part is divided into sections that are given both a number and a name. Each section may be further divided into headings (subtopics) that are given a letter and a name. Each heading may be further divided into subheadings that are given a number (lowercase roman numerals) and a name. Each section is divided into numbered paragraphs (not named) that provide the summary of the law, together with references to relevant cases and statutes.

The CED is updated regularly with supplemental sheets, found at the front of each subject title (printed on yellow or grey-edged paper). The supplemental sheets update case and statute references as well as other significant developments that have occurred since the publication date of the subject title. The paragraph numbers in the supplement correspond to the paragraph numbers in the main body of the text.

FINDING TOOLS

There are two separate finding tools to help you look for information in the CED:

- the Research Guide and Key, and

- the Index Key.

Research Guide and Key

The Research Guide and Key helps you find information in all the titles. It is found in a separate binder and contains three keys:

- the Contents Key,

- the Statutes Key, and

- the Rules and Regulations Key.

CONTENTS KEY

The **Contents Key** provides a list, in alphabetical order, of all the subject titles in the CED. It gives both the title number of the subject title and the volume number in which the subject title can be found.

STATUTES KEY

The **Statutes Key** provides a list, in alphabetical order, of all current federal and provincial statutes referred to in the various subject titles of the CED. It also provides the volume number, title number, and paragraph numbers where specific provisions of the statute are discussed or referred to.

RULES AND REGULATIONS KEY

The **Rules and Regulations Key** provides a list, in alphabetical order, of the rules of court (rules of civil procedure) and regulations referred to in the CED's subject titles. It also provides a reference to the relevant volume and paragraph numbers.

Index Key

The **Index Key** is a separate binder containing an alphabetical list of keywords, together with extensive cross-references within and among subject titles. It combines the individual indexes from all the titles.

The Index Key is the best place to start when you do not know what subject title your research topic falls under. By looking up keywords dealing with your research problem, you can easily find the relevant subject title. By looking under specific topics within the relevant subject title, you will be referred to the volume, title, and paragraph number that provides a general statement of law on your specific topic.

As we mentioned above, there is also a table of contents at the beginning of each subject title, as well as a subject index at the end of each subject title. Both provide yet another way to find increasingly more specific information on your research topic.

How To Use the CED

The approach you take with the CED will depend on whether you know the area of law that deals with the problem to be solved.

If you know your area of law:

1. Choose the volume that contains the appropriate subject title.

2. Look at the table of contents at the beginning of the title, or look at the index at the end of the title. Either will refer you to a paragraph number.

3. Find the useful paragraphs and read about your topic. It's usually a good idea to at least skim the entire section.

4. Write down what the law is and note which cases or statutes are referred to.

5. Update each relevant paragraph by looking at the supplemental sheets at the front of the title.

Contents Key
alphabetical list of all the subject titles in the CED

Statutes Key
alphabetical list of all current federal and provincial statutes referred to in the various subject titles in the CED

Rules and Regulations Key
alphabetical list of the rules of court and regulations referred to in the subject titles in the CED

Index Key
separate binder combining the individual indexes from all the titles and containing an alphabetical list of keywords, together with extensive cross-references within and among subject titles in the CED

If you don't know the area of law, use the Index Key, which combines the individual subject indexes from all the titles. This general index will refer you to a volume number, title number, and paragraph number.

Below we go into more detail about using the CED when you do and when you don't know your area of law.

AN EXAMPLE

The best way to learn how to use the CED is to work through an example. Assume that you have received a memo from a lawyer in your law firm that reads as follows:

> Our client in Toronto, Ontario has a cocker spaniel that barks constantly. One day last month, her neighbour went to her apartment to complain. When our client opened the door, the dog rushed out to attack the neighbour, who fell backwards and broke his leg. The neighbour is now suing your client for the injuries caused by the dog. Can our client be held legally responsible?

In order to advise your client, you will need to find a general statement of the law dealing with the issue whether a dog owner is responsible for the injuries caused by his or her dog.

Finding Your Topic When You Don't Know the Area of Law

If you do not know which area of law to look in, go to the Index Key. Find the relevant subject title by looking up keywords dealing with your problem. For example, if you look up the word "Dogs," you will be referred to the relevant subject title: "ANIMALS." See figure 8.1, which reproduces the relevant page of the Index Key.

Next, look in the Index Key for the heading "ANIMALS"; then look for your specific topic, in this case "Liability for Injuries Inflicted by Dogs" (under Part IX. Dogs). The entry refers you to the volume number, title number, and paragraph numbers for the specific topics under this general heading. See figure 8.2, which reproduces the relevant page of the Index Key dealing with "ANIMALS." Note that for information on "Dog Owners' Liability" under "Ontario" you are referred to 1A-6§388. These numbers tell you that the summary or general statement of the law on your research topic can be found in volume 1A of the CED, under subject title number 6 in paragraph number 388.

Finding Your Topic When You Know the Area of Law

If you already know something about this area of law, including the relevant subject title, you can start your research by looking at the List of Titles (in the Research Guide and Key) to find the relevant volume number and subject title for your specific topic. The relevant page of the List of Titles is reproduced in figure 8.3. The List of Titles tells you that "ANIMALS" is subject title number 6 and can be found in volume 1A of the CED.

Figure 8.1 CED General Index Key Showing "Dogs"

DIVORCE AND NULLITY VIII.3

3. Jurisdiction And Procedure . . . . .9–49§635
4. Commencement of Proceedings . . . . .9–49§638
5. Grounds For Declaration Of Nullity .9–49§639
   (a) Absence of Required Formalities . . . . .9–49§639
      (i) Provincial Competence in Solemnization of Marriage . . . . .9–49§639
      (ii) Effect of Non-Compliance with Statutory Formalities . . . . .9–49§641
      (iii) Requirement of Parental Consent for Minors . . . . .9–49§643
   (b) Absence of Capacity to Marry . . . . .9–49§645
      (i) Absence of Basic Biological Constitution . . . . . . .9–49§645
      (ii) Prior Subsisting Marriage . . . . .9–49§649
         A. General . . . . . . .9–49§649
         B. Remarriage Before Decree Effective . . . . . . .9–49§650
         C. Unrecognized Foreign Divorce . . . . .9–49§651
         D. Death or Disappearance of Former Spouse . . .9–49§652
         E. Proof of Prior Marriage or Divorce . . . . .9–49§654
      (iii) Prohibited Degrees of Consanguinity . . . . . .9–49§657
   (c) Absence of Freedom of Consent . . . . .9–49§658
      (i) General . . . . .9–49§658
      (ii) Insanity and Intoxication . . . . .9–49§659
      (iii) Duress . . . . .9–49§661
      (iv) Fraud and Mistake . . . . .9–49§663
      (v) Limited Purpose Marriages . . . . .9–49§665
   (d) Impotence . . . . .9–49§666
      (i) Definition and Elements of Impotence . . . . .9–49§666
      (ii) Refusal to Consummate . . . . .9–49§669
      (iii) Refusal to Undergo Medical Examination or Treatment . . . . .9–49§670
      (iv) Onus of Proof. . . .9–49§672
      (v) Plaintiff Pleading Own Impotence . . . . .9–49§673
      (vi) Bars to Decree Based on Impotence . . . . .9–49§674
         A. Delay and Approbation . . . . .9–49§674
         B. Insincerity . . . . .9–49§676
         C. Miscellaneous Bars . . . . .9–49§678
6. Decree of Nullity . . . . . . .9–49§680
   (a) Nature and Form of Decree . . . . .9–49§680
   (b) Effect of Decree . . . . .9–49§682
   (c) Alimony and Maintenance . . . . .9–49§684
   (d) Actions Arising Out of Invalid Marriages . . . . .9–49§686

DOCKS

See Shipping

DOCTORS

See Hospitals and Health Care; Negligence

DOCUMENTS

See Contracts; Deeds and Documents; Discovery; Evidence; Internet Law; Real Property; Sale of Land; Wills

DOGS

See Agriculture; Animals; Municipal Corporations; Negligence

248

Figure 8.2 CED Index Key Showing Topic "Liability for Injuries Inflicted by Dogs—Ontario—Dog Owners' Liability" (Under Part IX. Dogs)

ANIMALS VI.6(f)

22

Figure 8.3   CED List of Titles for Subject Title "Animals"

LIST OF TITLES

The following is a list of the subject titles in CED (Ont. 3rd), showing the volumes in which they appear and their respective title numbers.

Subject Title		Volume
1.	Absentees (4th Ed.)	1
1.1.	Access to Information and Protection of Privacy	1
2.	Actions (4th Ed.)	1
3.	Administrative Law	1
4.	Agency	1
5.	Agriculture	1A
6.	Animals (4th Ed.)	1A
7.	Annuities	1A
8.	Arbitration (4th Ed.)	1A
9.	Armed Forces	1A
10.	Associations and Not-for-Profit Corporations (4th Ed.)	1A
11.	Auctions	1A
12.	Aviation and Air Law	1A
13.	Bailment (4th Ed.)	2
14.	Banking	2
15.	Bankruptcy and Insolvency	2
16.	Barristers and Solicitors	3
17.	Bills of Exchange	3
18.	Bills of Sale	3
19.	Boundaries and Surveys (4th Ed.)	3
20.	Building Contracts (4th Ed.)	3
21.	Bulk Sales	3
22.	Burial and Cremation (4th Ed.)	3
23.	Carriers (4th Ed.)	4
24.	Charities	4
26.	Churches and Religious Institutions	4
27.01.	Companies' Creditors Arrangement Act (4th Ed.)	4
27.1	Condominiums (4th Ed.)	4A
28.	Conflict of Laws	4A
29.	Conspiracy (4th Ed.)	4A
30.	Constitutional Law (4th Ed.)	4A

April 2009

Alternatively, you can simply refer to the spine of the CED volumes to find the volume that contains your subject title. Each volume provides the volume number and the alphabetical range of subject titles contained in that volume. Once you find the right volume, you can simply refer to the tab that has your subject title name on it. To find more specific information within the title, use the table of classification found at the beginning of the subject title or the subject index found at the end of the title.

The table of classification breaks down the subject title into increasingly more topic-specific information, by dividing the title first into parts that are given both a number (uppercase roman numerals) and a name, and then into sections that are given both a number and a name. Sections may be further divided into headings (subtopics) that are given a letter (a, b, c) and a name, which may be further divided into subheadings that are given a number (lowercase roman numerals) and a name. Each section is divided into numbered paragraphs (not named) that provide the summary of the law. Figure 8.4 reproduces part of the table of classification for the subject title "ANIMALS."

The following table illustrates how the research topic in this problem is broken down within the subject title "ANIMALS."

	Number	**Name**
Subject title	6	ANIMALS
Part	IX	Dogs
Section	5	Liability for Injuries Inflicted by Dogs
Heading	(j)	Ontario
Subheading	(i)	Dog Owners' Liability
Paragraph	§388	

The subject index at the end of the title breaks down general topics into more specific topics using keywords and phrases, and refers you to the relevant paragraph numbers within the title that contain the general statement of law on your research topic. Figure 8.5 reproduces part of the subject index for the title "ANIMALS." Note that the subject index directs you to paragraphs 388 and 389 for general information about "injuries by dogs (Ontario)."

Finding and Reading the Text

Once you have identified your specific topic using one of the finding tools discussed above, read the relevant paragraph(s). In our example, we have been directed to paragraphs 388 and 389 of subject title 6 ("ANIMALS") in volume 1A of the CED. Those paragraphs are reproduced in figure 8.6.

Note how the paragraphs themselves contain a statement of the law. Paragraph 388 contains footnotes referring to the *Dog Owners' Liability Act*, the statute from which the statement of the law in that paragraph is drawn. Paragraph 389 also contains footnotes referring to cases from which the statement of the law in that paragraph is drawn.

Note also how the CED includes a cross-reference to the *Canadian Abridgment*. The *Canadian Abridgment* is discussed in Chapter 11.

Figure 8.4 CED Table of Classification for Subject Title "Animals" (1 of 2 pages)

ANIMALS

CED (4th) 6

Figure 8.4 CED Table of Classification for Subject Title "Animals" (2 of 2 pages)

TABLE OF CLASSIFICATION

(i) Dog Owners' Liability . . . . . §367
(ii) Seizure of Dangerous Dogs . . . . . §371
(h) Manitoba . . . . . §376
(i) Saskatchewan . . . . . §382
(j) Ontario . . . . . §388
(i) Dog Owners' Liability . . . . . §388
(ii) Search and Seizure . . . . . §398
(iii) Pit Bulls . . . . . §406
(iv) Protection of Livestock and Poultry . . . . . §418
6. Killing of Dogs . . . . . §421

X. Liability Regarding Animals . . . . . §435
1. General . . . . . §435
2. Negligence . . . . . §438
(a) General . . . . . §438
(b) Measure of Damages . . . . . §447
3. Scienter . . . . . §450
(a) General . . . . . §450
(b) Statutory Modification . . . . . §458
4. Trespass or Running at Large . . . . . §459
(a) Liability at Common Law . . . . . §459
(b) Driving Away Trespassing Animals . . . . . §467
(c) Defences . . . . . §470
(d) Measure of Damages . . . . . §472
(e) Apportionment of Liability . . . . . §475
(f) Distress Damage Feasant . . . . . §480
5. Animals on Highway . . . . . §492
(a) General . . . . . §492
(b) Rights and Duties of Animal Owners . . . . . §503
(c) Obligations of Motorists . . . . . §507
6. Wild Animals . . . . . §511
7. Injuries to Trespassers . . . . . §516

XI. Stray Animals . . . . . §518
1. General . . . . . §518
2. Alberta . . . . . §520

7 October 2008

Figure 8.5   CED Subject Index for Subject Title "Animals"

ANIMALS

- occupiers' liability (Alberta), 366
- police dogs, 353
- trespassing cattle, driving off, 354
- volenti non fit injuria, 355

injuries by dogs (Ontario)
- control orders, 393, 396
- damages, measure of, 389
- destruction orders, 392, 394, 396
- general, 388, 389
- "harbouring", 390
- livestock/poultry, 418–420
- occupiers' liability, 391
- offence, 388, 397
- "owner", 390
- pitbulls, 406–417
- proceedings re, 392, 393
- prohibition against owner, 395
- search/seizure, 398–405

injuries by dogs (parties liable), 339

injuries by dogs (Saskatchewan)
- fine not barring action, 384
- general, 382, 383, 386
- offence, 385
- police dogs, 387
- "protected animal", 382

injuries by dogs (scienter)
- Alberta, 365, 366
- British Columbia, 367
- barking at horses, 344
- elements of scienter, 340
- evidence of ferocious/savage nature, 341
- Manitoba, 376
- nuisance/negligence, effect of, 347
- running at large, 345
- sufficiency of precautions, 343

- volenti, 342, 343
- warning to strangers, sufficiency, 342

injuries by dogs (statutory remedies)
- British Columbia, 296, 370
- Manitoba, 348, 377–381
- Ontario, 349, 388–420
- Saskatchewan, 382–387

injuries by dogs (trespassers), 516, 517

injuries to animals, *see also* offences; prevention of cruelty
- apportionment of liability, 476, 478
- bailment situations, 31–47
- carriage of animals, 64–66
- cattle, 502
- damages, 448, 449
- defences, 471
- dogs, 46, 47, 296, 466, 476, 478
- highways, on or near, 499–501
- horses, 31–45, 64, 65
- livestock/poultry (Ontario), 418–420
- negligence by, 31, 35–37, 65, 499
- noise, 446
- overdriving, 38
- Saskatchewan, 382–387
- statutory compensation, 370
- trespassing animals, 354, 467–469, 471
- wrongful killing, 13, 432

inspections, *see* diseased animals; sale of animals

insurance, 26, 27, 28, 29, 359, 360

kennels, *see also* dogs
- Alberta, 293

CED (4th)   288

Figure 8.6   CED Volume 1A Showing Paragraphs That Contain the General Statement of the Law

PART IX — DOGS   §389

action substantive matter conferring vested rights; Rural Municipality Act, s. 222, not applying to actions arising before its enactment); *Gaudry v. Binning* (1996), 149 Sask. R. 250 (Sask. Q.B.) (under Urban Municipality Act, s. 135.6).

§387 A police officer is not negligent in using a police dog to take down a suspect if the level of force used is justified.[1]

  1 *Arnault v. Prince Albert (City) Police Commissioner* (1995), [1996] 4 W.W.R. 38 (Sask. Q.B.) (officer and dog pursuing suspect from break and enter where gun reported stolen; suspect acting in manner indicative of taking drugs; suspect twice warned to stop but continuing to run; suspect taken down by dog three times before being arrested; officer not negligent considering that theft of firearm reported; level of force used justified).

(j) — Ontario

(i) — Dog Owners' Liability

See Canadian Abridgment: TOR.XVI.10.a.iii Torts — Negligence — Liability of owner or possessor of animals — Injury by domestic animals — Injury by dog

§388 A dog owner must exercise reasonable precautions to prevent it from biting or attacking a person or domestic animal, or behaving in a manner that poses a menace to the safety of persons or domestic animals.[1] Failure to do so is an offence[2] and also exposes the owner to civil liability.[3]

  1 Dog Owners' Liability Act, R.S.O. 1990, c. D.16, s. 5.1 [en. 2005, c. 2, s. 1(15)].
  2 Dog Owners' Liability Act, R.S.O. 1990, c. D.16, s. 18 [en. 2005, c. 2, s. 1(16)]; **see also** §397.
  3 Dog Owners' Liability Act, R.S.O. 1990, c. D.16, s. 2.

§389 A dog's owner is liable for damages resulting from a bite or attack by the dog on another person or domestic animal.[1] Liability does not depend on knowledge of the propensity of the dog or fault or negligence on the part of the owner.[2] However, the court must reduce the damages awarded in proportion to the degree, if any, to which the plaintiff's fault or negligence caused or contributed to the damages.[3] An owner who is liable to pay damages is entitled to recover contribution and indemnity from any other person in proportion to the degree, if any, to which the other person's fault or negligence caused or contributed to the damages.[4]

  1 Dog Owners' Liability Act, R.S.O. 1990, c. D.16, s. 2(1); *Strom (Litigation Guardian of) v. White* (1994), 21 O.R. (3d) 205 (Ont. Gen. Div.) (general damages of $22,000 and special damages of $4,968 for

187   October 2008

Updating Your Research

As a final step, you must update your research by checking the relevant paragraph numbers in the supplemental pages found at the front of the subject title you are researching. If a paragraph is not mentioned, it means that there has been no change in the law as set out in that paragraph.

KEY TERMS

Contents Key

Index Key

Rules and Regulations Key

Statutes Key

CHAPTER 9

Finding and Updating Statutes

When you start to research a legal issue, the first thing you have to do is find out if there is a statute that is relevant to the issue. In Chapter 8 we saw that you may be able to find this out by looking in the *Canadian Encyclopedic Digest*, and there are other finding tools that we'll talk about in this chapter. Once you determine that there is a statute relevant to your problem, you also have to be able to locate the text of that statute.

This chapter discusses the following topics:

- how statutes are published,

- finding tools for statutes,

- finding the text of a statute,

- updating statutes, and

- legislative history and concording a statute.

HOW STATUTES ARE PUBLISHED

It is helpful to understand how statutes are published, in order to find the name of a statute that deals with the legal problem you have to solve, and then to find the text of that statute.

Acts passed by Parliament or by the provincial legislatures in any year are collected in a series for that year. They appear in a bound annual volume that is designated by year—for example, S.C. 1992 (*Statutes of Canada, 1992*) contains only statutes passed in 1992. Statutes are given chapter numbers in the volume according to the order in which they were passed in that particular year.

The federal statutes and some provincial statutes are revised every number of years. Producing a set of revised statutes means collecting all the statutes that are in force at the date of the revision and publishing them in a format that incorporates any amendments that have been made to each statute since the previous revision.

The most recent federal revision was in 1985; the one before that was in 1970. Until recently, Ontario statutes were revised every 10 years. However, the most recent revision of Ontario statutes was published in 1990. The current trend is to consolidate statutes (by incorporating subsequent amendments) on a continuing basis rather than to revise them at regular intervals. This has become possible in the last few years because governments are now able to maintain statutes by computer and publish them in computerized format on their websites.

FINDING TOOLS FOR STATUTES

Often the challenge of dealing with statute law is not locating the text of the statute itself, but finding out whether there is a statute on the subject you are researching. There are several different ways of finding whether a relevant statute exists. You can

- ask someone,

- look for a statute directly,

- work from the general to the specific, or

- use a provincial case report series.

Each of these methods is discussed below.

Ask Someone

This is an obvious but frequently overlooked answer. Ask a lawyer who has experience in the subject area, or a law librarian.

Look for a Statute Directly

Revised statute series and consolidated statutes have index volumes, arranged by subject matter, that may be useful; however, note that index volumes are often out of date or have disappeared from the shelf because someone else is using them.

If you cannot locate an index volume, look through the table of statutes or table of public statutes of the revised or consolidated statutes for the name of a statute that looks relevant. If you suspect that you may be dealing with a statute passed since the last revision occurred or before the consolidation has been updated, look through the table of public statutes at the end of the most recent annual volume of statutes. Be very careful when relying on this method alone to find relevant statutes. Often, the names of the statute can be misleading. You may not be able to find a statute that is relevant to your particular problem, or you may find a statute whose name sounds like it is relevant to your particular research topic, but, in fact, is not. For example, if you are researching a question about adoption, you might expect to find a statute called the *Adoption Act*, but there is no such statute. Adoption is dealt with under a statute called the *Child and Family Services Act*, the name of which offers no hint that it deals with adoption.

For new statutes, you will need to use an "index to current bills" in order to locate bills that have been enacted recently. For federal and provincial bills, use *Canadian Current Law: Legislation*, "Progress of Bills." For federal bills only, you can instead check the *Canada Legislative Index* under the "Titles Index." For Ontario only, look at the *Ontario Legislative Digest Service* under "Acts Affected." You can also find the status of current bills using the statute citators.

Work from the General to the Specific

Instead of starting with statutes, find information on the general subject in which you are interested in

- a text,

- an encyclopedia entry, or

- an article.

If a statute figures prominently in the area, the source you are using almost certainly will mention it. A table of statutes is sometimes all you need and is usually found at the front of the text or encyclopedia entry.

The *Canadian Encyclopedic Digest* (CED, discussed in Chapter 8) is an excellent research tool, perhaps the best tool for finding relevant statutes. Once you find the general statement of law dealing with your particular topic, the CED will refer you to the relevant statute governing that area of law, if there is one.

You also can look for articles in the bibliography contained at the front of *some* titles of the CED. They are usually arranged in reverse chronological order—that is, the most recent titles appear first. Conference and seminar materials, which are collections of articles on a single topic, may be more useful to you than an isolated journal article.

NOTE: Do not look for articles until you have looked at a text or an encyclopedia entry. Articles usually have a narrow focus—make sure you know that you want a particular, narrow focus before you spend the time.

Use a Provincial Case Report Series

If you are in a hurry and resources are limited—for example, if you work in a small law office with a meagre library—you might look in the index of your provincial case report series, such as the *Ontario Reports*, or in the index of the *Dominion Law Reports*, under the subject that interests you. Look at the case digests under the subject heading; if a statute figures prominently in the area, it likely will be mentioned in a case digest.

FINDING THE TEXT OF A STATUTE

Once you find the name of the statute that deals with your research problem, you will need to find the text of that statute, and, in particular, the section or sections of the statute that apply to your situation. To do this, it is helpful to understand both how statutes are published (see above) and statutory citations.

Statutory Citations

The citation of a statute gives you essential information about the statute, including where to find it. A citation is made up of the following four components:

| 1 | 2 | 3 | 4 |

Business Corporations Act,   R.S.O. 1990,   c. B.16,   s. 2

1. NAME OF THE STATUTE

The short title of the statute is used, omitting the word "the." (The short title is usually found at the end of the statute and is prefaced by the words "this act may be cited as.") The name of the statute is italicized and is followed by a comma.

2. VOLUME TITLE ABBREVIATION

This tells you the name of the statute series in which the statute appears, including the year of publication. It is followed by a comma. Statutes are published in either an annual volume or a revised series of volumes. Annual volumes are abbreviated as

- S.C. (Statutes of Canada), and
- S.O. (Statutes of Ontario).

Revised volumes are abbreviated as

- R.S.C. (Revised Statutes of Canada), and
- R.S.O. (Revised Statutes of Ontario).

In the citation in the example above, the statute is shown as being published in the Revised Statutes of Ontario, 1990 revision.

The following are some additional examples of volume title abbreviations:

- S.C. 1989 (Statutes of Canada for 1989)
- S.O. 1993 (Statutes of Ontario for 1993)
- R.S.C. 1985 (Revised Statutes of Canada, 1985 revision)
- R.S.O. 1990 (Revised Statutes of Ontario, 1990 revision)

3. CHAPTER NUMBER

The chapter number tells you the specific number assigned to the statute in the volume. It is followed by a comma. In annual statute volumes, the statutes are put in alphabetical order and then numbered from 1 onward, using numbers only—for example, c. 46. In revised statute volumes, the statutes are put in alphabetical order and then numbered using an alphanumeric—for example, c. A.10, c. B-16, or c. C.32. The uppercase letter in an alphanumeric chapter number is drawn from the title of the statute. So in "c. C.32," the uppercase "C," part of the alphanumeric, means that the statute name begins with the letter "C"; the lowercase "c" just means "chapter number."

In the citation in the example above, the "B" is drawn from the *Business Corporations Act.* Revised Ontario statutes use a period in the alphanumeric (c. A.10). Revised federal statutes use a hyphen in the alphanumeric (c. B-16).

4. SECTION NUMBER

The section number tells you which section number or numbers in the Act are being referred to. The abbreviation "s." stands for section. The abbreviation "ss." stands for sections.

If a statute has been amended, the citation is slightly different. The original statute is cited first, followed by the words "as am. by," and then the citation of the amending statute. The name of the amending statute is included only if it is different from that of the original statute. For example, *Employment Standards Act*, R.S.O. 1990, c. E.14, as am. by S.O. 1991, c. 16 and S.O. 1991, c. 43, s. 2.

Sometimes a statute is amended to add new sections. Sections that have been added to the statute by amendment and before the statute series has been revised are squeezed into existing sections by adding .1, .2, and so on to the immediately preceding section or subsection number. For example, *Regulated Health Professions Act, 1991*, S.O. 1991, c. 18, as am. by S.O. 1993, c. 37, s. 43.1.

Using the Statutory Citation To Find the Text of the Statute

The statutory citation gives you the information you need to find the text of the statute in the official provincial or federal annual or revised statute volumes.

The volume title abbreviation will direct you to either the revised statute volumes or the annual statute volumes.

If you are directed to the revised statute volumes, remember that all the statutes are organized in alphabetical order and divided into volumes. Look on the spine of the various volumes until you find the volume containing the alphanumeric chapter number of your statute.

If you are directed to the annual volumes, look for the volume or volumes for the year indicated in the volume title abbreviation. The statutes for that year will be organized in alphabetical order. If there is more than one volume for the year, look on the spine of the various volumes until you find the volume containing the numeric chapter number of your statute.

Where Else Can You Find the Text of the Statute?

The statutory citation tells you where to find the statute in the annual volumes or revised volumes. However, there are additional sources for and editions of statutes. These include

- consolidated versions,

- annotated versions, and

- office consolidations.

Choose the one that is most recent to shorten your updating time.

Consolidated versions and annotated versions of important statutes are published by commercial legal publishers, often annually. If you can find the statute edition for the present year, it will shorten the work involved in checking for amendments. These commercial editions of statutes are not the "official" version of the statute (the official text is contained only in the revised statutes or annual statute volumes and, in some cases, the consolidated statutes), but are usually reliable. If you are researching a statute that will be relied on in court, use the revised statutes for the text, plus the annual volumes of statutes for the text of amendments.

Canada and most provinces publish office consolidations of some or all of their statutes. An office consolidation of a statute sets out the text of the statute as amended (that is, with provisions of the statute either changed or "repealed," which means deleted) to the date of printing. An office consolidation is usually not the authoritative version of the statute, although it is useful for research. If you are researching a statute that will be relied on in court, use the revised statutes for the text in addition to the annual volumes of statutes for the text of amendments.

Finding the Text of Bills and Recent Statutes

bills
proposed statutes that are before Parliament or a provincial legislature but have not yet been passed

Proposed statutes that are before Parliament or a provincial legislature but have not yet been passed are called **bills**. The text of federal bills is available through the federal bills subscription service; the text of provincial bills is usually available through the various provincial bills subscription services. You can find federal bills and the bills of your own province in most provincial law libraries; many law firms subscribe to the provincial bills service.

Statutes may have come into existence through receiving royal assent, but may not yet have been bound into an annual volume of statutes. In that case, you'll have to go to another source. Federal statutes are published initially in the *Canada Gazette Part III*. Provincial statutes are initially available in provincial bills subscription services (such as the *Ontario Statute Citator Current Bills Service*), which can be found in most law libraries and in many law firms.

UPDATING STATUTES

Once you've found the text of a statute, you have to update the statute to find out whether any part of it has been amended. If you're dealing with a recently enacted statute, you may also need to find out whether it has actually come into effect—that is, been "proclaimed in force." Some statutes that have received royal assent sit on the books for a while before anyone has to obey them.

Updating Federal Statutes

Start with the most recent version of the statute that you can find—a government-published office consolidation or a privately published consolidated or annotated version of the statute in question. If a consolidated version is not available, start with the *Revised Statutes of Canada, 1985* and supplements, or the annual volumes of the *Statutes of Canada*, depending on the date of the statute. Note that R.S.C. 1985 did not come into force until December 12, 1988; the supplements contain legislation passed between 1985 and 1988. The annual volumes contain legislation passed since 1988.

For amendments, check one of the following sources:

- *Canada Statute Citator,*
- *Canadian Current Law: Legislation,* or
- table of public statutes.

The *Canada Statute Citator* is a loose-leaf service published by Canada Law Book, organized alphabetically by statute short title. It gives the full citations of all statutes in R.S.C. 1985 and later statutes to date, and sets out the text of all amendments to those statutes. Check under the individual statute and in the "Monthly Bulletin" (the green pages at the front).

Canadian Current Law: Legislation is part of Carswell's *Canadian Abridgment.* Check under "Statutes Amended, Repealed or Proclaimed in Force." Note that *Canadian Current Law: Legislation* has been published only since 1989–90, and it does not provide a cumulative overview of amendments. If you are looking for more than the most recent amendments, you will have to go through each annual volume as well as the pamphlets, which are published regularly throughout the year.

If neither of the above is available, look in the table of public statutes in the most recent annual volume of the *Statutes of Canada,* update with the cumulative table in *Canada Gazette Part III,* and then with individual issues of *Canada Gazette Part III* published since the date of the cumulative table.

A federal statute that has received royal assent, including a statute that amends another statute, has no official authority until it has been proclaimed in force. For proclamation dates of new statutes or amending statutes, check the proposed date of proclamation in force in the statute itself (usually at the end of the statute); the actual date of proclamation in force in *Canadian Current Law: Legislation,* under "Statutes Amended, Repealed or Proclaimed in Force" in the *Canada Statute Citator* under individual statutes; and in the "Monthly Bulletin" (the green pages at the front). You may also look in the latest annual volume of the *Statutes of Canada* in the "Proclamations of Canada" tables, but this approach will require more work to update.

For proclamations more recent than the date of whichever source you are using, look in the table of proclamations either in *Canada Gazette Part III* or in the quarterly index of *Canada Gazette Part I.* For the most recent information on proclamations, check individual issues of *Canada Gazette Part I,* where they are announced.

Updating Ontario Statutes

Start with the most recent version of the statute that you can find—a government-published office consolidation or a privately published consolidated or annotated version of the statute in question. If a consolidated version is not available, start with the *Revised Statutes of Ontario, 1990,* or the annual volumes of the *Statutes of Ontario,* depending on the date of the statute.

For amendments, check one of the following sources:

- *Ontario Statute Citator,*
- *Canadian Current Law: Legislation,* or
- table of public statutes.

The *Ontario Statute Citator* is a loose-leaf service published by Canada Law Book organized alphabetically by statute short title. It gives the full citations of all statutes in R.S.O. 1990 and later statutes to date, and sets out the text of all amendments to those statutes. Use the *Ontario Statute Citator* to check for amendments. Note the useful "Consequential Amendments to Acts" heading in the pink "Weekly Bulletin Service."

Canadian Current Law: Legislation is part of Carswell's *Canadian Abridgment*. Check under "Statutes Amended, Repealed or Proclaimed in Force" under Ontario. Note that *Canadian Current Law: Legislation* has been published only since 1989–90 and it does not provide a cumulative overview of amendments. If you are looking for more than the most recent amendments, you will have to go through each annual volume, as well as through the pamphlets.

If you do not have access to *Canadian Current Law: Legislation* or to the *Ontario Statute Citator*, you can look for amendments in the table of public statutes in the most recent annual volume of the *Statutes of Ontario*. You must then update by checking for new and amending statutes since the date of the annual volume in the *Ontario Statute Citator Current Bills Service*.

A provincial statute has no official authority until it has been proclaimed in force. For proclamation in force dates of new statutes and amendments, look for the proposed date of proclamation in the statute itself, and for the actual date of proclamation in any of the following sources:

- *Canadian Current Law: Legislation* under "Statutes Amended, Repealed or Proclaimed in Force" (Ontario);

- the *CCH Provincial Legislative Record*, under Ontario;

- the *Ontario Legislative Digest*;

- the *Ontario Statute Citator*—the pink "Weekly Bulletin Service" pages at the front of the volume; or

- individual issues of the *Ontario Gazette*.

LEGISLATIVE HISTORY AND CONCORDING A STATUTE

In successive revisions of the statutes of Canada or of a province, the same statute may appear under a different chapter number and the same statutory provision may appear under a different section number. It may be important when reading cases that interpret a provision to compare the provision in different revisions in order to find out if it has been amended. If the wording of the provision is different in the present revision, the case law interpreting an earlier provision may not be useful.

legislative history
given at the end of each provision in a statute

The **legislative history** of a provision is given at the end of each provision in a statute. This history gives the section number of the provision in the previous revision or (if the provision has been amended or newly created between revisions) the year of and the chapter and section in the statute that amended or created the provision. Looking at the legislative history will permit you to find the *previous* section number of a provision for which you know the present section number.

In order to find the *present* section number of a provision if you only know the section number in the previous revision, you will have to consult a **concordance**. A concordance will also show you the previous section number if you know the present section number. Concordances focus on two adjacent revisions of a statute series.

concordance
a tool for finding corresponding sections in either an earlier or a later version of a statute

Concordance for Statutes of Canada

The *Revised Statutes of Canada, 1985* has a companion volume called *Table of the History and Disposal of Acts* (1995) that concords statutes enacted to December 1, 1988. Look in the "former legislation" column after you have located the statute by name. Similar tables exist for the revisions of 1970 (in the Second Supplement to R.S.C. 1970); 1952 (in the Appendixes volume of R.S.C. 1952); 1927 (in the Appendixes volume of R.S.C. 1927); 1906 (in the Appendixes volume of R.S.C. 1906); and 1886 (in volume 2 of R.S.C. 1886).

Concordance for Statutes of Ontario

Use the *Canadian Encyclopedic Digest (3d)*'s *Ontario Statutes Concordance 1980–1990*; or, in the *Revised Statutes of Ontario, 1990*, volume 12 (Appendix), look at Schedule B, "Table of Disposition."

KEY TERMS

bills

concordance

legislative history

Exercises

Where would you look for

1. a federal bill or a bill of your provincial legislature, if you know the bill number;

2. whether the wording of a given statutory provision was different in the previous revision of statutes;

3. the text of a statute of your provincial legislature whose name you know;

4. whether a statute of your province or a federal statute has been amended;

5. the text of a federal statute whose name you know;

6. whether there's a statute of your province or a federal statute on a given subject;

7. whether a statute of your province or federal statute has been proclaimed in force yet?

CHAPTER 10

Finding and Updating Regulations

Regulations are as important as statutes and sometimes may be more important. It is therefore vital to look for regulations after you have found out that there is a statute relevant to the area of law you are researching. Once you determine that there is a regulation relevant to your problem, you must be able to locate the text of the regulation.

Finding and updating regulations using paper sources is difficult, but this chapter sets out how to get through the task with as little pain as possible (which is not to say that there is no pain at all).

This chapter discusses the following topics:

- when regulations come into force,

- finding and updating federal regulations,

- finding and updating Ontario regulations, and

- regulatory citations.

WHEN REGULATIONS COME INTO FORCE

Regulations can come into force upon "filing," "registration," or "publication"; the wording differs in each jurisdiction. Federal regulations come into force on the day specified in the regulation or on the date of registration (recorded at the top of the text of the regulation). You can refer to a province's *Regulations Act* for more information about the coming into force of provincial regulations.

FINDING AND UPDATING FEDERAL REGULATIONS

The last consolidation of federal regulations was made in 1978, so the regulations contained in it are not up to date. You may find the text or amended text of the regulation you are looking for not in the consolidation but in the individual issues of *Canada Gazette Part II*, which is where regulations are published. Federal regulations are included in the general term **statutory instruments**.

statutory instrument
general term that includes federal regulations

1. To find out whether a regulation exists, check the following:

   - *Consolidated Index of Statutory Instruments* (part of *Canada Gazette Part II*). Consolidated semi-annually. Look at Table I for regulations by name of regulation; look at Table II for regulations by name of authorizing statute; look at Table III for statutes whose regulations are exempt from publication. (You guessed it—you will not be able to find regulations for Table III statutes.)

   - Carswell's *Canada Regulations Index*. A monthly consolidated index to all Canadian regulations and statutory instruments currently in force that allows you to find the citation of a specific regulation. You can then use the citation to locate the text of the regulation in the 1978 *Consolidated Regulations of Canada* or subsequent issues of the *Canada Gazette Part II*, depending on the date of the regulation.

2. Update with

   - Carswell's *Canada Regulations Index*,

   - *Canadian Current Law: Legislation* under "Regulations," and

   - *Consolidated Index of Statutory Instruments* (part of *Canada Gazette Part II*). Quarterly cumulation (look at Table I for regulations by name of regulation; look at Table II for regulations by name of authorizing statute; look at Table III for statutes whose regulations are exempt from publication).

                          AND

3. Update to the present with current issues of *Canada Gazette Part II* published since the date of the source you used.

FINDING AND UPDATING ONTARIO REGULATIONS

You have to first find out whether there are any regulations published under the "enabling" statute—the statute under which the regulation is made—and then locate the text of the regulation.

To find out whether a regulation exists under the enabling statute, look under the name of the statute in

- the *Ontario Gazette Index to Regulations*—published twice a year;

- Carswell's *Ontario Regulations Service*—a monthly subscription service that provides all regulations and amendments published each month, together with an annual consolidated index;

- the table of regulations at the back of each annual volume of the *Statutes of Ontario*.

The text of Ontario regulations is published in the *Revised Regulations of Ontario, 1990*. These regulations have been changed and new regulations have been added in

- the annual supplements to the Revised Regulations (made up of bound issues of the *Ontario Gazette*), and

- the individual issues of the *Ontario Gazette.*

Update by looking in

- Carswell's *Ontario Regulations Service* (updated by the yellow pages), or

- *Canadian Current Law: Legislation* under "Regulations" (Ontario). When you are using *Canadian Current Law: Legislation* to find regulations, remember that (1) it has been published only since 1989–90, and (2) it does not provide a cumulative overview of regulations. If you are looking for more than the most recent regulations, you will have to go through annual volumes as well as the monthly pamphlets.

Update to the present by looking for regulations in the individual volumes of the *Ontario Gazette* published since the date of the source you are using. In some law libraries, check the loose-leaf binder that is kept to update regulations as each *Ontario Gazette* release is received.

REGULATORY CITATIONS

You must be able to read a regulatory citation correctly in order to find the text of the regulation. Regulations are usually cited by year and number—the year in which the regulation was made, and the chronological number of the particular regulation in that year. Regulations of Canada are identified by "SOR," which stands for "Statutory Orders and Regulations." (If you see "SI," it means "Statutory Instrument," which is a broader term than regulation; it may include, for example, rules of court.) Regulations of the provinces are identified by an abbreviated name of the province plus "Reg." for Regulation—for example, B.C. Reg., O. Reg., and Nfld. Reg.

Examples

- SOR/95-18—look in the *Canada Gazette Part II* for 1995 and turn to regulation 18.

- O. Reg. 22/97—look in the *Ontario Gazette* for 1997 and turn to regulation 22.

Regulations of Canada may also appear in the 18-volume *Consolidated Regulations of Canada, 1978*, which includes all regulations in force on December 31, 1977. The citation will look like this:

- SOR Cons./78, Vol. 3, 208—look in volume 3 of the 1978 consolidation at page 208.

Regulations of Ontario are revised when the statutes are revised. If an Ontario regulation appears in the multi-volume *Revised Regulations of Ontario, 1990*, the citation will look like this:

- R.R.O. 1990, Reg. 601—the citation doesn't include the volume, but the spine of each volume shows the numbers it contains.

KEY TERMS

statutory instrument

Exercises

1. a. How would you find out whether there are regulations made under your provincial corporations act?

    b. How would you update those regulations?

2. a. How would you find out whether there are regulations made under the federal *Environmental Protection Act*?

    b. How would you update those regulations?

CHAPTER 11

Finding and Updating Cases

After determining whether there are any statutes or regulations relevant to the issue you are researching, you must then find out whether there is any relevant case law. In Chapter 8 we saw that you may be able to do this by looking in the *Canadian Encyclopedic Digest*, but there are other finding tools as well. If you determine that there is case law relevant to your problem, you must be able to locate the text of the cases.

This chapter discusses the following topics:

- how cases are published;

- finding tools—are there any relevant cases?;

- looking for cases about a subject—*Canadian Abridgment Case Digests*;

- looking for cases interpreting a statute;

- looking for cases considering a word or a phrase;

- treasure hunting—looking for a case using a partial or incorrect citation;

- looking for unreported cases;

- looking for the text of a case—understanding a case citation; and

- updating cases.

HOW CASES ARE PUBLISHED

It is helpful to understand how cases are published, in order to find the name of a case that deals with your research problem and then to find the text of that case.

As we said in Chapter 4, a case is the written record of a judge's reasons for deciding a legal dispute. Judges (and other judicial officers) deal with many matters: motions, trials, and appeals. At the end of the matter, the judge must make a decision. Often the judge's decision is given to the parties and their lawyers orally and then "endorsed on the record" (written on the back of the court documents sent to the judge by the court office). If the reasons for the decision are lengthy or complex, the judge will give his or her decision and reasons in writing. Only some of these written decisions wind up being published, or **reported**, in a law report series—usually the more important ones. Many cases are **unreported**—not published in a law report series.

reported case
judge's decision and reasons about a case published in a law report series

unreported case
case not published in a law report series

There are many different series of law reports. Some are organized by court level, such as the *Supreme Court Reports*, which contain only decisions of the Supreme Court of Canada. Others are organized by region or geographical area, such as the *Ontario Reports*, which contain decisions of the Ontario courts; the *Western Weekly Reports*, which contain decisions from the western provinces; and the *Dominion Law Reports*, which contain decisions from all over Canada. Still others are organized by subject area, such as the *Reports of Family Law* and *Canadian Criminal Cases*.

Some of these law report series are considered official because they are authorized by a particular court or province. The *Ontario Reports* and the *Supreme Court Reports* are official reports; the *Reports of Family Law* is not official. A case may be reported in more than one case report series. For example, an Ontario family law case that goes to the Supreme Court of Canada may be reported in the *Ontario Reports*, the *Supreme Court Reports*, and the *Reports of Family Law*.

FINDING TOOLS: ARE THERE ANY RELEVANT CASES?

There are a number of different secondary sources that you can use to find case law on the issue you are researching. The source you use will depend on the reason you are looking for case law. Ask yourself the following questions:

1. Are you looking for case law dealing with a specific subject or legal issue? If so, you should use the *Canadian Abridgment Case Digests*.

2. Are you looking for cases that have interpreted a statute or a section of a statute? If so, you should use *Canadian Statute Citations* (part of the *Canadian Abridgment*) or a Canadian or provincial statute citator.

3. Are you looking for case law considering a word or a phrase? If so, you should use *Words and Phrases Judicially Defined in Canadian Courts and Tribunals* (also part of the *Canadian Abridgment*).

4. Are you treasure hunting—that is, trying to find a case using a partial or incorrect citation? If so, you should use the *Consolidated Table of Cases* or the *Canadian Case Citations* volumes of the *Canadian Abridgment*.

5. Are you looking for an unreported case? If so, you should use a digest service such as *All Canada Weekly Summaries*.

LOOKING FOR CASES ABOUT A SUBJECT: CANADIAN ABRIDGMENT CASE DIGESTS

Many secondary sources will refer you to the leading cases on a subject, such as

- the *Canadian Encyclopedic Digest* (see Chapter 8),

- a text on the subject, or

- a loose-leaf service on the subject.

To find a text or loose-leaf service, check in the library catalogue under the subject name. Loose-leaf services are updated on a regular basis and are therefore more likely to cite recent decisions, but they tend to be less organized than texts.

If you want to move beyond the leading cases, the most comprehensive research tool for finding case law on a subject is Carswell's *Canadian Abridgment Case Digests*. The *Case Digests* is a multi-volume publication that collects **case digests**, or summaries of cases from all Canadian courts and many tribunals, and organizes them by subject area. Each digest provides a brief summary of how a legal issue was decided in a particular case, together with a summary of all necessary background facts and the reasons for the decision. Each digest covers only a single legal issue. If a case deals with several legal issues, there is a separate digest for each issue.

case digest
summary of how a legal issue was decided in a particular case

Organization of the Case Digests

The third edition of the *Case Digests* contains 55 subject titles. These subject titles are contained in a set of grey hardcover volumes organized alphabetically by broad subject area. Each volume is numbered. Each hardcover volume is updated by a softcover supplement volume. The supplement volumes are issued annually. Each new annual supplement is "cumulative"—that is, it incorporates the contents of each previous supplement—and replaces the previous supplement. As a result there is only one supplement volume for each hardcover volume. The supplements are further updated by monthly softcover editions of *Canadian Current Law: Case Digests*.

Within the hardcover and supplement volumes, the digests are organized by subject and arranged according to a multi-level classification system, called the **key classification system**. Each digest is classified under one of the *Case Digests*' subject titles. Each subject title is given a name and broken down into increasingly more specific levels. Main topics within the subject title are identified by a roman numeral, subtopics by numbers, and sub-subtopics by letters. For example, CIVIL PRACTICE AND PROCEDURE is a subject title. CIVIL PRACTICE AND PROCEDURE III.2.d is:

key classification system
multi-level classification system

> CIVIL PRACTICE AND PROCEDURE
>   III. Institution of Proceedings
>   2. Writ of Summons
>   d. Issuance

Each individual digest has a key classification number and a specific case digest number.

Finding Tools

Two main tools help you to locate all the digested cases on a particular issue in the *Case Digests*: the key and research guide and the general index. Both will direct you to the relevant case digests dealing with your legal issue or topic, but only the key and research guide uses the key classification system.

The **key and research guide** is really an elaborate table of contents. It groups subjects together according to the key classification system. You start by looking up a term that describes your issue. You will be referred to relevant subject titles and

key and research guide
one of two finding tools to locate digested cases that uses the key classification system

their subtitles according to the key classification system. From there you will be referred to the digests falling under those titles and subtitles in the relevant permanent volume and supplement. The key and research guide thus allows you to locate your issue within the classification scheme and then look through all the digests falling under the appropriate title and subtopic. It also provides the classification number to use throughout your search in any part of the *Canadian Abridgment*. In the third edition of the *Case Digests*, some subject titles are so large that they are spread out over more than one volume. When that happens, the classification table indicates the volume number in which each main topic of the subject title appears.

general index
one of two finding tools to
locate digested cases

The **general index** arranges terms and key words alphabetically. Each entry is followed by the location of the relevant case digests by reference to the volume number and case digest numbers. The general index does not give you the classification number.

How To Use the Case Digests

Follow these steps when using the *Case Digests*:

1. Look in the general index or key and research guide to find where the relevant case digests are located.

   ■ The general index will give you the relevant volume number and digest numbers.

   ■ The key and research guide will give you the relevant volume numbers and key classification numbers.

2. Find the hardcover volume that contains your subject title. Look at the digest numbers from the general index or the classification number from the key and research guide.

   ■ Scan the digests under the appropriate subject title and classification number, and make a note of the names and citations of important cases.

   ■ Within each classification number, the digests are set out in reverse chronological order. The most recent case comes first. Each digest is identified by the key classification number of the subject title, subtitle, and sub-subtitle it belongs to. This number is found in the upper right hand corner of the digest entry. Each digest is also given a digest number, found in the upper left hand corner of the digest entry. The digest entries are numbered consecutively within each volume.

3. Look in the corresponding supplement volume for cases reported after the cut-off date of the hardcover volume. It contains digests from the cut-off date of the main volume to the end of the year shown on the cover of the volume. Find the subject title, and then look at the digests under the key classification number.

4. Consult *Canadian Current Law: Case Digests* to find cases reported after the cut-off date for the supplement.

    ■ These softcover booklets are published monthly.

    ■ To find the digests in these booklets, look up your topic in the index found at the back of each monthly issue. The subject titles are set out in alphabetical order.

    ■ The March, June, September, and December issues contain a cumulative index of all digests that have appeared to that date during the year, so begin your search with the most current volume that contains a cumulative index. Then check each subsequent monthly issue.

    ■ You can also use the case law update section provided in the general index to direct you. The "scope note" at the start of the case law update section sets out the *Canadian Current Law: Case Digests* issues covered in the update section. Look for the subject title and classification number.

An Example

The best way to learn how to use the *Case Digests* is to work through an example. Assume that you are continuing to work on the memo discussed in Chapter 8. It reads as follows:

> Our client in Toronto, Ontario has a cocker spaniel that barks constantly. One day last month, her neighbour went to her apartment to complain. When our client opened the door, the dog rushed out to attack the neighbour, who fell backwards and broke his leg. The neighbour is now suing your client for the injuries caused by the dog. Can our client be held legally responsible?

In Chapter 8, we used the *Canadian Encyclopedic Digest* to find a general statement of the law relating to injuries caused by dogs, and we found both case law and statute law there. Now we want to find case law using the *Case Digests* instead.

USING THE GENERAL INDEX TO FIND THE RELEVANT CASE DIGESTS

Start by looking up the word "Dog" in the index. You will be referred to the main topic "Animals." This part of the index is set out in figure 11.1. Next, look up the word "Animals" in the general index. You will be referred to all the topics and subtopics under this main topic. The topic "Injury by animals" tells you to refer to the main topic "Negligence" and the subtopic "Liability of owner or possessor of animals," as illustrated in figure 11.2. Next, look up the word "Negligence." This part of the index is set out in figure 11.3. Note the following:

■ "Negligence" is the main topic. "Liability of owner or possessor of animals" is a main subtopic under this main topic. "Injury by domestic animals" is a more specific subtopic and "Injury by dog" is an even more specific subtopic.

■ Bullets are used to identify the level of each subtopic under the main topic "Animals." Main subtopics have one bullet, subtopics under this main subtopic have two bullets, and sub-subtopics under this subtopic have three bullets.

Figure 11.1　Case Digests General Index Showing "Dog"

General Index　　　　　　　　　　　　Domestic contracts and settlements

• •　Change in purpose of beneficiary, **EST 35.**1483-1486; **EST 35Supp.**214

• •　Impracticability of carrying out purpose

• • •　General principles, **EST 35.**1494-1503; **EST 35Supp.**215-216

• • •　Insufficient funds, **EST 35.**1504-1509; **EST 35Supp.**217

• •　Miscellaneous circumstances, **EST 35.**1516-1519

• •　Non-existent beneficiary, **EST 35.**1437-1460; **EST 35Supp.**211

• •　Obsolescence of purpose, **EST 35.**1487-1493

• •　Sale of devised property, **EST 35.**1510

• •　Surplus funds, **EST 35.**1511-1515

•　When doctrine not applicable

• •　Absence of general charitable intent, **EST 35.**1520-1533; **EST 35Supp.**218

• •　Continuing possibility of original application, **EST 35.**1534-1538; **EST 35Supp.**219

Documentary evidence, *see* Children in need of protection; Evidence; Motor vehicles, Evidence

Dog, *see* Animals

Domestic animals, *see* Agricultural products, Property in domestic animals

Domestic contracts

•　Effect of contract

• •　On spousal support

• • •　Effect on application under dependants' relief legislation, *see* Dependants' relief legislation

•　Marriage settlements, *see* Domestic contracts and settlements

•　Variation of terms

• •　By inconsistent disposition in will, *see* Estates

Domestic contracts and settlements

•　Effect of contract

• •　Miscellaneous issues, **FAM 43.**3100-3144; **FAM 43Supp.**1566-1584

• •　On child support, **FAM 43.**2700-3010; **FAM 43Supp.**1464-1533

• •　On custody and access, **FAM 43.**3011-3099; **FAM 43Supp.**1534-1565

• •　On division of family property

• • •　General principles, **FAM 43.**1756-1962; **FAM 43Supp.**1275-1317

• • •　Matrimonial home, **FAM 43.**1963-2055; **FAM 43Supp.**1318-1332

• • •　Pensions, **FAM 43.**2056-2087; **FAM 43Supp.**1333-1349

• •　On spousal support

• • •　Terms regarding cost of living adjustments, **FAM 43.**2696-2699

• • •　Under Divorce Act, **FAM 43.**2088-2601; **FAM 43Supp.**1350-1445

• • •　Under provincial legislation, **FAM 43.**2602-2695; **FAM 43Supp.**1446-1463

•　Enforcement

• •　Effect of death, **FAM 43.**3689-3706; **FAM 43Supp.**1762-1764

• •　Effect of divorce, **FAM 43.**3669-3688

• •　Effect of electing alternate remedy, **FAM 43.**3750-3766

• •　Effect of reconciliation, **FAM 43.**3707-3744; **FAM 43Supp.**1766

• •　Effect of release against estates, **FAM 43.**3745-3749

• •　General principles, **FAM 43.**3479-3566; **FAM 43Supp.**1695-1735

• •　Jurisdiction of courts, **FAM 43.**3568-3603; **FAM 43Supp.**1736-1744

• •　Practice and procedure, **FAM 43.**3604-3668; **FAM 43Supp.**1745-1761

•　General principles, **FAM 43.**1115-1143; **FAM 43Supp.**1089-1095

•　Incorporation into divorce decree or court order, **FAM 43.**3767-3806; **FAM 43Supp.**1767-1776

•　Interpretation, **FAM 43.**3145-3241; **FAM 43Supp.**1585-1614

•　Marriage settlements, **FAM 43.**3807-3853

•　Miscellaneous issues, **FAM 43.**3864-3873; **FAM 43Supp.**1789-1805

•　Settlements between counsel, **FAM 43.**3854-3863; **FAM 43Supp.**1777-1788

•　Termination, **FAM 43.**3242-3264; **FAM 43Supp.**1615-1618

•　Validity

• •　Essential validity and capacity

• • •　Duress, fraud, undue influence and unconscionability, **FAM 43.**1338-1591; **FAM 43Supp.**1149-1209

• • •　General principles, **FAM 43.**1144-1314; **FAM 43Supp.**1096-1144

• • •　Lack of disclosure, **FAM 43.**1616-1650; **FAM 43Supp.**1227-1240

Figure 11.2   Case Digests General Index Showing "Animals"

General Index   Annulment

- In charities, *see* Charities, Uncertainty
- In contract, *see* Contracts, Construction and interpretation
- In municipal by-law, *see* Municipal law, Attacks on by-laws and resolutions
- In statutes, *see* Statutes, Interpretation
- In will, *see* Estates

Amicus curiae, *see* Barristers and solicitors, Relationship with client

Amortization, *see* Mortgages

Ancillary letters probate, *see* Estates

Animals
- Diseases of animals
- • Compensation, **PER 85**.369-385; **PER 85Supp.**9-12
- • Destruction of animals, **PER 85**.351-367; **PER 85Supp.**8
- • General principles, **PER 85**.348-350
- • Miscellaneous, **PER 85**.386-390; **PER 85Supp.**13
- Injury by animals, *see* Negligence, Liability of owner or possessor of animals
- Injury to animals
- • By railway, **PER 85**.100-265
- • Cattle, **PER 85**.266-276
- • General principles, **PER 85**.1-7; **PER 85Supp.**1
- • Malicious injury, **PER 85**.277-329
- • Miscellaneous, **PER 85**.330-347; **PER 85Supp.**2-7
- • On streets and highways
- • • Duty of motorist, **PER 85**.33-87
- • • Miscellaneous, **PER 85**.88-99
- • Stray animals, **PER 85**.8-32
- Miscellaneous, **PER 85**.405-413; **PER 85Supp.**14-26
- Stray animals, **PER 85**.391-404

Annuities
- Abatement of annuity, **INS 57**.2933-2937
- Ademption, *see* Estates
- Apportionment of annuity on annuitant's death, **INS 57**.2930-2932
- Attachment of annuity, **INS 57**.2938-2941
- Conditional annuity, **INS 57**.2942-2945
- General principles

- • Annuity distinguished from other payments, **INS 57**.2858-2862
- • Definitions, **INS 57**.2854-2857
- • Term of annuity, **INS 57**.2863-2868
- Government annuity, **INS 57**.2946-2952
- Miscellaneous issues, **INS 57**.2953-2954; **INS 57Supp.**2256-2257
- Payment of annuity
- • Annuity charged on fund, **INS 57**.2909-2910
- • Annuity charged on land
- • • General principles, **INS 57**.2875-2896
- • • Rights of bona fide purchaser in due course, **INS 57**.2897-2901
- • Annuity in lieu of dower, **INS 57**.2902-2908
- • General principles, **INS 57**.2869-2874
- • Rights of residuary legate, **INS 57**.2928-2929
- • Where annuity in arrears
- • • General principles, **INS 57**.2917-2921
- • • Interest on arrears, **INS 57**.2922-2927
- • Whether corpus chargeable
- • • Where annuity charged on income only, **INS 57**.2911-2913
- • • Where corpus generally chargeable, **INS 57**.2914-2916

Annulment
- Decree or judgment, **FAM 44**.34-57; **FAM 44Supp.**1
- Effect of annulment on family rights
- • Property, **FAM 44**.58
- Essential validity
- • Consanguinity and affinity, **FAM 43**.4043-4054
- • Impotence
- • • Evidence, **FAM 43**.4024-4042
- • • General principles, **FAM 43**.3969-4009; **FAM 43Supp.**1811
- • • Practice and procedure, **FAM 43**.4010-4023
- • Lack of parental consent, **FAM 43**.3907-3923
- • Lack of party's consent
- • • Effect of deception, **FAM 43**.3937-3942
- • • Effect of duress or coercion, **FAM 43**.3943-3949; **FAM 43Supp.**1808-1809

Figure 11.3　Case Digests General Index Showing "Negligence"

Negligence　　　　　　　　　　　　　　　　　　　　　　　　General Index

• • •　Application of principles, **TOR** 114.3321-3335

• • •　Miscellaneous, **TOR** 114.3336-3342; **TOR 114Supp.**191

• •　Common practice, **TOR** 114.3215-3224; **TOR 114Supp.**187-188

• •　Exculpatory clauses, **TOR** 114.3184-3214; **TOR 114Supp.**185-186

• •　Inevitable accident

• • •　Application of principles, **TOR** 114.3225-3288; **TOR 114Supp.**189

• • •　Miscellaneous, **TOR** 114.3289-3320; **TOR 114Supp.**190

• •　Mental illness, **TOR 115.**147-149

• •　Miscellaneous, **TOR 115.**164-178; **TOR** 115Supp.6

• •　Plaintiff's carelessness as sole cause of injury, **TOR 115.**151-163; **TOR** 115Supp.2-5

• •　Volenti non fit injuria

• • •　Intoxicated driver, **TOR 115.**33-128

• • •　Knowledge and appreciation of risk, **TOR 114.**3343-3384

• • •　Miscellaneous, **TOR 115.**146

• • •　Sporting events, **TOR 115.**129-145

• • •　Statutory breach, **TOR 114.**3488-3495

• • •　Voluntary acceptance of risk, **TOR** 114.3386-3459; **TOR 114Supp.**192-196

• • •　Waiving right of action, **TOR 114.**3460-3487; **TOR 114Supp.**197

• • •　Willing passengers, **TOR 115.**1-32; **TOR 115Supp.**1

•　Duty and standard of care

• •　After accidents, **TOR 113.**1679-1688

• •　Duty of care, **TOR 113.**1033-1362; **TOR** 113Supp.118-181

• •　Emergencies, **TOR 113.**1597-1651; **TOR** 113Supp.249

• •　Exercise of statutory powers, **TOR** 113.1707-1731; **TOR 113Supp.**252-255

• •　Fiduciary duty, **TOR 113.**1756-1781; **TOR** 113Supp.261-279

• •　Gratuitous undertakings, **TOR 113.**1689-1706

• •　Gross negligence, **TOR 113.**1732-1743; **TOR 113Supp.**256-258

• •　Intoxication, **TOR 113.**1744-1755; **TOR** 113Supp.259-260

• •　Miscellaneous, **TOR 113.**1782-1836; **TOR** 113Supp.280-285

• •　Rescue, **TOR 113.**1652-1678; **TOR** 113Supp.250-251

• •　Standard of care, **TOR 113.**1363-1596; **TOR 113Supp.**182-248

•　Effect of wrongful conduct, **TOR 113.**2411-2423; **TOR 113Supp.**392

•　Fatal Accidents Acts, *see* Fatal accidents acts

•　General principles, **TOR 113.**998-1032; **TOR** 113Supp.113-117

•　Liability for environmental damage, *see* Environmental law

•　Liability of owner or possessor of animals

• •　Criminal liability, **TOR 114.**2814-2830; **TOR 114Supp.**148-150

• •　Distress damage feasant, **TOR 114.**2765-2813

• •　Injury by domestic animals

• • •　At common law, **TOR 114.**2436-2469

• • •　Injury by dog, **TOR 114.**2476-2605; **TOR 114Supp.**139-147

• • •　On highway, **TOR 114.**2606-2698

• • •　Under by-law or statute, **TOR 114.**2470-2475; **TOR 114Supp.**138

• •　Injury by wild animals, **TOR 114.**2699-2706

• •　Liability for nuisance, **TOR 114.**2831-2845; **TOR 114Supp.**151

• •　Miscellaneous, **TOR 114.**2874-2881; **TOR 114Supp.**155-159

• •　Regulation of dangerous animals, **TOR** 114.2846-2873; **TOR 114Supp.**152-154

• •　Trespass by animals, **TOR 114.**2707-2764

•　Miscellaneous, **TOR 115.**1764-1844; **TOR** 115Supp.153-155

•　Motor vehicles, *see* Motor vehicles

•　Occupiers' liability

• •　Definitions

• • •　Contractual entrant, **TOR 114.**964-966

• • •　Invitee, **TOR 114.**967-999

• • •　Licensee, **TOR 114.**1000-1017

• • •　Occupier, **TOR 114.**905-963; **TOR** 114Supp.40-48

• • •　Trespasser, **TOR 114.**1018-1033; **TOR** 114Supp.49

• •　Duties and obligations

• • •　Contractual, **TOR 114.**1044-1064; **TOR** 114Supp.53-54

360

The index gives you the relevant volume number and case digest numbers in those volumes that deal with your specific topic. For cases dealing with the liability of an owner for injuries caused by his or her dog, you are referred to TOR 114 2476-2605 and TOR 114 Supp. 139-147.

TOR refers to the subject title abbreviation for the relevant subject title, "Torts." 114 refers to the volume number of the *Case Digests* that contains the subject title "Torts." 114 Supp refers to the corresponding supplement volume. 2476-2605 refers to the case digest numbers of the case digests in the hardcover volume that deal with your specific topic. 139-147 refers to the case digest numbers of case digests in the corresponding supplement volume.

USING THE KEY AND RESEARCH GUIDE TO FIND THE RELEVANT CASE DIGESTS

The *Case Digests* divides the law into main subject titles, and every topic falls under one of these subject titles. If you look up a word or topic that is not an actual subject title, you will be referred to the subject title under which your word or topic falls.

A subject titles table, found at the beginning of the key and research guide, lists all the subject titles in the *Case Digests* and refers you directly to the pages in the key that contain information about each title. If you already know that "Torts" is the subject title relevant to your issue, you can look at the subject titles table; it refers you to page 2-719 of the key (see figure 11.4). If you don't know the subject title, use the index portion of the key to look up "Dogs." It refers you to the subject titles that contain information about "dogs," and provides the relevant main topic and subtopic of each subject title. In our example, the relevant subject title is "Torts." The relevant main topic is topic XVI, and the relevant subtopic is section 10 (see figure 11.5). Look at page 2-719 of the key, set out in figure 11.6. It tells you that topic XVI (Negligence) is dealt with in volumes 113-115. Next, look at section 10 of topic XVI in the table of classification for the subject title "Torts," set out in figure 11.7. The table of classification breaks down, or "classifies," the subject title into increasingly more specific subtopics.

You will find topic section 10 of topic XVI (XVI.10) broken down into subtopics and sub-subtopics, as follows:

    10. Liability of Owner or Possessor of Animals
        a. Injury by domestic animals
            i. At common law
            ii. Under by-law or statute
            iii. Injury by dog
                A. At common law
                B. Under by-law or statute
                C. Injury to other animals

Using this information, you can "classify" your topic. In our example, you are looking for cases dealing with a dog owner's liability under the relevant Ontario statute. The classification number for this specific topic is XVI.10.a.iii.B. All the case digests dealing with this specific topic will have the same classification number. Find the volumes that contain the subject title "Torts" and then find the volume that contains this classification number. Note that when a subject title is contained in more than one volume of the *Case Digests*, the table of classification for the subject title will indicate which classifications appear in each volume.

Figure 11.4   Case Digests Subject Titles Table Showing "Torts" (1 of 2 pages)

SUBJECT TITLES TABLE

> **EDITOR'S NOTE:** The list of subject titles below is supplemented in the Key by an extensive system of cross-references. The cross-references appear in bold-face and may be of assistance in locating specific topics or related issues. In addition, each subject title includes a Scope Note describing its contents and the location of related issues in other subject titles.

Figure 11.4   Case Digests Subject Titles Table Showing "Torts" (2 of 2 pages)

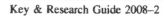

Figure 11.5   Case Digests Key and Research Guide Showing "Dogs"

DUPLICITY

DISTRESS — *see Commercial law III, IV.7 ; Criminal law V.8; Municipal law XXI.7.f; Public law I; Real property V.18*

DISTRIBUTION — *see Bankruptcy and insolvency XIV; Estates and trusts I.6.l*

DISTURBANCE DAMAGES — *see Real property VI.9*

DITCHES — *see Natural resources V; Real property IX*

DIVIDED SUCCESS *effect on costs — see Civil practice and procedure XXIII.6.c*

DIVIDENDS — *see Bankruptcy and insolvency XIV; Business associations III.2.b*

DIVISION OF PROPERTY — *see Family law III*

DIVORCE — *see Conflict of laws; Constitutional law; Family law*

DNA TESTING — *see Criminal law; Evidence II.8.j.v, XVI.5.b.iv; Family law XIV.3.d.vi*

DOCKS — *see Maritime and admiralty law VII; Natural resources V.3.d*

DOCTORS — *see Health law III.2.o*

DOCUMENTARY EVIDENCE — *see Criminal law VI.21.c.iv.C; Evidence VII; Motor vehicles XI.1.a.i*

DOCUMENTS — *see Civil practice and procedure X.2; Contracts; Criminal law VI.49, VI.55.d.i.A, VI.55.g.i.A; Evidence VII*

DOGS — *see Personal property I; Torts XVI.10*

DOMAIN NAME — *see Information technology II*

DOMESTIC CONTRACTS — *see Family law III*

DOMESTIC TRIBUNALS — *see Administrative law*

DOMICILE — *see Business associations III.5.a; Conflict of laws*

DOMINANT TENEMENT — *see Real property VIII*

DONATIO MORTIS CAUSA — *see Estates and trusts I.15.d.iii, IV.1.b*

DOUBLE ASPECT — *see Constitutional law VII.5.d; Public law I*

DOUBLE JEOPARDY RULE — *see Criminal law IV.23*

DOUBLE POSSIBILITIES — *see Estates and trusts IX.2*

DOWER — *see Civil practice and procedure XXII.3.b.ii; Family law II.8; Real property VII*

DRIVING WHILE DISQUALIFIED — *see Criminal law VI.113*

DRUGGISTS — *see Health law III.2.n*

DRUGS — *see Criminal law XVIII*

DRUNKENNESS — *see Criminal law V.12, VI.98.c.iii, VI.125.b.iv.A; Equity IV.1.c*

DUE DILIGENCE — *see Environmental law II.1.c*

DUMPING — *see International trade and customs II*

DUPLICITY — *see Criminal law VI.21.b.ii, VI.113.b.i, VII.6.f.ii.B, VIII.11.b.ii.B, XII.1.b.i.D*

Figure 11.6 Case Digests Key and Research Guide, Page 2-719 Showing the Contents of the Subject Title "Torts"

TORTS
THIRD EDITION

CONTENTS

RELATED TITLES

- Tort of passing off — see INTELLECTUAL PROPERTY III.10
- Injunctions to restrain tortuous conduct generally — see REMEDIES II
- Injunctions as remedy for nuisance — see REMEDIES II.2.a.ix.A, II.2.f.i
- Limitation of actions in tort — see CIVIL PRACTICE AND PROCEDURE XXII.5
- Damages for assault and battery — see REMEDIES I.5.a.ii.C
- Exemplary, punitive and aggravated damages for assault and battery — see REMEDIES I.7.c.i

2-719 Key & Research Guide 2007-1

Figure 11.7   Table of Classification for Topic XVI.10 of "Torts"

TORTS XVI.8.a.ii   Can. Abr. (3rd)

ii. Contractual entrant
iii. Invitee
iv. Licensee
v. Trespasser
b. Duties and obligations
  i. General principles
  ii. Contractual
  iii. Invitee
    A. Extent of invitation
    B. Unusual danger
      1. Knowledge of danger
      2. Duty to warn
      3. Miscellaneous
    C. Invitors by legal compulsion
    D. Miscellaneous
  iv. Licensee
  v. Trespasser
    A. Duty to fence premises
    B. Miscellaneous
  vi. Statutory duty
  vii. Miscellaneous
c. Particular situations
  i. Amusement or other public parks
  ii. Swimming areas
  iii. Sporting facilities
  iv. Hotels and taverns
  v. Stores
  vi. Ice and snow
  vii. Landlord and tenant
  viii. Construction sites and excavations
  ix. Property abutting on highway
  x. Roofs
  xi. Doors
  xii. Walls
  xiii. Racetracks
  xiv. Mines
  xv. Miscellaneous
d. Miscellaneous
9. Hotels and inns

a. Definitions
  i. Guest
  ii. Inn or hotel
  iii. Innkeeper or hotelkeeper
b. Duties and rights of innkeepers and guests
  i. Guest
  ii. Innkeeper
  iii. Guest registration
c. Loss of property
10. Liability of owner or possessor of animals
a. Injury by domestic animals
  i. At common law
  ii. Under by-law or statute
  iii. Injury by dog
    A. At common law
    B. Under by-law or statute
    C. Injury to other animals
  iv. On highway
b. Injury by wild animals
c. Trespass by animals
d. Distress damage feasant
e. Criminal liability
  — criminal offences generally, see CRIMINAL LAW
f. Liability for nuisance
g. Regulation of dangerous animals
h. Miscellaneous
11. Fires
a. Determination of liability
  i. Breach of statutory duty
  ii. Breach of contractual duty
  iii. Fire departments
  iv. Agriculture and cultivation
  v. Miscellaneous
b. Defences
  i. Statutory authorization
    A. Accidental fire
    B. Compliance with issued permit
    C. Miscellaneous
  ii. Miscellaneous

Key & Research Guide 2007-1   2-738

FINDING AND READING THE TEXT

Once you have identified your specific topic using one of the finding tools discussed above, locate the appropriate volume—that is, 114—and refer to the digest numbers (2476-2605 in the main volume and 139-147 in the supplement volume) obtained from the general index, or the key classification number (XVI.10.a.iii.B) obtained from the key and research guide.

Scan the appropriate digests, and write down the names and citations of important cases.

If you used the general index, look for appropriate case digest numbers in the upper left corner of each digest. From your research of this issue in the *Canadian Encyclopedic Digest* (see Chapter 8), you know that there is statute law, the *Dog Owners' Liability Act*, governing this issue. As a result, you can go directly to the digest entries dealing with liability under statute law. The first digest under this heading is number 2526. If you used the key and research guide, look for the key classification number that appears at the upper right hand corner of each digest. All the case digests dealing with your research topic will be under classification number XVI.10.a.iii.B. The relevant digests are reproduced in figure 11.8.

UPDATING YOUR RESEARCH

Look in the supplement volume of the *Case Digests* for digests of any cases that may have been reported after the cut-off date of the permanent volume. As noted above, if you used the general index as your finding tool, it will provide the digest numbers in the supplement volume, if any, for your research topic—in this case 139-147. If you used the key and research guide, find your subject title—in this case Torts—and then look under the relevant classification number—in this case XVI.10.a.iii.B.

To update beyond the supplement's cut-off date (the end of the previous calendar year), check each monthly softcover issue of *Canadian Current Law: Case Digests*, starting with January of the current calendar year. To find the digests in these issues, look up "Torts" in the index found at the back of each monthly issue. The subject titles are set out in alphabetical order. The March, June, September, and December issues contain a cumulative index of all digests that have appeared to that date during the year, so begin your search with the most current volume that contains a cumulative index. Then check each subsequent monthly issue. You can then refer to the relevant case digests contained in these issues.

LOOKING FOR CASES INTERPRETING A STATUTE

You can consult a number of different sources to find cases that have interpreted or applied a statute, including

- the *Canadian Abridgment Canadian Statute Citations*,
- statute citators, and
- annotated statutes.

Figure 11.8   Case Digests for Classification Number XVI.10.a.iii.B

XVI.10.a.iii.A   TORTS   [2524–2529]

jury by dog — At common law —— Vicious propensities of dog — Owner's knowledge — Scienter — Damages.

Action was brought for damages for injuries inflicted by a dog owned or harboured by defendant. It was shown that the dog was formerly owned by a man in defendant's employ, who lived at defendant's house. The man went away and left the dog with defendant's son to be kept until sent for. The dog went every day with defendant or defendant's son to defendant's place of business. On two occasions, the dog's savage disposition was shown in evidence to have been exhibited, once in the presence of defendant and once in the presence of defendant's son. **Held:** There was ample evidence for the jury that defendant harboured the dog with knowledge of its vicious propensities.

Vaughan v. Wood (1890), 18 S.C.R. 703, 1890 CarswellNB 70 (S.C.C.); affirming (1889), 28 N.B.R. 472, 1889 CarswellNB 36 (C.A.).

2525.   (XVI.10.a.iii.A)

Negligence — Liability of owner or possessor of animals — Injury by domestic animals — Injury by dog — At common law —— Dog biting person — Evidence of previous and subsequent attacks by dog — Admissibility thereof — Owner's knowledge of dog's vicious propensity — Negligence.

In an action brought for an injury inflicted by a dog, it is necessary to allege and prove that defendant had knowledge of the animal's vicious propensity. As soon as that knowledge is shown, the same responsibility attaches to the owner to keep him from doing mischief, as the keeper of an animal, naturally ferocious, would be subject to, and there is no necessity for proving negligence. Plaintiff was bitten by defendant's dog. In an action for damages, 1 witness testified that he had been bitten by the dog one year previously and that he informed defendant of it and another witness testified that he had been bitten by the same dog subsequently to the action having been brought. **Held:** The evidence with reference to the dog's biting on the occasion subsequent to the action having been started, was improperly received, but since the trial Judge expressly withdrew it from the consideration of the jury, the verdict should not be interfered with.

Wilmot v. Vanwart (1877), 17 N.B.R. 456, 1877 CarswellNB 58 (C.A.).

B. *Under by-law or statute*

2526.   (XVI.10.a.iii.B)

Negligence — Liability of owner or possessor of animals — Injury by domestic animals — Injury by dog — Under by-law or statute.

Crichton v. Noon (2005), 2005 CarswellOnt 4899, Searle D.J. (Ont. S.C.J.).

2527.   (XVI.10.a.iii.B)

Negligence — Liability of owner or possessor of animals — Injury by domestic animals — Injury by dog — Under by-law or statute.

Graham (Litigation Guardian of) v. 640847 Ontario Ltd. (2005), 2005 CarswellOnt 3866, Belleghem J. (Ont. S.C.J.).

2528.   (XVI.10.a.iii.B)

Negligence — Liability of owner or possessor of animals — Injury by domestic animals — Injury by dog — Under by-law or statute.

R. v. Callero (2005), 2005 CarswellOnt 3943, 2005 ONCJ 381, De Morais J.P. (Ont. C.J.).

2529.   (XVI.10.a.iii.B)

Negligence — Liability of owner or possessor of animals — Injury by domestic animals — Injury by dog — Under by-law or statute —— Dog jumped onto fence and lunged at victim, injuring her lip — Accused owner of dog was charged under s. 8(4) of Dangerous Dog By-law for owning dog that, "without provocation, attacked, assaulted, wounded, bit, injured or killed person or domestic animal" — Crown provided specific particulars, namely that dog "bit lady on right side upper lip" — Justice of peace acquitted owner, finding reasonable doubt existed as to whether victim's injury was consequence of bite per se, and not accident — Crown appealed — Appeal dismissed — Contrary to Crown's contention that justice of peace erred in finding there was provocation, justice of peace in fact made no finding of provocation, nor did he address legal test for provocation, as no evidence existed on issue — In choosing to charge accused as being owner of dog that "without provocation ... bit ... person", Crown had to prove dog bit victim, not merely injured or wounded victim as was open to Crown in drawing information — Justice of peace correctly focused upon offence of dog bite — Sufficient evidence existed to support justice of peace's conclusion.

R. v. Florness (2005), 273 Sask. R. 173, 2005 SKQB 517, 2005 CarswellSask 856, Sandomirsky J. (Sask. Q.B.).

564

Canadian Statute Citations

Canadian Statute Citations is part of the *Canadian Abridgment* and contains citations of cases that interpret both federal and provincial statutes. Federal and provincial statutes are located in separate volumes. First, locate the hardcover volumes for Canada or the province in which you are interested; then find the name of the statute. Look up the statutory provision by statute name and then by section number. Cases considering statutes as a whole appear at the beginning of the entry for that statute under the heading "generally." The statutes are listed alphabetically and then, within that order, chronologically by statute revision. Make sure that you look under the correct revision of the statute (1990, 1980, 1970, etc.). You will have to concord the statutory revision (see Chapter 9) to find cases that were decided under earlier revisions of the statute. After looking in the hardcover volume of *Canadian Statute Citations*, check the corresponding supplement volume to find cases decided after the cut-off date of the permanent volume. You should check the corresponding supplement volume even if you don't see the name of the statute or the section of the statute you are looking for in the hardcover volume, since cases may have been decided after the cut-off date of the hardcover volume. Complete your search by consulting the monthly issues of *Canadian Statute Citations*.

Each case citation is preceded by a code inside a small circle that indicates the court's treatment of the statute. See figure 11.9.

FIGURE 11.9 Treatment Symbols for Statutes

Symbol	Meaning
(U)	**Unconstitutional:** The case decided that a section of the statute was unconstitutional or invalid.
(C)	**Considered:** The case analyzed or interpreted a section of the statute.
(P)	**Pursuant to:** The case was brought pursuant to a section of the statute.
(R)	**Referred to:** The case mentions a section of the statute in passing, but does not consider it directly.

Statute Citators

Statute citators provide another way of looking for cases interpreting a statute or a specific provision of a statute. The citator will refer you to important cases dealing with a statute. For cases involving federal statutes, consult the *Canada Statute Citator*. For cases involving Ontario statutes, consult the *Ontario Statute Citator*. Cases are listed under the statutory provision to which they are related. The citator is not comprehensive and should be used only with another source.

Annotated Statutes

There is also a third way of looking for cases interpreting a statute. A commercially published annotated version of the statute will list relevant cases under the section of the statute that the cases considered.

LOOKING FOR CASES CONSIDERING A WORD OR PHRASE

The *Canadian Abridgment* has a set of volumes called *Words and Phrases Judicially Defined in Canadian Courts and Tribunals*. Use this source to find cases that have considered particular legal terms or phrases. Words and phrases are arranged alphabetically in the volumes. Each entry includes an extract from the judgment in which the word or phrase was considered. It also gives you the name, citation, and jurisdiction for each case. First check the hardcover volumes of *Words and Phrases Judicially Defined in Canadian Courts and Tribunals*; next look in the supplement volumes to update your search for cases reported after the cut-off date of the hardcover volume.

TREASURE HUNTING

Sometimes you can't find a case that you're looking for because you have been given a wrong or partial citation.

Finding a Case When You've Been Given the Wrong Citation

One of the most tedious aspects of legal research is that, when looking for a case, chances are about 50–50 that you have an incorrect citation. Either you have copied it down wrong, the person who gave you the citation copied it down wrong, or the text from which you got the citation contains a misprint that was not caught by a proofreader. What do you do when you track down the case report volume in the citation you've been given and the case you're looking for is nowhere to be found?

To find the correct case name, try looking in either the *Consolidated Table of Cases* or the *Canadian Case Citations* volumes of the *Canadian Abridgment*. Cases are arranged alphabetically by name and are cross-referenced by alternate case names and by the defendant's name.

If you cannot find the name of a case in the hardcover volumes, check the supplement volumes. It may be that the case you are looking for was decided or reported after the cut-off date of the main volume.

 NOTE: Before you do the above, you may wish to check (1) the table of cases in the case report volume you pulled that was *supposed* to contain the case but didn't, and/or (2) the index volume of that case report series. Incorrect citations are often a matter of a wrong page number or volume number.

If the above steps do not work, recheck the source of the citation, because you may have the wrong name.

"Find me this case—I think it's called Smith, or maybe it's Jorgensen"

Another tedious aspect of legal research is dealing with lawyers who expect a case to be found given little information. Here's a suggestion. Look up the supposed name of the case in the *Consolidated Table of Cases* or *Canadian Case Citations* permanent volumes and all supplements.

If you still cannot find the correct name, you probably have been given a completely wrong name reference. Find out exactly the subject of the case, and proceed to research the matter as you would research a subject. You eventually may come across the case under a variation of the originally suggested name.

"Find me a case that says . . ."

Research the matter as you would research a subject.

LOOKING FOR UNREPORTED CASES

Many more cases are decided than are reported. Lawyers used to think that an unreported case was not worth showing to the court, but that has now changed, partly because so many decisions are handed down that not all the important ones can be reported, and partly because computer databases have made it possible to find more and more unreported decisions.

Unreported cases may be found in digest services or legal newspapers.

Digest Services

Digest services are published on a weekly or monthly basis and contain summaries of recent cases of interest. An unreported decision is usually available on request from the publisher of the service. There are various digests available:

- General digests—*Canadian Current Law: Case Digests, Dominion Report Service*, and *Canadian Weekly Law Sheet.*

- Civil cases digests, from all jurisdictions—*All Canada Weekly Summaries* (A.C.W.S.).

- Topical digests, with cases from all jurisdictions—for example, the *Family Law Digest*, the *Weekly Criminal Bulletin* (W.C.B.), and the *Weekly Digest of Civil Procedure* (W.D.C.P.).

- Supreme Court digests—*Supreme Court of Canada Bulletin, Supreme Court of Canada Summaries, Supreme Court of Canada Reports Service*, and *Supreme Court of Canada Decisions.*

Legal Newspapers

Unreported decisions are available from legal newspapers on request; the digest section of each paper provides phone and fax numbers of the newspaper. *The Lawyers Weekly* covers all of Canada and contains news articles about recent decisions and case digests in every issue; it produces *The Lawyers Weekly Reports* as a supplement, which gives the full text of selected recent decisions that have not yet been reported. The *Law Times*, published weekly, covers Ontario cases only and, as with *The Lawyers Weekly*, prints both articles about decisions and case digests.

LOOKING FOR THE TEXT OF A CASE: UNDERSTANDING A CASE CITATION

Once you have found the name and citation of relevant cases, you still need to find the text. To do this, you must understand case citations.

Case Citations

A correct legal citation of a case consists of several parts as illustrated in the following examples, explained below:

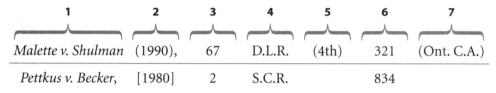

	1	2	3	4	5	6	7
Malette v. Shulman	(1990),	67	D.L.R.	(4th)	321	(Ont. C.A.)
Pettkus v. Becker,	[1980]	2	S.C.R.		834	

1. STYLE OF CAUSE OR GENERAL HEADING

style of cause
names of the parties in an action

The **style of cause** of the citation sets out the names of the parties (last names only). The names of *all* the parties to the action are not always included in the citation. In a reported case, the editors of the report series will have given the case a short style of cause as well as the complete one if it is long. The names of the parties are separated by "v." (which is Latin for "versus," meaning against) and are italicized.

2. YEAR

The year in which the case is decided or reported—that is, published in a report series—follows the style of cause and will be in either round or square brackets.

Some report series number their volumes sequentially no matter what the year, and it is not essential to know the year in which the case was reported in order to find it in the report series. In that case the year is placed in round brackets—( )—and is followed by a comma.

Other report series start a new set of volume numbers each calendar year, and it is essential to know the year in order to find the case in the report series. In this case, the year appears in square brackets—[ ]—and is preceded by a comma. For example, in each calendar year, the first volume of the *Supreme Court Reports* is volume 1. To find a case that is located in volume 1, you must know the year in which the case was reported to find the appropriate volume 1.

3. LAW REPORT VOLUME NUMBER

This number tells you the volume number of the report series in which your case can be found. Some law report volumes are identified simply by volume number (as in the first example above), while others are identified also by the year in which the volume was published. More than one volume may be published in one year as illustrated in the second example above. If the report series starts a new sequence of volume numbers each year, then you must make sure you look for the volume number for the correct year. In the example of *Pettkus v. Becker* above, you are looking for volume 2 for the year 1980.

4. NAME OF THE LAW REPORT SERIES

This part of the citation tells you the name of the law report series in which the case is reported. Abbreviations are generally used. In the example of *Malette v. Shulman* above, D.L.R. stands for the *Dominion Law Reports*. In the example of *Pettkus v. Becker*, S.C.R. stands for the *Supreme Court Reports*.

See the appendix for a list of standard abbreviations covering most Canadian report series.

5. LAW REPORT SERIES NUMBER

Many reports will not continue past a certain number of volumes. When the report reaches, for example, volume 75 or volume 100, that series ends and a new one begins. Subsequent editions are identified by 2d, 3d, 4th, and so on (*not* 2nd, 3rd). If a series or edition number is provided in a citation, be sure that you have the right series as well as the right volume number of the report. In the *Malette v. Shulman* citation above, the case can be found in the 67th volume of the 4th series of the D.L.R.

6. PAGE NUMBER

This number tells you the page number on which the case begins in the report volume. In a correct citation no abbreviation such as p., pp., or pg. is used before the page number.

7. JURISDICTION AND COURT

The abbreviation for jurisdiction and the level of court is found in round brackets following the page number of the case. This information is omitted if the jurisdiction and/or court level is obvious from the name of the report series.

If the citation refers to a report series that includes cases for one province only, such as the *Ontario Reports* or the *British Columbia Reports*, only the level of court is set out. For example, the citation of a Court of Appeal case published in the *Ontario Reports* will end with (C.A.). The citation for the same case in the *Dominion Law Reports* (which publishes cases from across Canada) will end in (Ont. C.A.).

If the citation refers to a report series for one court only, the level of court will not be included in the citation. For example, the *Supreme Court Reports* cover only Supreme Court of Canada decisions. Therefore a citation for that report series will omit both the jurisdiction and level of court, as illustrated in the example of *Pettkus v. Becker* above.

Sometimes the name of the judge or judges who decided the case is included in the citation. For example (Ont. C.A.—Robins J.). The J. stands for judge or justice; it is not the initial of the judge's first name. JJ. stands for justices and JJ.A. stands for justices of appeal. C.J. stands for Chief Justice. A judge's own initial is used only if it is necessary to distinguish between two judges with the same last name, for example R.E. Holland J. and J. Holland J.

Parallel Citations

Cases may be reported in more than one report series, in which case "parallel" citations are given. A parallel citation tells you about other reports where the same case report can be found. The citation for any official report series is given first. For example:

> *R. v. Carosella*, [1997] 1 S.C.R. 80, 142 D.L.R. (4th) 595, 112 C.C.C. (3d) 289.

This citation means that the case can be found in the *Supreme Court Reports*, the *Dominion Law Reports*, and *Canadian Criminal Cases*. Parallel citations are separated by commas.

When parallel citations are given, you need to choose only one of the report series to find the text of the case. However, if the case has been reported in an official report series, you should read and copy the case from that report series, if it is available to you.

Using the Case Citation
To Find the Text of the Case

The citation of a case contains all the information you need to find the actual case report, by providing the name and volume numbers of the report series in which the case has been published.

Start your search for a cited case by finding the law report series, including the correct series number. Then look for the appropriate volume number. Finally, turn to the page number set out in the citation. The case starts on that page.

UPDATING CASES

Once you find relevant case law, you must make sure that it is current, by updating each case to find out

appeal history
history of a case—for example, whether the case has been confirmed or overturned on appeal and the name of the highest court that reviewed the decision

- the case's **appeal history** or case history—has it been confirmed or overturned on appeal; what was the highest court that reviewed the decision; and

- how has the case been treated by other judges—has it been followed or not; has it been distinguished?

A case in your favour is useless if it has been reversed on appeal; a case that has not been followed by other judges has less persuasive value than one that has been followed consistently.

If a case has been appealed to higher courts, the citation you have in hand may include a complete appeal history or case history of the journey of the case through the court system. For example:

> *Queen v. Cognos Inc.*, [1993] 1 S.C.R. 87, rev'g. (1990), 74 O.R. (2d) 176 (C.A.),
> aff'g. (1987), 63 O.R. (2d) 389 (H.C.J.).

This citation tells you that the 1993 Supreme Court of Canada decision reversed the 1990 decision from the Ontario Court of Appeal, but affirmed the 1987 decision of the Ontario High Court of Justice.

If you don't have a full citation showing the case history, or if you think the case may still be in play so the citation is not complete, use either the *Consolidated Table of Cases* or the *Canadian Case Citations* (both series are part of the *Canadian Abridgment*) to find the history of the case. *Canadian Case Citations* may be slightly more thorough in listing cases. For either series, look in both the hardcover main volumes and the paperback supplementary volumes. To find out whether a case has been followed by other judges, use *Canadian Case Citations*.

Figure 11.11 reproduces a page from *Canadian Case Citations*. Note how the cases are listed alphabetically with parallel citations. If a case has been mentioned in other cases, those cases are listed at the end of the entry. Each case is preceded by an explanatory letter in a circle, as shown in figure 11.10.

FIGURE 11.10   Treatment Symbols for Cases

Symbol	Meaning
(F)	**Followed:** This case followed the principle of law in the cited case.
(D)	**Distinguished:** This case distinguished the cited case—that is, the principle of law was not applied because of a difference in facts or law.
(N)	**Not Followed/Overruled:** This case ruled that the cited case was wrongly decided.
(C)	**Considered:** This case considered or mentioned the cited case.

KEY TERMS

appeal history

case digest

general index

key and research guide

key classification system

reported case

style of cause

unreported case

Figure 11.11   Canadian Case Citations Sample Page

(1961), 38 C.R. 19 (B.C. Co. Ct.)

Stewart v. R.
(March 11, 1902)
(1902), 32 S.C.R. 483 (S.C.C.)

Cases citing S.C.C.
Ⓕ Lawson v. W.R. Carpenter Oversea Shipping Ltd., [1945] 1 W.W.R. 5 (B.C. C.A.)
© Klimack Construction Ltd. v. Belleville (City), [1951] O.W.N. 705 (Ont. H.C.)

Stewart v. R.
(1901), 7 Ex. C.R. 55 (Can. Ex. Ct.)

Cases citing Can. Ex. Ct.
© Klimack Construction Ltd. v. Belleville (City), [1951] O.W.N. 705 (Ont. H.C.)

Stewart; R. c., see R. c. Stewart

Stewart; R. v., see R. v. Stewart

Stewart v. R. (No. 2)
(1977), 35 C.C.C. (2d) 281 (Ont. C.A.)

Cases citing Ont. C.A.
Ⓕ Myers v. R. (1991), 65 C.C.C. (3d) 135 (Nfld. C.A.)
Ⓓ R. v. Pearson (1978), 7 C.R. (3d) 175 (Que. S.C.)
© Desbiens v. Québec (Procureur général), [1986] R.J.Q. 2488 (Que. S.C.)
© R. v. Skogman, [1984] 2 S.C.R. 93 (S.C.C.)
© Stolar v. R. (1983), 32 C.R. (3d) 342 (Man. C.A.)
© Bourget v. Northwest Territories (1982), 47 A.R. 220 (N.W.T. S.C.)

Stewart v. Ray
(October 27, 1941)
[1941] 3 W.W.R. 881, [1941] 4 D.L.R. 718 (Sask. C.A.)

Stewart v. Reavell's Garage
[1952] 2 Q.B. 545, [1952] 1 All E.R. 1191 (Eng. Q.B.)

Cases citing Eng. Q.B.
Ⓓ Walsh Insurance & Real Estate Ltd. v. Trans North Holdings Ltd. (1978), 20 A.R. 108 (Alta. T.D.)
Ⓕ Raiche's Steel Works Ltd. v. J. Clark & Son Ltd. (1977), 16 N.B.R. (2d) 535 (N.B. Q.B.)
Ⓕ Scott Maritimes Pulp Ltd. v. B. F. Goodrich Canada Ltd. (1977), 19 N.S.R. (2d) 181 (N.S. C.A.)

Stewart v. Rempel
(November 5, 1991), Doc. Vancouver B880462
[1991] B.C.W.L.D. 2603 (B.C. S.C.)

Stewart v. Rennie
(1836), 5 U.C.Q.B. (O.S.) 151

Stewart v. Rhodes
[1900] 1 Ch. 386 (Eng. Ch. Div.)

Cases citing Eng. Ch. Div.
© Jacobson Brothers v. Anderson (1962), 48 M.P.R. 29 (N.S. C.A.)

Stewart v. Richard
(1885), 3 Man. R. 610 (Man. Q.B.)

Cases citing Man. Q.B.
Ⓕ Canada Settlers Loan Co. v. Fullerton (1893), 9 Man. R. 327 (Man. C.A.)
Ⓓ Morris (Rural Municipality) v. London & Canadian Loan & Agency Co. (1890), 7 Man. R. 128 (Man. C.A.)

Stewart v. Richardson
(February 18, 1870)
(1870), 17 Gr. 150

Stewart v. Richardson Securities of Canada
(February 12, 1982), Doc. GDC-3210
(1982), 35 Nfld. & P.E.I.R. 325, 99 A.P.R. 325 (P.E.I. S.C.)

Stewart v. Richardson Sons & Co.
(June 10, 1920)
[1920] 3 W.W.R. 134, 30 Man. R. 481, 53 D.L.R. 625 (Man. C.A.)

Stewart; Robertson v., see Robertson v. Stewart

Stewart; Robichaud v., see Robichaud v. Stewart

Stewart v. Rogers
(June 30, 1905)
(1905), 6 O.W.R. 195 (Ont. H.C.)

Stewart v. Roop
(1983), 58 N.S.R. (2d) 407, 123 A.P.R. 407 (N.S. T.D.)

Stewart v. Ross
Doc. Q.B. J.C.R. 4226/86
(1988), 64 Sask. R. 271 (Sask. Q.B.)

Stewart v. Rounds
(1882), 7 O.A.R. 515

Cases citing 1st level
Ⓕ Weaver v. Sawyer & Co. (1889), 16 O.A.R. 422 (Ont. C.A.)
© Bate v. Canadian Pacific Railway (1888), 15 O.A.R. 388

Stewart v. Routhier
(December 21, 1971)
(1971), 4 N.B.R. (2d) 340 (N.B. Q.B.)
affirmed / confirmé (March 9, 1972) (1972), 4 N.B.R. (2d) 332, 26 D.L.R. (3d) 752 (N.B. C.A.)
which was reversed / qui a été infirmé (1973), [1975] 1 S.C.R. 566, 7 N.B.R. (2d) 251, 45 D.L.R. (3d) 383, 1 N.R. 183 (S.C.C.)
which was varied / qui a été modifiée (April 2, 1974) (1974), [1975] 1 S.C.R. 588, 7 N.B.R. (2d) 558, 53 D.L.R. (3d) 77, 1 N.R. 630 (S.C.C.)

and which was reversed / et qui a été infirmé (1973), [1975] 1 S.C.R. 566, 7 N.B.R. (2d) 251, 45 D.L.R. (3d) 383, 1 N.R. 183 (S.C.C.)
which was varied / qui a été modifiée (April 2, 1974) (1974), [1975] 1 S.C.R. 588, 7 N.B.R. (2d) 558, 53 D.L.R. (3d) 77, 1 N.R. 630 (S.C.C.)

Cases citing S.C.C.
Ⓕ Bate v. Kileel Enterprises Ltd. (1976), 14 N.B.R. (2d) 204 (N.B. C.A.)
Ⓕ Brekka v. Reid (1975), 14 N.S.R. (2d) 677 (N.S. C.A.)
Ⓕ Lessard v. Paquin, [1975] 1 S.C.R. 665 (S.C.C.)
Ⓓ Lewis Realty Ltd. v. Skalbania (1980), 25 B.C.L.R. 17 (B.C. C.A.)

Cases citing S.C.C.
Ⓓ Canadian Aero Service Ltd. v. O'Malley (1975), 10 O.R. (2d) 239 (Ont. H.C.)

Stewart v. Rowlands
(1864), 14 U.C.C.P. 485

Stewart v. Rowsom
(1892), 22 O.R. 533

Stewart v. Royal Bank
(1930), 1 M.P.R. 302, [1930] 2 D.L.R. 617 (N.S. C.A.)
reversed / infirmé (June 11, 1930), [1930] S.C.R. 544, [1930] 4 D.L.R. 694 (S.C.C.)

Cases citing N.S. C.A.
© Laidlaw Waste Systems Ltd. v. C.U.P.E., Local 1045 (1993), 37 L.A.C. (4th) 146 (Ont. Arb. Bd.)
© Landymore v. Hardy (1991), 21 R.P.R. (2d) 174 (N.S. T.D.)
© Landymore v. Hardy (December 23, 1991), Doc. S.H. 77533/91 (N.S. T.D.)

Cases citing S.C.C.
Ⓕ El-Zayed v. Bank of N.S. (1988), 87 N.S.R. (2d) 171 (N.S. T.D.)
Ⓕ Booth Fisheries Canadian Co. v. Banque provinciale du Canada (1972), 7 N.B.R. (2d) 138 (N.B. Q.B.)
© Levasseur v. Banque de Montréal, [1978] C.S. 1157

Stewart; Royal Bank v., see Royal Bank v. Stewart

Stewart; Royal Trust Co. v., see Royal Trust Co. v. Stewart

Stewart v. Royds
(1904), 118 L.T. 176

Cases citing 1st level
Ⓕ Richardson v. McCaffrey (1919), 45 O.L.R. 153 (Ont. C.A.)

Stewart v. Rundle
(April 13, 1940)

CHAPTER 12

Library Exercises

Now that you know more than you want to about paper-based legal research, it's time to apply your knowledge to research in a law library.

Below are sample questions, but an exercise is not useful unless it involves looking for recent changes to the law *and* takes into account the available materials. Therefore, ask your professor for an exercise that requires you to update statutes, regulations, and cases and includes questions that require you to find the following:

- a provincial or federal statute on a given subject;

- whether a specific provincial or federal statute has yet come into force;

- whether a regulation has been made under a specific provincial or federal statute;

- whether a specific statutory provision has been repealed or amended;

- whether a specific statutory provision has been interpreted by case law;

- whether a specific case has been cited in other cases; and

- a specific case that has been given to you as an incorrect citation.

SAMPLE QUESTIONS

Read the questions below, and for each one

- identify the kind of information you're being asked for (a statute, a regulation, a case, an update, or other?);

- decide which research tool(s) you will need;

- in the library, find out which tools are available; and

- answer the question. Cite correctly any statute, regulation, or case that you are asked to find.

1. Is there an Ontario statute that governs transplanting of human organs after death?

   a. What kind of information are you being asked for?

   b. Which research tools will you need?

   c. Which tools are available in your library?

   d. Your answer to the question.

2. Find the federal statute that deals with the sentencing of young offenders.

   a. What kind of information are you being asked for?

   b. Which research tools will you need?

   c. Which tools are available in your library?

   d. Your answer to the question.

3. The federal *Tobacco Products Control Act* is no longer in force. On what date was it repealed and by what statute?

    a. What kind of information are you being asked for?

    b. Which research tools will you need?

    c. Which tools are available in your library?

    d. Your answer to the question.

4. Find the *Criminal Code* section that deals with possession of prohibited weapons and update it to the present.

    a. What kind of information are you being asked for?

    b. Which research tools will you need?

    c. Which tools are available in your library?

    d. Your answer to the question.

5. Are there any cases in your province that followed the Supreme Court of Canada decision in *Crocker v. Sundance Northwest Resorts Ltd.*, [1988] 1 S.C.R. 1186?

   a. What kind of information are you being asked for?

   b. Which research tools will you need?

   c. Which tools are available in your library?

   d. Your answer to the question.

6. Was the 1992 Ontario case *Dunn v. Dunn Estate* appealed? If so, what happened on appeal?

   a. What kind of information are you being asked for?

   b. Which research tools will you need?

   c. Which tools are available in your library?

   d. Your answer to the question.

7. Find two recent texts on torts that are available in the library in which you are working. Give the author's name, book title, publisher, and date of publication.

   a. What kind of information are you being asked for?

   b. Which research tools will you need?

   c. Which tools are available in your library?

   d. Your answer to the question.

8. Are there any Manitoba Court of Appeal cases dealing with renewal of franchising contracts?

   a. What kind of information are you being asked for?

   b. Which research tools will you need?

   c. Which tools are available in your library?

   d. Your answer to the question.

9. Choose a specific provision of the Ontario *Limitations Act* and then find out if that provision has been cited in case law. Remember that you may have to concord the provision to trace the same section back through previous statute revisions.

   a. What kind of information are you being asked for?

   b. Which research tools will you need?

   c. Which tools are available in your library?

   d. Your answer to the question.

10. Are there any cases that have cited s. 181(2) of the 1985 federal *Bankruptcy and Insolvency Act*?

    a. What kind of information are you being asked for?

    b. Which research tools will you need?

    c. Which tools are available in your library?

    d. Your answer to the question.

11. Find the Ontario statute that provides information about who may adopt infants and children. Are there any regulations made under it?

   a. What kind of information are you being asked for?

   b. Which research tools will you need?

   c. Which tools are available in your library?

   d. Your answer to the question.

12. Your firm's client resides in British Columbia. She recently defaulted in her mortgage payments and the mortgagee is suing for a final order for foreclosure. Which B.C. statute provides information about the effect of a final order for foreclosure? Find the text of this statute.

   a. What kind of information are you being asked for?

   b. Which research tools will you need?

   c. Which tools are available in your library?

   d. Your answer to the question.

13. There is a 1982 Alberta Court of Appeal case involving Holt Renfrew and another corporation. Find the name and citation of this case. Locate the case report and provide the names of all the judges.

a. What kind of information are you being asked for?

b. Which research tools will you need?

c. Which tools are available in your library?

d. Your answer to the question.

PART V

Computer-Assisted Legal Research

In part IV of this book you learned about using paper sources for legal research. By the time you got from the beginning of Chapter 7 to the end of Chapter 12, you felt as though a library shelf full of books had fallen on top of you—and you were thinking (if not shouting) that there must be an easier way to do legal research.

Well, there *is* another way, and it is often an easier way, although it's not always the best way. In this part of the book, we explain how to use a computer to do legal research.

As with paper sources, there are usually several different ways to find answers to your questions when you do your research using a computer. You may be used to thinking of access to information via computer as free—but many of the computerized legal research sources are "subscription" sources, for which a library or a law firm has to pay. So, once again, you may find you won't have a lot of choice about which tool to use—there may be one computerized tool in the office or library for finding statutes, one for regulations, and one for cases, and you won't know which one until you get to the library or office. Just as with paper sources, you need to know something about all the available computerized sources. Then, when you sit down to work, you'll know how to deal with whatever tools are available.

CHAPTER 13

An Overview of Computerized Sources

When you conduct legal research using computerized sources, your purpose is the same as when you conduct legal research using paper sources—to find binding law that is relevant to a legal problem you need to solve. The law that you are looking for will be in the form of statutes, regulations, and/or cases. These primary sources, whether in paper or computerized form, are not especially user-friendly, and it is usually wise to start your research with secondary sources, using them to gain an understanding of the law and as finding tools to direct you to the primary sources that actually create the law.

This chapter begins to examine the process of finding law that is binding, using computerized primary and secondary sources. We will look at the various computerized legal research sources according to the purpose they serve or the job that they do and discuss the following topics:

- finding tools,

- primary sources,

- updating tools, and

- categories of computerized sources.

The various sources are discussed more fully in Chapters 14, 15, 16, and 17.

FINDING TOOLS

Generally speaking, you will start your computerized legal research using secondary sources we call "finding tools." Finding tools are used to help you find

- a general statement of the law,

- specific statutes,

- specific regulations, and

- specific cases.

General Statement of the Law

When you use computerized sources, just as when you use paper sources, it is best to start your research by looking for a general statement of the law as it applies to the problem to be solved. As we said in Chapter 7, legal encyclopedias such as the *Canadian Encyclopedic Digest*, or CED, not only provide you with a summary of the law, but refer you to the relevant statutes, regulations, and cases from which the principles of law are derived, so they are a good place to begin.

Looking for a general statement of the law with the computerized version of the CED is discussed in more detail in Chapter 14.

Specific Statutes and Regulations

Some computerized finding tools are designed specifically to help you find statutes and/or regulations on a particular subject or area of law. These finding tools include

- the Index to Federal and Ontario Statutes Online,

- government website search templates,

- Westlaw Canada's LawSource,

- LexisNexis®Quicklaw™ ("Quicklaw"), and

- the Canadian Legal Information Institute (CanLII) website.

Looking for statutes using computerized sources is discussed in more detail in Chapter 15.

Looking for regulations using computerized sources is discussed in more detail in Chapter 16.

Specific Cases

Legal encyclopedias, textbooks, and articles refer you only to the leading cases on a particular subject. When you want to find additional cases, there are computerized finding tools designed specifically to help you. The two main finding tools are the *Canadian Abridgment*'s *Canadian Case Digests* (CCD) and Quicklaw, both of which can be used to find

- cases dealing with a specific subject or legal issue,

- cases that have interpreted a statute or a section of a statute,

- cases considering a word or a phrase,

- cases when you have only a partial or incorrect citation (treasure hunting), and

- unreported cases.

Looking for cases using computerized sources is discussed in more detail in Chapter 17.

PRIMARY SOURCES

You cannot rely on secondary sources alone. Use them to gain an understanding of the law and as finding tools to direct you to the primary sources that actually create the law. Finding tools will give you the names of relevant statutes, regulations, and cases and sometimes a summary of their provisions. You must then go to the primary sources they refer you to, read them, and understand what they say.

Looking for the text of statutes using computerized sources is discussed in Chapter 15. Looking for the text of regulations using computerized sources is discussed in Chapter 16. Looking for the text of cases using computerized sources is discussed in Chapter 17.

UPDATING TOOLS

Once you have found the relevant statutes, regulations, and/or cases, you must make sure that the statutes and regulations have not been amended or repealed and that the cases have not been overturned on appeal and their legal principles changed by subsequent cases. You do this using secondary sources that we call "updating tools."

The following computerized sources will help you update statutes:

- Canada or Ontario Citator Service,
- *Canada Gazette* website (for federal statutes only),
- Library of Parliament website (for federal statutes only), and
- Legislative Assembly of Ontario website (for Ontario statutes only).

These updating tools are discussed more fully in Chapter 15.

The following computerized sources will help you update regulations:

- *Canada Gazette* website (for federal regulations only), and
- *Ontario Gazette* website (for Ontario regulations only).

These updating tools are discussed more fully in Chapter 16.

The following computerized sources will help you update cases:

- Quicklaw's QuickCite, and
- LawSource's KeyCite.

These updating tools are discussed more fully in Chapter 17.

CATEGORIES OF COMPUTERIZED SOURCES

As you can see, you can use computerized sources to do anything that you can do using paper sources. Before starting to work with computerized sources, however, you must know a little bit about their categories.

Computerized sources can be categorized by

- format,

- organization, and

- function.

Format

Computerized sources come in a variety of different formats.

Sources available in CD-ROM format include:

- *Canadian Encyclopedic Digest*, and

- *Canadian Case Digests*—the CD-ROM equivalent of the *Canadian Abridgment Case Digests*.

Sources available through free-access websites include:

- Canada and Ontario government websites for statutes and regulations—the online equivalents of the *Revised Statutes of Canada, Statutes of Canada, Canada Gazette, Revised Statutes of Ontario, Statutes of Ontario*, and *Ontario Gazette*;

- various court websites providing access to the text of case reports; and

- the Canadian Legal Information Institute (CanLII) website.

Sources available through pay-for-use subscription services include:

- Westlaw Canada's LawSource, which includes access to the *Canadian Encyclopedic Digest* and the *Canadian Case Digests*,

- Quicklaw, and

- Ontario Citator Service and Canada Citator Service—the online version of the statute citators.

Organization

Human editors have organized the information in the paper sources that we have looked at in various ways, be it by topic or chronologically. When you work with paper sources, you retrieve information by browsing through the source or by using an index or table of contents.

Computerized sources may or may not be edited. Information in all computerized sources is stored in databases. If the source is not edited, its information is stored randomly and you can retrieve it only by searching through the database for specific words. If the source is edited, you can also browse through it and use a table of contents.

Function

Computerized research sources serve the same functions as paper research sources. They may act as finding tools, primary sources, or updating tools, and you have seen examples of each listed above. In addition, online services such as Westlaw Canada's LawSource and Quicklaw combine secondary-source finding tools with access to the primary-source texts of statutes and case reports as well as updating tools.

KEYWORD SEARCHING

Computerized research sources will provide you with the same information as paper sources. However, although the information is the same in both print and computerized sources, the methods of getting access to the information differ for the two types of sources.

Information in paper sources is edited and organized, usually by topic. A researcher uses an index or table of contents to locate information. So, when you work with paper sources, you must analyze the facts of your legal research problem in an attempt to identify categories of law and/or legal concepts that may be relevant to your problem. You then use those categories and concepts to locate the information you are looking for in an index or table of contents.

Computerized sources store information randomly in databases. A researcher "asks" the computer to locate information in the database by searching for words that we call **keywords**. A computerized search is a request for all documents that contain requested keywords. When the researcher enters the keywords, the computer searches the entire database for appropriate matches.

Computerized sources usually use Boolean logic (named for a British mathematician, George Boole) to locate documents. In a **Boolean search**, the computer hunts through thousands of documents to locate requested combinations of words or phrases. Because information is not arranged in a database by subject, the only way the computer can locate a document is to locate words within the document.

When you work with computerized sources, you must analyze the facts of your legal research problem in an attempt to identify keywords that are likely to appear in the statutes, regulations, or court decisions that deal with your problem. It is important to understand that when you conduct a keyword search, you will get only what you ask for. The quality of your research will depend on how well you choose your keywords. You will not be able to see the surrounding material about your subject that would jump out at you from a print source.

keywords
words by which researchers search computerized sources for information stored randomly in databases

Boolean search
method by which the computer hunts through thousands of documents to locate requested combinations of words or phrases

The Role of Legal Knowledge and Analysis

When you do computerized legal research you are asking the computer to find cases that are relevant to your particular legal issue by searching the database for statutes, regulations, or court decisions that contain the keywords you have identified. In order to choose your keywords you must have some idea of the words that are likely to be found in a judge's decision in a case or a statute or regulation that deals with your issue. This means that you must know enough about the law to identify the legal issue(s) involved, and you must be familiar enough with the wording of statutes and the language of cases to be able to choose useful keywords.

The first step in this process is to place your legal problem within the relevant area of the law. Each area of law has terms and expressions that are commonly used, and you must know enough about the area of law you are researching to know what keywords to use. If you use inappropriate keywords, you risk retrieving far too many documents and/or missing what you are looking for entirely. Once you retrieve some statutes, regulations, and/or cases, you must review them to decide whether they are relevant to the issue you are researching.

Here's an example. Your client wants to sue her doctor. She went to the doctor because she had a broken arm, and the doctor made the break worse. You have to conduct a keyword search for relevant cases. If you don't know the relevant area of the law, your choice of keyword is limited to *arm*, *broken*, and *doctor*. A search using these terms will retrieve every case that contains those words in it, regardless of the area of law the case deals with. You'll get criminal cases about assault victims with broken arms who were examined by the doctor, and you'll get product liability cases about broken armrests in doctored automobiles. If you know that the area of law is tort law, you can be more specific and add terms such as *medical malpractice* or *negligence* to your keyword search that will reduce the number of unwanted cases that you retrieve.

Coming Up with Keywords

In a Boolean search, you are asking the computer to search for statutes, regulations, or case decisions containing keywords you have chosen. You have to guess what words the documents you're looking for might contain. In order to choose useful keywords, try thinking about common words or phrases used within this area of law, either from your general knowledge of law or from research you have done using secondary sources.

Usually there are several possible keywords you can try. For example *drunk driving* is also known as *impaired driving*, *operating a motor vehicle while impaired*, or *driving over 80*. If you choose just one keyword, you will not retrieve any of the cases that have referred to the matter in a different way. You increase your chances of getting the most accurate results when you search using a range of keywords.

For example, in a Boolean search involving medical malpractice in the setting of a broken arm, you might start off with the keywords *doctor*, *medical malpractice*, and *broken arm*. However, the computer will search only for these specific words or phrases. If a case on the same subject uses different words or phrases instead, such as *physician* or *surgeon* instead of *doctor*, or *negligence* instead of *malpractice*, the computer will *not* find the case. So you want to search for cases that contain the word *doctor*, *physician*, OR *surgeon* PLUS the word *arm*, *radius*, OR *ulna* PLUS the words *medical malpractice*, *negligence*, *negligent*, or *negligently*. You have to look for all these synonyms because it is impossible to know in advance whether a particular written decision spoke of a *doctor* who was *negligent* in splinting a *radius* or of *medical malpractice* involving a *surgeon* who did not set an *arm* properly.

KEYWORD EXAMPLE

Marsha Steward had a party at her cottage, Loon Hill, in Muskoka. During the party, one of her guests slipped on the staircase leading from the dock to the cottage. In keeping with the theme of her party—decorating with butter—Marsha had placed butter carvings of Ontario birds all along the stairs. Unfortunately, the carvings melted in the heat, making the staircase slippery. The guest has sued Marsha, and Marsha wonders whether she will be held liable. She would like you to give her some advice. You decide you will research relevant case law.

1. What area of law does this case involve?

   Tort law.

2. What kind of torts decisions are you looking for?

   Cases dealing with negligence generally, but in particular with occupier's liability.

3. What words might you expect to find in a decision about occupier's liability? Think of all the synonyms and variations of each term.

   a. occupier's liability;

   b. negligent, negligence, negligently;

   c. owner, homeowner, occupier;

   d. guest, invitee; and

   e. slip, fall, trip.

Boolean Connectors

When you conduct a Boolean search using keywords, it is not enough simply to come up with the correct keywords. You must also think about the combinations of the words that interest you. Do you want to see case decisions that contain *any* of your keywords, or only those decisions that contain *all* of your keywords?

Boolean searching is based on principles of Boolean logic—the logical relationship among search terms. Boolean searching uses three basic connectors:

- OR,

- AND, and

- NOT.

These connectors allow you to direct the computer to search for any of your keywords or for all of your keywords.

THE OR CONNECTOR

The OR connector directs the computer to search for documents that contain either term or both (or all) terms. For example, if you're looking for information about incarceration, you can search for two terms, *jail* OR *prison*. This search will retrieve documents in which at least one of the search terms is present—documents with either *jail* or *prison* or both in them. In figure 13.1, the shaded circle with the word *jail* represents all the documents that contain the word *jail*; the shaded circle with the word *prison* represents all the documents that contain the word *prison*; and the shaded overlap area represents all the documents that contain both *jail* and *prison*. An OR search will retrieve all these documents.

Figure 13.1   OR Search with Two Terms

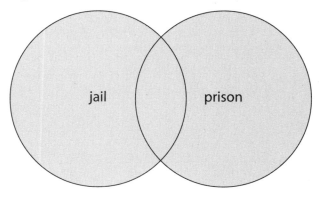

The OR connector is most commonly used to search for different ways of saying the same thing. The more terms or concepts combined in a search with the OR connector, the more documents the search will retrieve. For example, you can search for *jail* OR *prison* OR *penitentiary*, as illustrated in figure 13.2. This search will retrieve documents that contain any one, any two, or all three words.

Figure 13.2   OR Search with Three Terms

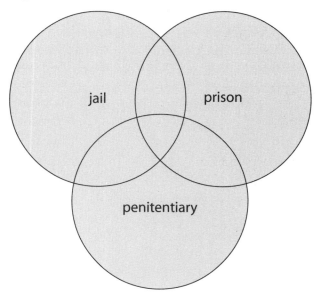

THE AND CONNECTOR

The AND connector directs the computer to search only for documents that contain both or all search terms. For example, if you're interested in researching the relationship between alcohol and abuse, you would search *alcohol* AND *abuse*.

This search will retrieve only documents in which BOTH of the search terms are present. In figure 13.3 this is represented by the shaded area in which the two circles overlap. The search will not retrieve documents containing only *alcohol* or only *abuse*.

Figure 13.3   AND Search with Two Terms

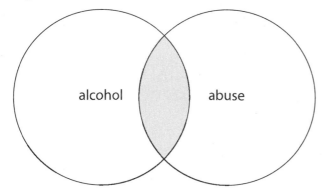

The more terms or concepts you combine in a search with the AND connector, the fewer documents you will retrieve. For example, you can search for *alcohol* AND *abuse* AND *gender*, as illustrated in figure 13.4. This search will retrieve documents that contain all three terms.

Figure 13.4   AND Search with Three Terms

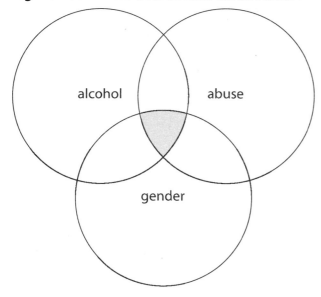

THE NOT CONNECTOR

The NOT connector is used when you want to retrieve documents that include one term, but not if the documents also include a second term. For example, if you want to see information about support, but want to avoid seeing anything about interim support, you would search *support* NOT *interim*. The search will retrieve documents in which *only* the word *support* is present. In figure 13.5, the circle on the left represents all the documents that include the word *support*. The area of overlap represents documents that include the words *support* and *interim*. The shaded area represents the documents that contain the word *support* but not the word *interim*.

Figure 13.5   NOT Search

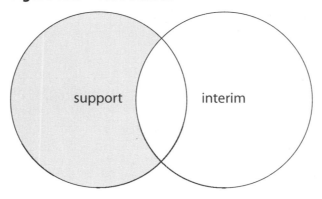

The NOT connector excludes documents from your search results. You must be careful when using the NOT connector because the term you are searching for may be present in relevant documents that also contain the word you wish to avoid.

More Advanced Boolean Searching

Once you have the hang of the simple connectors, you can move on to somewhat more complicated search methods.

SEARCHING FOR A PHRASE

None of the Boolean connectors discussed above will retrieve documents containing a phrase—a series of words in a given order. To search for a phrase, most computerized sources require you to enclose the phrase in quotation marks. For example, if you search for "*child support*" you will retrieve only documents that contain that specific phrase.

PROXIMITY CONNECTORS

When you're doing a Boolean search, to make sure you retrieve cases that are really about your topic, you may need to specify that certain words be close together.

If you are looking for cases on sexual harassment, for example, you can ask for cases where *sexual* and *harassment* both appear by joining the two words with the AND connector. A search query for *sexual* AND *harassment* will bring up cases where both words appear in the case, but those words may appear anywhere in the document. For example, you may retrieve a case in which there was a criminal sexual assault on a victim who also claimed there was harassment by the investigating police officers. You can retrieve cases where *sexual* and *harassment* are joined as a phrase by putting the phrase in quotation marks: "*sexual harassment.*"

You can also ask for cases where words are not beside each other in a phrase, but appear reasonably close to each other in the document. If you are searching for cases on the right to counsel under the *Charter of Rights and Freedoms*, for example, you would want cases that contain the phrase "*right to counsel*" but you would probably also want cases that contain the words *right to retain counsel* and *right to contact and obtain advice from counsel*. Proximity connectors allow you to limit your search to documents in which the terms you are searching for appear close to each other—for example, within 10 words of each other or within the same paragraph.

SUBSTITUTION AND TRUNCATION

Most computerized sources use substitution and truncation symbols (sometimes referred to as "expanders") to make the job of searching all possible search terms a little easier.

Substitution

Because your keywords may be spelled in more than one way (*offence* and *offense*), you can ask the computer to search for the word spelled either way by using a **substitution symbol**—for example, "*" (an asterisk) for the letters that may change: *offen*e.*

substitution symbol
symbol used in a computerized search that replaces a single letter to find keywords spelled in more than one way

Truncation

Because your keywords may have different endings (*dismiss, dismissing, dismissed,* and *dismissal*), you can ask the computer for all these words by using a **truncation symbol**—for example, "!" (an exclamation mark): *dismiss!*

truncation symbol
symbol used in a computerized search to find all possible endings of a root word

CONNECTOR PRIORITY

If you are using multiple Boolean and/or proximity connectors, you must determine in what order your search will be processed. Depending on connector priority, searches can be processed in different ways. For example, consider the following Boolean search: *child /5 support* AND *divorce* OR *separation.*

If a computerized source processes this search from left to right, it will first find documents in which the word *child* appears within 5 words of *support*, and then combine the result with all documents containing the word *divorce*. It will then combine that result with all documents containing the word *separation*. If, however, the source processes this search based on its default connector priority, the search may be processed differently. For example, it could find documents in which the word *child* appears within 5 words of *support* as one result, then find documents containing the word *divorce* or *separation*, or both, as another result, and then find all documents that contain both of these results.

If you are not sure of a source's connector priority, or, if you want to change its connector priority, use brackets to force the order of processing you desire. Connectors within parentheses will have priority over and operate before connectors outside the parentheses.

For example, the search *(support AND access) /5 child* will first look for all documents that contain the words *support* and *access*. It will then find all documents that contain the word *child* within 5 words of that result.

Each computerized source has its own connector priority. You must determine this priority before developing your Boolean search.

SEARCH SYNTAX

All the sources you will use for computerized legal research rely on the same Boolean logic, and all require you to have the same skills in determining and combining the appropriate keywords. But different sources may have different "search syntax"—that is, different proximity connectors, truncation symbols, substitution symbols, and rules for setting up the search. You will find that Boolean logic is used in one of three ways, depending on the source:

- Full Boolean logic with the use of connectors. You must use the connectors OR, AND, or NOT between your search terms.

- Implied Boolean logic. You enter search terms, but you don't use Boolean connectors. The space between the keywords defaults to either OR or AND, depending on the source. This is what is most commonly found in Internet searching. Many well-known search engines traditionally defaulted to OR but as a rule are moving away from that practice and defaulting to AND.

- Predetermined language. Some sources offer a search template that sets out connectors for you to choose from a drop-down menu.

Each computerized source has its own default implied Boolean logic that you must learn before you use the source. You must find out whether the words you enter

- are searched as a phrase,

- are searched as though there were an OR between them,

- are searched as though there were an AND between them, or

- require the Boolean connectors to be keyed in.

When using a computerized source, you must also learn what, if any, proximity connectors and truncation symbols are used by that source. In other words, you must learn the search syntax for that source. For example, the substitution symbol for one source is a question mark "?" while for other sources, it is an asterisk "*." Most sources use the proximity connector /n, where "n" is replaced with the number that specifies how far apart your keywords must be from each other. For example, *child /3 support* will find documents where the words *child* and *support* are up to 3 words apart from each other (have a maximum of 2 words between them). To find words within the same paragraph, most sources require you to connect the words by using /p. Each computerized source will explain the search syntax that is used by that source. Most computerized sources also contain a help feature that explains how to develop a Boolean search using that source. Here are some general guidelines for developing an effective Boolean search:

- Familiarize yourself with the search syntax of the source you are using. Make sure you know the proximity connectors, substitution and truncation symbols, and connector priority.

- Choose appropriate keywords for your research topic (as discussed earlier in this chapter).

- Consider whether any of your keywords should be joined as a phrase and use the appropriate "phrase" syntax (for most sources, you must surround the words in quotation marks).

- Combine your keywords logically, using the appropriate connectors (and parentheses, if necessary).

- Consider whether there are any synonyms for any of your keywords, and add them to your search using the OR connector.

- Identify keywords that may have alternate spellings or variant letters, and replace variant letters with the appropriate substitution symbol.

- Identify the keywords that have alternate endings and truncate these words using the appropriate truncation symbol.

Here's a Boolean search using the medical malpractice situation set out earlier in this chapter. To find cases that contain the word *doctor, physician,* or *surgeon* PLUS the word *medical malpractice, negligent,* or *negligence* PLUS the word *arm, radius,* or *ulna,* use the following Boolean language:

> doctor OR physician OR surgeon AND "medical malpractice" OR negligen! AND arm OR radius OR ulna

KEY TERMS

Boolean search

keywords

substitution symbol

truncation symbol

CHAPTER 14

Finding a General Statement of the Law: The Canadian Encyclopedic Digest

The general approach to legal research using computerized sources is the same as that for paper sources. It is best to start your research by using a secondary source, such as a legal encyclopedia, to find a general statement of the law as it applies to the legal problem you need to solve.

As we said in Chapter 8, the *Canadian Encyclopedic Digest*, or CED, is an excellent place to begin your research. In Chapter 8 we talked about the print version of the *Canadian Encyclopedic Digest*. In this chapter we discuss the computerized version of the CED.

WHAT IS THE CED?

The CED is a legal encyclopedia that provides a general overview of most areas of law. It's an excellent starting point for your research when you know very little about the area of law that you are researching. The CED is available in two computerized formats: CD-ROM and online. Both are organized in the same way as the print version.

The computerized versions of the CED are made up of over 220 subject titles, arranged alphabetically, and they combine the contents of the Ontario and Western editions of the CED in print. The subject titles are broad topics or general areas of law—for example, animals, contracts, evidence, and income tax. Each subject title contains parts, sections, subsections, and sub-subsections, breaking the title down into increasingly more topic-specific areas of information.

THE CED ONLINE

The CED is available on the Internet as part of LawSource, a subscription service offered by Westlaw Canada.

There are two main tools for finding information in the online version of the CED:

1. the table of contents, and
2. custom search templates.

Table of Contents

The table of contents lists all the subject titles in the CED in alphabetical order. It has several levels and each new level can be reached by clicking on the + sign next to a heading.

Access the table of contents by clicking on the CED link under the heading "Browse Tables of Contents" on the left-hand side of the home page. Figure 14.1 illustrates how the subject title "Animals" is broken down in the table of contents.

When you find your specific research topic, the following information is displayed in blue text:

1. the number of the part, section, heading and subheading of your topic (classification); and
2. the paragraph number(s) in the CED that deal with your topic.

Click on the text to view the entire paragraph(s). The text of the relevant paragraph(s) will be displayed in a separate window, together with a cross-reference to the *Canadian Abridgment*. Figure 14.2 illustrates the text of paragraphs 388–397 displayed in a separate window.

Figure 14.1 Online CED Table of Contents for the Subject Title "Animals"

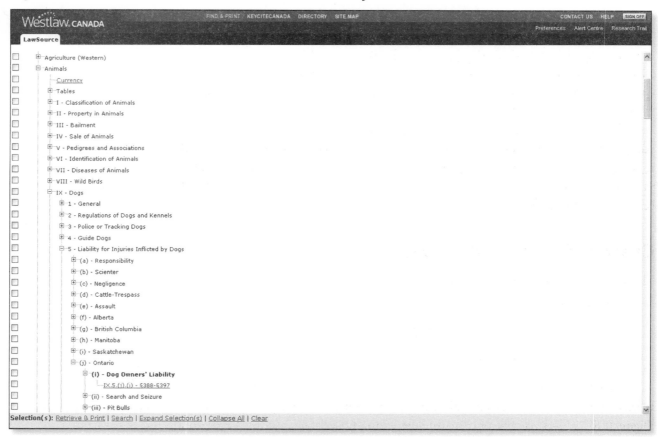

Figure 14.2   Text of Paragraphs 388–397 Displayed in a Separate Window

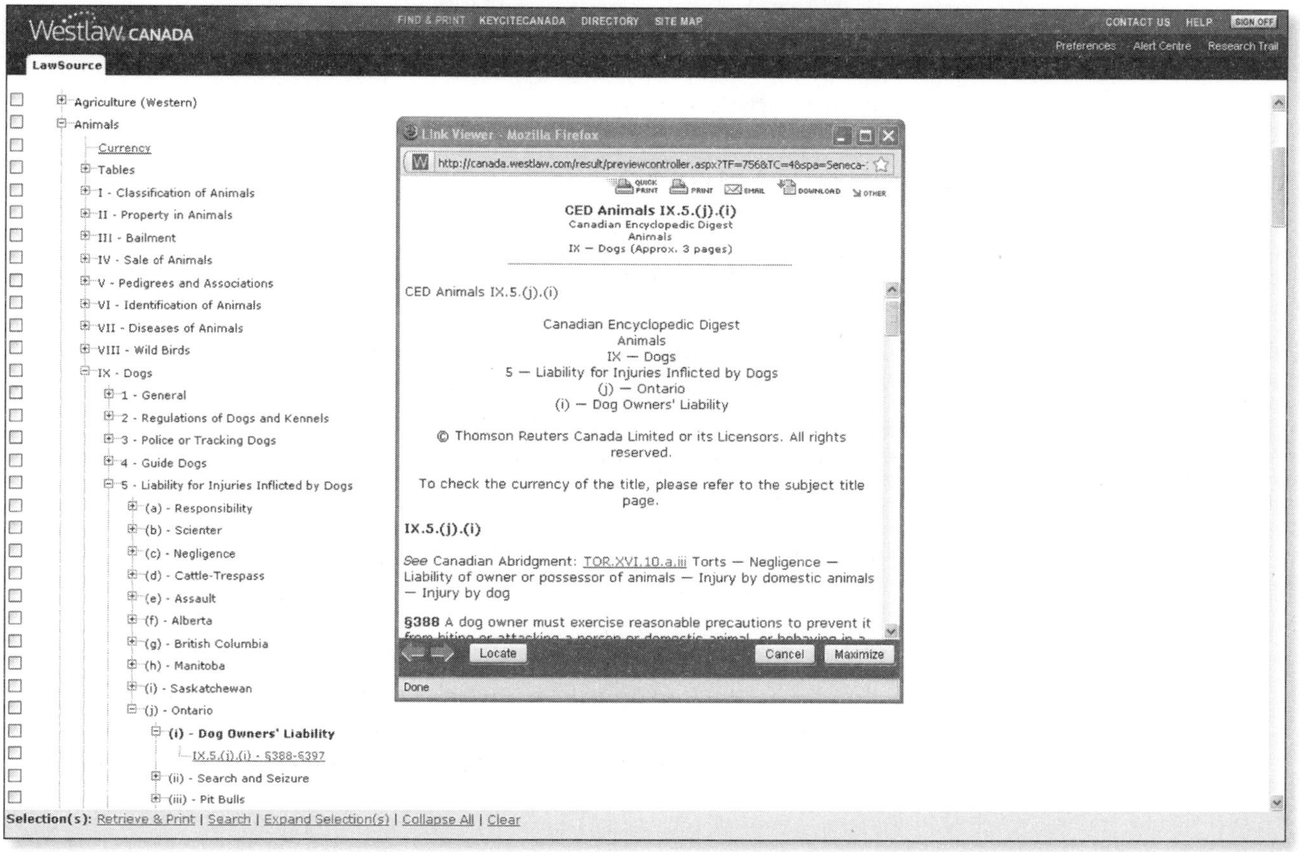

Note that the link to the relevant classification number in the *Canadian Abridgment Digests*. The *Canadian Abridgment Digests* is discussed in Chapter 17. See also Chapter 8 for a complete discussion of the table of classification in the CED, and Chapter 11 for a complete discussion of the key classification system in the *Canadian Abridgment*.

Click on the Maximize button to view a full-screen version of the text of the paragraphs. In the full-screen version, you will be able to look at paragraphs of adjoining classifications, by clicking on previous or next, at the top of the screen. Figure 14.3 illustrates the full screen version of the text of paragraphs 388–397 (classification IX.5.j.i).

Custom Search Templates

There are three custom search templates available:

1. standard search,

2. terms and connectors search, and

3. natural language search.

The **standard search** template allows you to search for information using keywords. You get access to this template by clicking on the "Canadian Encyclopedic Digest (CED)" link on the right-hand side of the home page, under the heading

standard search
allows you to search for information using keywords and a connector that is selected from the drop-down menu

Figure 14.3   Full-Screen Version of the Text of Paragraphs 388–397

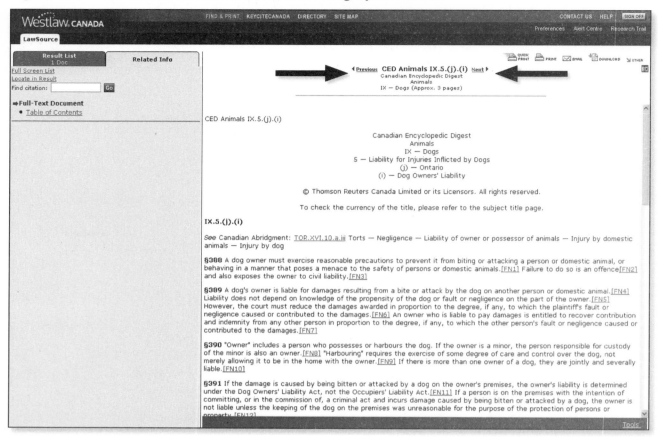

"Custom Search Templates." Enter the keywords and then select the desired connector from the drop-down menu within the template. You can search for

- any of the keywords you entered,

- all the keywords you entered,

- the exact phrase you entered,

- all the keywords you entered within five words of each other,

- all the keywords you entered in the same sentence, or

- all the keywords you entered in the same paragraph.

The template also allows you to search the entire CED or to limit your search to a specified subject title, classification, or citation. Figure 14.4 illustrates the standard search template.

The **terms and connectors search** template allows you to construct a Boolean search using keywords and your own Boolean connectors and expanders. It is, therefore, not as limiting as the standard search template. Access this search tool by clicking on the "Terms and Connectors Search" link at the top right-hand side of the standard search template screen. You can use it to search the entire CED or you can limit your search to parts of the CED by adding field and date restrictions to your search.

Figure 14.5 illustrates the terms and connectors search screen.

terms and connectors search
not as limiting as the standard search template; allows you to construct a Boolean search using keywords and your own Boolean connectors and expanders

Figure 14.4   Online CED Standard Search Template

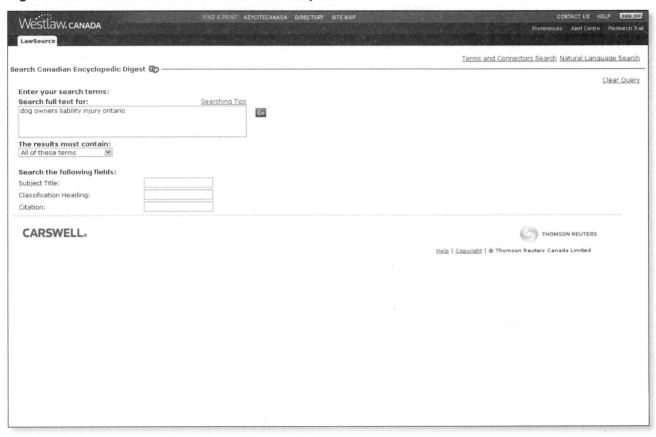

Figure 14.5   Online CED Terms and Connectors Search Template

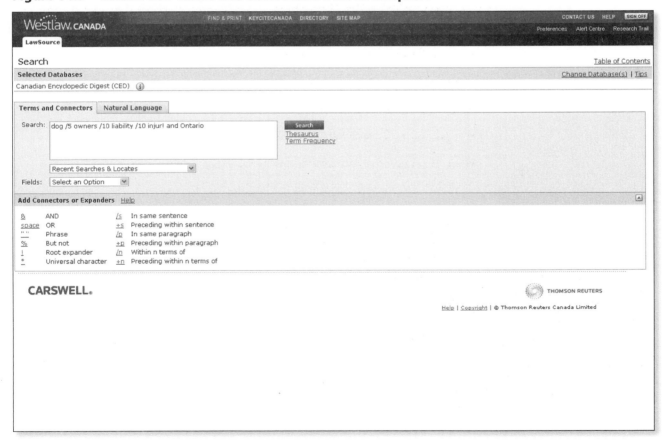

As we said in Chapter 13, each computerized source has its own search syntax, which will be explained by the source. The search syntax for the online version of the CED is set out below the terms and connectors search window, as illustrated in figure 14.5.

The terms and connectors search template contains a built-in thesaurus that provides related terms for all the keywords you enter. It also contains a term frequency option that lets you specify how many times your keyword must appear. There is a link to both these features beside the terms and connectors search window.

natural language search
allows you to search for
information by asking
your question using
plain language

The **natural language search** allows you to search for information by asking your question using plain language. You get access to this search tool by clicking on the "Natural Language Search" link at the top right-hand side of the standard search template screen. You can also get a link to this search template by clicking on the Natural Language tab while you are in the terms and connectors search template. You simply enter your question in the description box. You do not need to use any operators or connectors. "Are dog owners in Ontario liable for injuries caused by their dog?" is an example of a natural language search.

Figure 14.6 shows the natural language search template. By default, LawSource will select which terms to include in the search. To get the best results, use the "require/exclude terms link" (at the bottom of the natural language search template screen) to specify which of these terms you require to be present in your search and which terms (if any) may be excluded. In our example, the term "caused" may be excluded from the search.

Figure 14.6   Online CED Natural Language Search Template

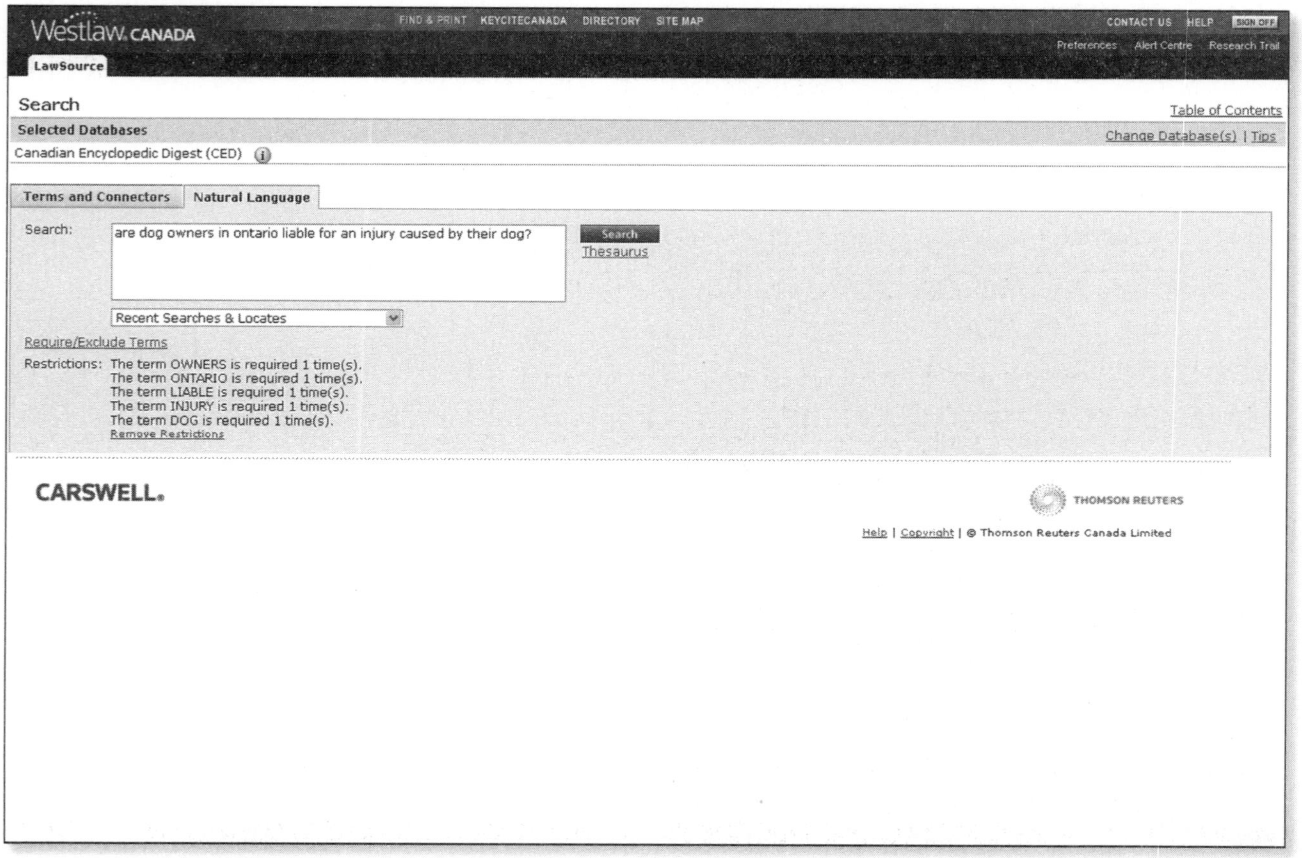

The natural language search template, like the terms and connectors search template, contains a built-in thesaurus.

Linking to the Text

Using any of the above search methods will lead you to the paragraph(s) in the CED that provide an overview or summary of the relevant law. Results are displayed on the left-hand side of the screen. Each result provides an excerpt from the paragraph with the search keywords highlighted. Results are numbered and provide the subject title, part, section(s), and paragraph number. Figure 14.7 illustrates the results of a natural language template search for the following research question: are dog owners in Ontario liable for an injury caused by their dog? (with the term "caused" excluded from the search).

Each result number is a hyperlink to the text of the entire paragraph. To view the text of the paragraph, click on the number in the result list that contains the paragraph you want to read. Figure 14.8 shows the text of one of the paragraphs from the results of the natural language search described above.

Each paragraph includes a reference to the relevant legislation and leading cases. The paragraphs also provide a hyperlink to the text of the cases. By clicking on the hyperlink, you can retrieve the full text of the case.

Figure 14.7   Results of a Natural Language Search

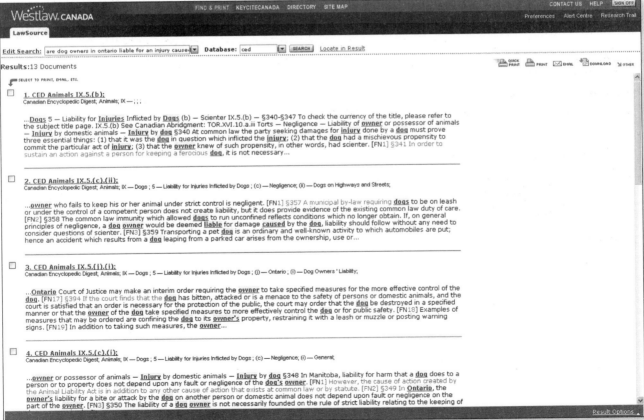

Figure 14.8   Paragraph from the Results of a Natural Language Search

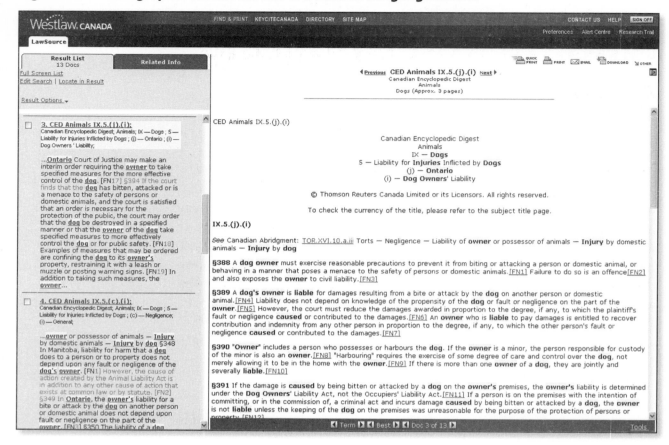

KEY TERMS

natural language search

standard search

terms and connectors search

CHAPTER 15

Finding and Updating Statutes

When you are doing legal research using computerized sources, your first priority is to find out whether there is a statute that is relevant to the issue. In Chapter 14 we saw that you may be able to do this by looking in the *Canadian Encyclopedic Digest*. There are also computerized finding tools, which we'll talk about in this chapter. Once you determine that there is a statute relevant to your issue, you have to be able to locate the text of that statute, which we'll also discuss.

This chapter addresses the following topics:

- how statutes are published in computerized format,
- computerized finding tools for statutes,
- finding the text of the statute using the computer,
- updating statutes using the computer, and
- legislative history.

HOW STATUTES ARE PUBLISHED IN COMPUTERIZED FORMAT

In Chapter 9, we discussed how statutes are published in paper format by both the federal and provincial governments and noted that the official text of the statutes is contained in the government revised statutes or annual statute volumes. The federal and Ontario (as well as other provincial) governments also publish their statutes on their websites. Copies of statutes that are obtained from both the Ontario and the federal government sites are official copies of the law.

Federal Statutes

You can find federal statutes at the federal Department of Justice website: http://laws.justice.gc.ca/en/. This site contains consolidated versions of the federal statutes, organized alphabetically by title. "Consolidated" means that the version incorporates all amendments that have been made to the text of the statute, to the most recent update. The "current-to" date is provided at the beginning of each consolidated statute. Statutes are updated on an ongoing basis and are generally current to within a few weeks.

The Department of Justice website also

- provides access to different consolidated versions of a statute as they read during earlier points in time ("point-in-time");

- provides direct links to related resources including the Constitution, the Charter, and federal bills and regulations;

- provides access to the text of a statute as originally enacted (not the consolidated version) (dating back to 2002);

- contains a table of private acts (a historical index showing all private acts of Canada, other than those dealing with divorces, that have been enacted since 1867); and

- contains a table of public statutes (a historical index with information on specific statutes, such as the dates of enactment and the responsible ministers as well as a detailed listing of amendments, including repealed sections).

The site contains several search tools, which are discussed further below under the heading "Computerized Finding Tools for Statutes."

Figure 15.1 shows the home page for the website as of July 6, 2009.

Figure 15.1   Department of Justice Laws Home Page

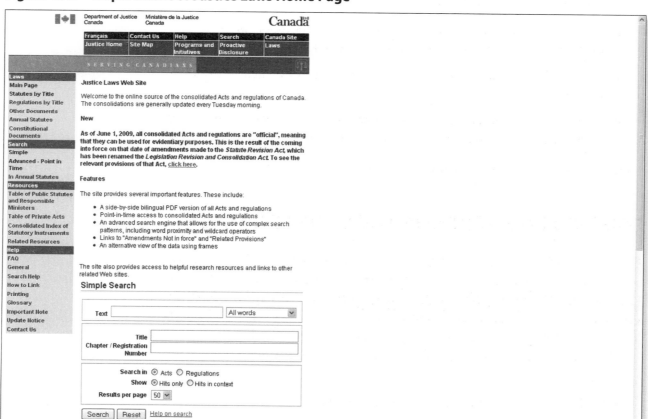

Ontario Statutes

You can find Ontario statutes at the Ontario government's e-Laws website: http://www.e-laws.gov.on.ca. This website contains the current consolidated version of most of Ontario's public statutes (the statutes that don't appear are listed in the site's table of unconsolidated and unrepealed public statutes).

The statutes are organized alphabetically by name. At the beginning of each consolidated statute, there is a notice of currency, which provides the consolidation period for the statute. The consolidation period for most statutes is up to date to the "e-Laws currency date." Click on the "e-Laws currency date" link in the notice of currency to see the e-Laws currency date for the statute. The government's goal is to provide consolidated statutes that are up to date within three business days of enactment of a new law or amendment of an existing law. A "notice of additional information" may appear at the beginning of a consolidated statute, stating whether there are outstanding amendments or coming-into-force events that affect the consolidated statute. These amendments and events will be incorporated into a subsequent consolidation of the statute. Grey-shaded text is included to provide commencement information about provisions that are not yet in force. In addition to consolidated statutes, the website also contains:

- Public and private statutes as enacted, dating back to January 1, 2000 (referred to as "source law")—these include new statutes and amending, repealing, or revoking statutes. They are organized first by the year in which the statute was enacted, and then alphabetically by name.

- Consolidated versions of a statute as they read during different periods in time (referred to as "period in time" or "PIT" law).

- Historical versions (a consolidated version of a statute as it read immediately before a change) of statutes amended since January 1, 2004.

- A list of all public statutes that were enacted during a specified year (dating back to 2000).

- The text of many repealed statutes, if the statute was in the *Revised Statutes of Ontario, 1990* or enacted after 1990 and repealed on or after January 1, 2004.

Figure 15.2 shows the home page for the website as of July 25, 2007.

COMPUTERIZED FINDING TOOLS FOR STATUTES

As we noted in Chapter 9, the challenge with respect to statute law is not so much finding the text of the statute as it is finding whether, in fact, a relevant statute exists. The easiest way to find whether a relevant statute exists is by researching your subject using the CED. When you find the general statement of the law dealing with your specific topic, it will refer you to the relevant legislation, if any.

There are other computerized ways to find whether a relevant statute exists, including

- the Index to Federal and Ontario Statutes Online, and

- government website search templates.

Figure 15.2   e-Laws Home Page

Government Website Search Templates

Both the federal Department of Justice and the Ontario e-Laws websites include search templates that allow you to search for current consolidated statutes using keywords—that is, by entering words that may appear in either the title or text of a statute. This method is not always easy or reliable because you may find more than one statute containing the keywords you entered. You will then have to scan each statute carefully to determine whether it is in fact relevant to your research topic.

The Department of Justice site contains two search templates for finding current consolidated statutes:

- The simple search template allows you to search for keywords in the text of a statute. It provides a drop-down menu of default connectors for the keywords you enter. You can choose to search "all words," "any word," or an "exact phrase." The simple search template also provides "Title" and "Chapter/Registration Number" fields. These two fields can be used alone or together with a text field search (to narrow the results).

- The advanced search (point-in-time) template allows you to search for keywords in the text of a statute using Boolean connectors.

The Ontario e-Laws site contains a standard search template that allows you to search for keywords within the titles alone of all the consolidated statutes or within the contents, including titles, of all the consolidated statutes. You can use the connector links provided or insert your own connectors and operators using the appropriate search syntax.

FINDING THE TEXT OF A FEDERAL STATUTE

Once you know the name of the federal statute that is relevant to the issue you are researching, it is easy to find the text of the statute. Use any of the following sources:

- the Department of Justice website,
- Westlaw Canada's LawSource,
- LexisNexis®Quicklaw™ ("Quicklaw"), or
- the Canadian Legal Information Institute (CanLII) website.

Department of Justice Website: http://laws.justice.gc.ca

When you know the name of the statute you are looking for, you can browse by title for the text of the consolidated version of that statute. Click on the link "Statutes by Title" (under the heading "Laws" on the left-hand side of the home page). Select the letter of the alphabet that corresponds to the first letter of the name of the statute you are looking for. All statutes that begin with that letter are displayed. Scroll down the list until you find your statute and then click on its name. Figure 15.3 is a copy of the Browse by Title page for the letter "A."

Figure 15.3   Browse Statutes by Title Page

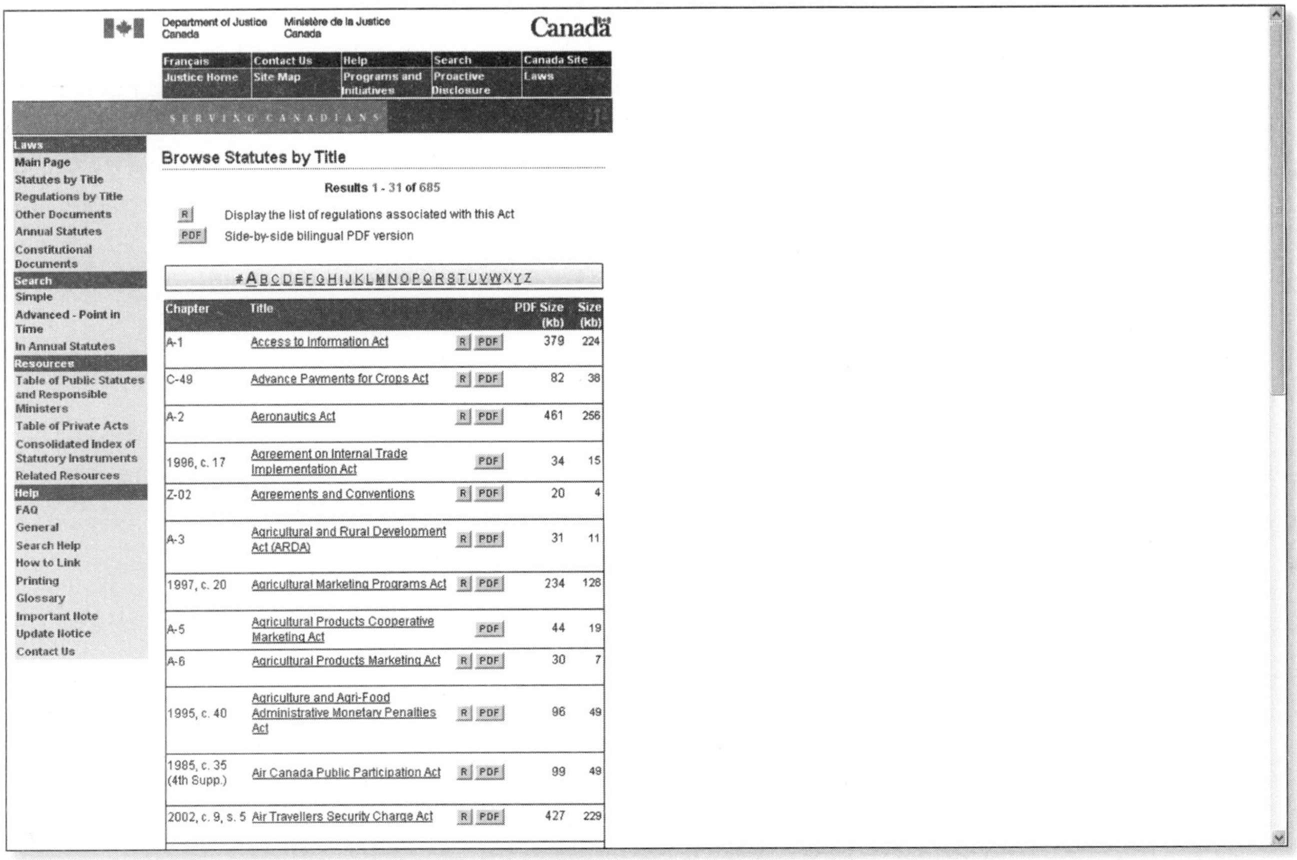

Assume, for example, that you want to find the text of the *Canada Health Act.* Click on the letter "C" and then click on the name of the statute. You are taken to the Table of Contents page for the statute. From this page, you can then link either to the text of the entire Act (by clicking the "Full Document for Printing" link) or to a specific section only (by clicking on the desired heading). When you select a desired heading, you will be taken into the "Document View" for that selection. In this view, only selected segments (parts and sections of the statute) are displayed. You can move to different segments of the statute by using the drop-down menu at the top and bottom of each segment.

From the Table of Contents page, select the "Frames View" option to see both the content of the statute together with its table of contents.

The search also generates a link to related regulations and related information. Figure 15.4 illustrates the Table of Contents view of the search results for the *Canada Health Act.* Figure 15.5 illustrates the Frames View of the search results for the *Canada Health Act.*

Westlaw Canada's LawSource

The text of federal statutes is available on the Internet as part of LawSource, a subscription service offered by Westlaw Canada. If you know the name of the statute you are looking for, you can use the "Legislation" fields of the "Find/KeyCite a Document" template on the bottom of the LawSource home page.

Figure 15.4   Table of Contents View of the Search Results for the Canada Health Act

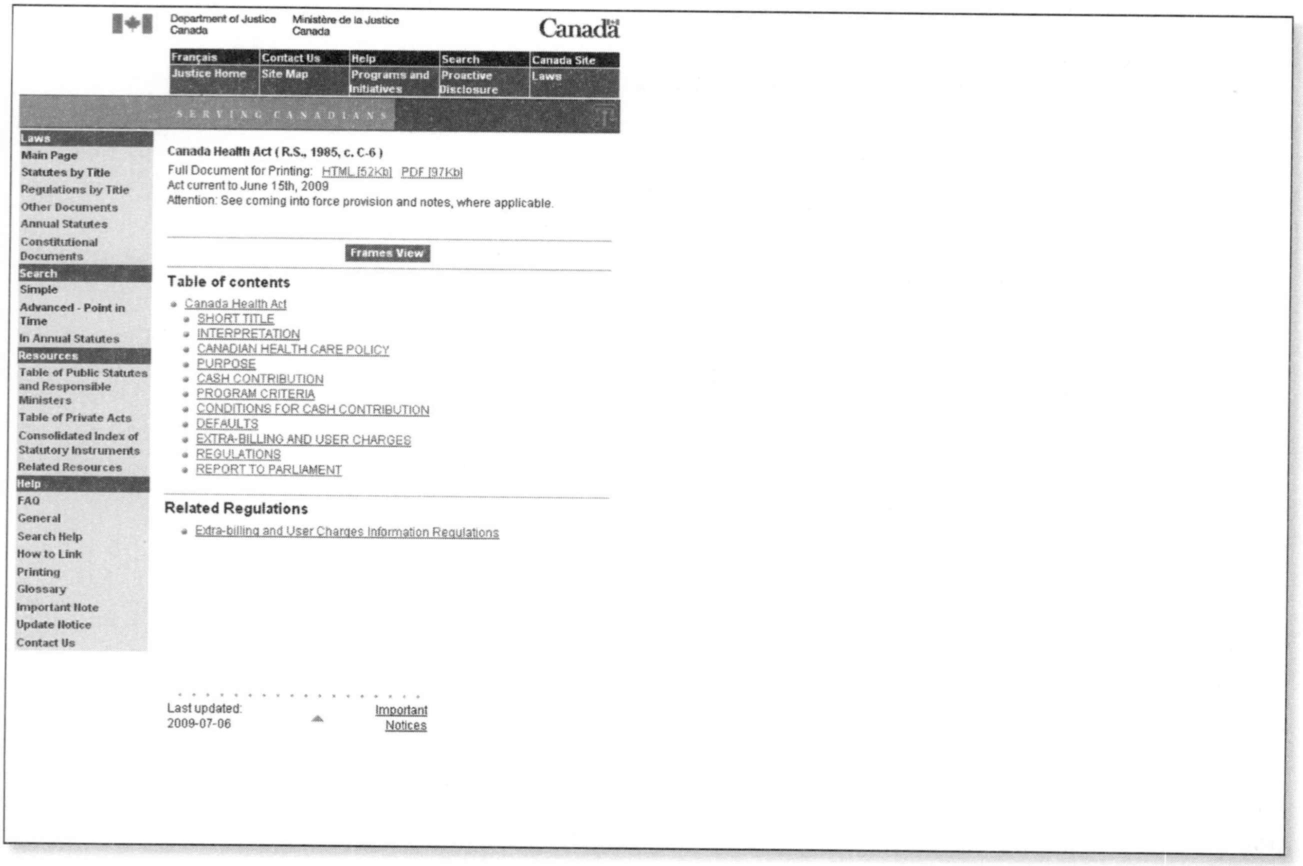

Figure 15.5   Frames View of the Search Results for the Canada Health Act

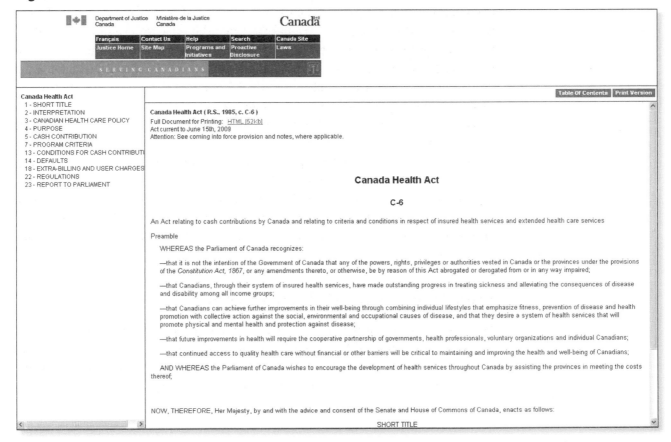

For example, to find the *Canada Health Act*, enter "Canada Health Act" under "Title" and choose "Federal" for jurisdiction. You can also include a section number to find a specific section of the statute. Figure 15.6 shows the completed Find/Key-Cite a Document template for finding the text of the *Canada Health Act*. Figure 15.7 shows the results of the search for the *Canada Health Act*.

Click on the section of the Act that you want to look at. LawSource displays the text of statutes by sections only; you cannot view the text of the entire statute at once. The letter "c" next to a section indicates that citing references for that section are available, in which case you can link directly to case law citing that section. Figure 15.8 illustrates the text of s. 2 of the *Canada Health Act*.

You can also find the text of federal statutes by browsing the Tables of Contents. Select "Legislation" under the heading "Browse Tables of Contents" (on the left-hand side of the home page). Expand "Canada" (by clicking the + sign) and then expand "Federal (English)." Click on "Statutes" and then browse the alphabetical list of statutes to find the name of the statute you are looking for.

LexisNexis®Quicklaw™ ("Quicklaw")

The text of federal statutes is also available on the Internet as part of the Quicklaw subscription service. The easiest way to find the text of the current consolidation of a federal statute is to use the legislation search template. Click on the "Legislation" tab on the home page and choose "Search" under the heading "Current Consolidations." Select the appropriate source (for example, "All Canadian Statutes") and

Figure 15.6 Completed Find/KeyCite a Document Template

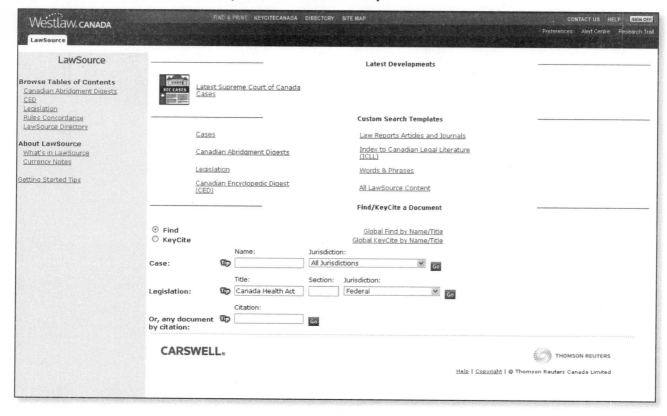

Figure 15.7 Result of Search for the Canada Health Act

Figure 15.8 Text of Section 2 of the Canada Health Act

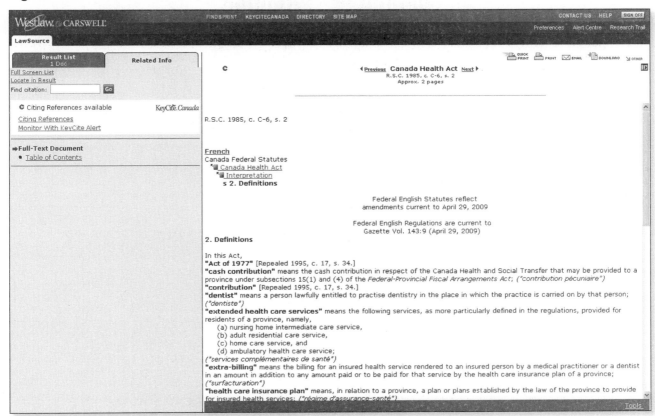

enter the name of the statute you are looking for in the "Legislation Title" field. You can also include a section number to find a specific section of the statute. In the "Legislation Type" field, choose "Acts." Results are displayed by sections of the statute—click on the section you want to see the text of. To see the text of the entire statute, select "Show Document Options" from the View drop-down menu at the top of the section you are viewing. Click on the name of the statute in the "View More" box at the top right-hand side of the document.

You can also browse by title for federal statutes. Click on the "Legislation" tab on the home page and choose "Browse" under the heading "Current Consolidations." Select the appropriate source and then browse the alphabetical list of statutes to find the name of the statute you are looking for.

Canadian Legal Information Institute (CanLII): http://www.canlii.org

The Canadian Legal Information Institute (CanLII) maintains a website at http://www.canlii.org. This website provides access to the text of federal statutes. Choose "Federal" under the heading "Databases" and then enter the name of the statute in the "statute name" field box of the search template. Or, choose "Federal" and then click on "Statutes and Regulations" under the heading "Legislation." Select the letter that is the first letter of the name of the statute you are looking for (under the heading "Consolidated Statutes of Canada") to link to the text of the statute. For example, to find the text of the *Divorce Act*, select the letter "D" to see a list of all federal statutes starting with that letter.

Figure 15.9 illustrates the list of consolidated federal statutes beginning with the letter "D."

Click on the name of the statute to link to its text. Figure 15.10 illustrates the first page of the text of the *Divorce Act*. As you can see in figure 15.10, CanLII provides three additional options, which appear at the top of the page containing the text of the statute you selected. You can choose to link directly to the regulations associated with the statute, note-up the statute, or compare different versions of the statute, if available, by clicking on the appropriate tab. For example, to compare the current version of the statute with the earliest version, check the boxes beside these two versions. The two requested versions are displayed side-by-side on your screen. Figure 15.11 illustrates the results of this request.

FINDING THE TEXT OF AN ONTARIO STATUTE

Once you know the name of an Ontario statute, it is easy to find the text of the statute. Use any of the following sources:

- the Ontario e-Laws website,
- Westlaw Canada's LawSource,
- Quicklaw, or
- the Canadian Legal Information Institute (CanLII) website.

Figure 15.9 Consolidated Federal Statutes Beginning with the Letter "D" (CanLII)

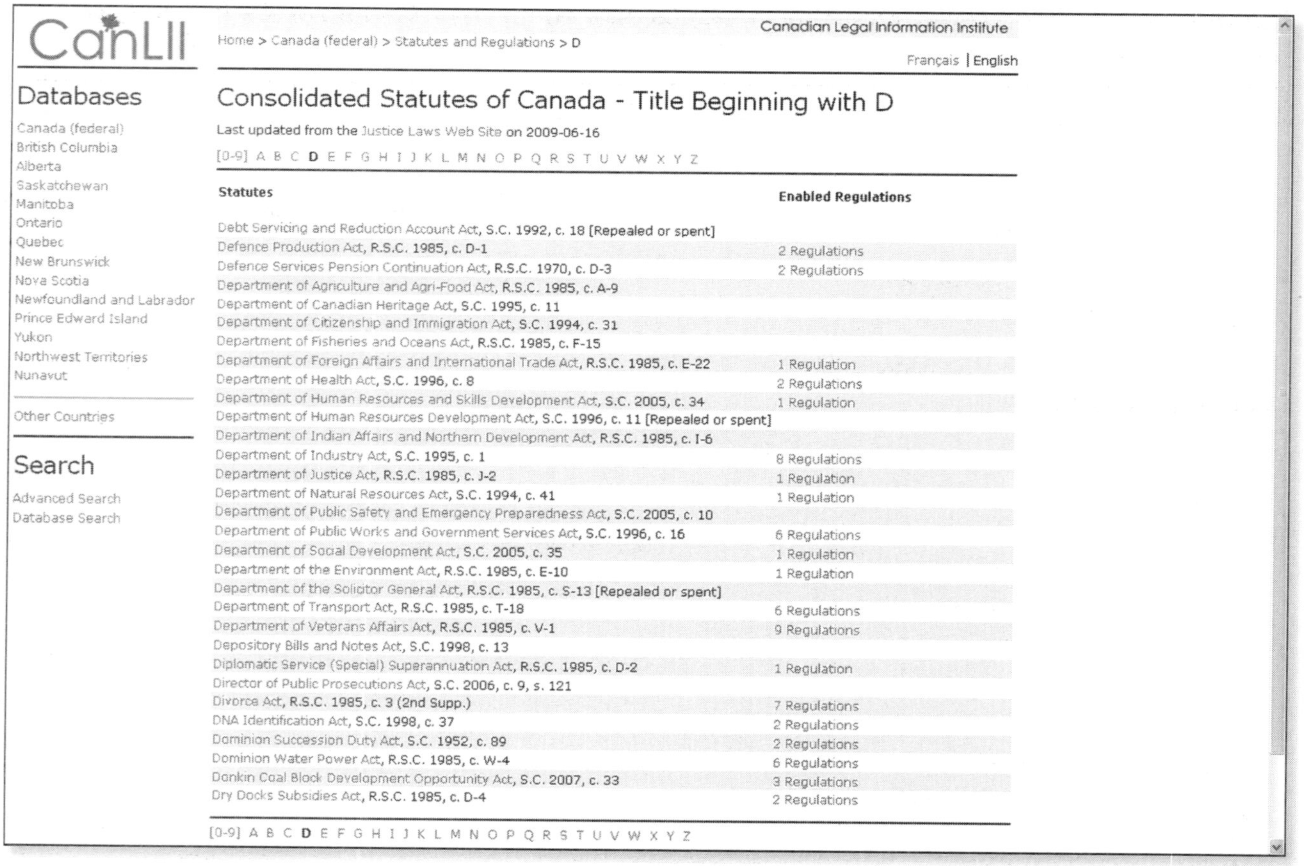
CanLII

Home > Canada (federal) > Statutes and Regulations > D

Canadian Legal Information Institute

Français | English

Databases

Canada (federal)
British Columbia
Alberta
Saskatchewan
Manitoba
Ontario
Quebec
New Brunswick
Nova Scotia
Newfoundland and Labrador
Prince Edward Island
Yukon
Northwest Territories
Nunavut

Other Countries

Search

Advanced Search
Database Search

Consolidated Statutes of Canada - Title Beginning with D

Last updated from the Justice Laws Web Site on 2009-06-16

[0-9] A B C D E F G H I J K L M N O P Q R S T U V W X Y Z

Statutes	Enabled Regulations
Debt Servicing and Reduction Account Act, S.C. 1992, c. 18 [Repealed or spent]	
Defence Production Act, R.S.C. 1985, c. D-1	2 Regulations
Defence Services Pension Continuation Act, R.S.C. 1970, c. D-3	2 Regulations
Department of Agriculture and Agri-Food Act, R.S.C. 1985, c. A-9	
Department of Canadian Heritage Act, S.C. 1995, c. 11	
Department of Citizenship and Immigration Act, S.C. 1994, c. 31	
Department of Fisheries and Oceans Act, R.S.C. 1985, c. F-15	
Department of Foreign Affairs and International Trade Act, R.S.C. 1985, c. E-22	1 Regulation
Department of Health Act, S.C. 1996, c. 8	2 Regulations
Department of Human Resources and Skills Development Act, S.C. 2005, c. 34	1 Regulation
Department of Human Resources Development Act, S.C. 1996, c. 11 [Repealed or spent]	
Department of Indian Affairs and Northern Development Act, R.S.C. 1985, c. I-6	
Department of Industry Act, S.C. 1995, c. 1	8 Regulations
Department of Justice Act, R.S.C. 1985, c. J-2	1 Regulation
Department of Natural Resources Act, S.C. 1994, c. 41	1 Regulation
Department of Public Safety and Emergency Preparedness Act, S.C. 2005, c. 10	
Department of Public Works and Government Services Act, S.C. 1996, c. 16	6 Regulations
Department of Social Development Act, S.C. 2005, c. 35	1 Regulation
Department of the Environment Act, R.S.C. 1985, c. E-10	1 Regulation
Department of the Solicitor General Act, R.S.C. 1985, c. S-13 [Repealed or spent]	
Department of Transport Act, R.S.C. 1985, c. T-18	6 Regulations
Department of Veterans Affairs Act, R.S.C. 1985, c. V-1	9 Regulations
Depository Bills and Notes Act, S.C. 1998, c. 13	
Diplomatic Service (Special) Superannuation Act, R.S.C. 1985, c. D-2	1 Regulation
Director of Public Prosecutions Act, S.C. 2006, c. 9, s. 121	
Divorce Act, R.S.C. 1985, c. 3 (2nd Supp.)	7 Regulations
DNA Identification Act, S.C. 1998, c. 37	2 Regulations
Dominion Succession Duty Act, S.C. 1952, c. 89	2 Regulations
Dominion Water Power Act, R.S.C. 1985, c. W-4	6 Regulations
Donkin Coal Block Development Opportunity Act, S.C. 2007, c. 33	3 Regulations
Dry Docks Subsidies Act, R.S.C. 1985, c. D-4	2 Regulations

[0-9] A B C D E F G H I J K L M N O P Q R S T U V W X Y Z

Figure 15.10   First Page of the Text of the Divorce Act (CanLII)

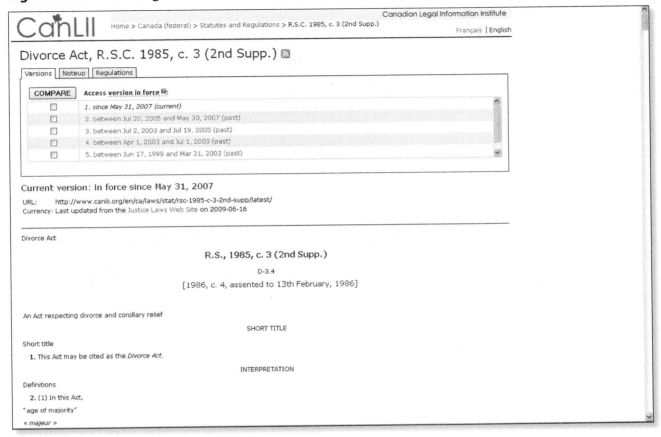

Figure 15.11   Side-by-Side Comparison of the Current and Earliest Version of the Divorce Act

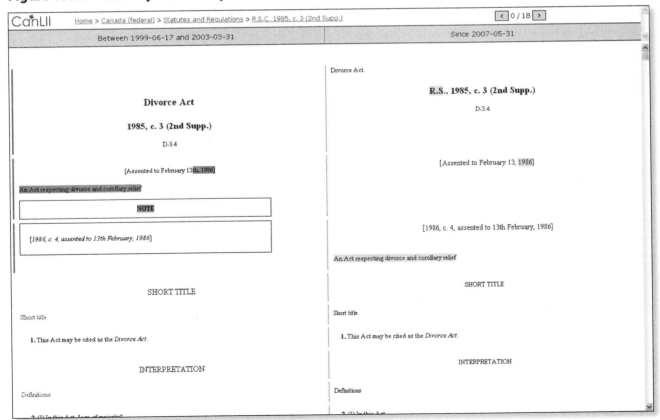

Ontario e-Laws Website: http://www.e-laws.gov.on.ca

To find the text of the current consolidation of a statute, select "Search or Browse Current Consolidated Law" (in the centre of the home page) or "Current Consolidated Law" (on the left-hand side of the home page). Both links will take you to the same page. Under the heading "Browse Current Consolidated Law," click on the letter that is the same as the first letter of the name of the statute you want to find to see all current consolidated statutes beginning with that letter. For example, to find the text of the *Dog Owners' Liability Act*, click on the letter "D" and scroll down to the name of the statute. Click on the name of the statute to view the text of the entire statute. Figure 15.12 illustrates the "Browse Current Consolidated Law" page. Figure 15.13 illustrates how the text of the statute is displayed. The consolidation period appears at the top of the page indicating whether there are any amendments yet to be consolidated into the statute and the date those amendments will come into force. Amendments that have been passed but have not yet come into force will be displayed in greyed-out text in the statute.

Westlaw Canada's LawSource

The text of Ontario statutes is available on the Internet as part of LawSource, a subscription service offered by Westlaw Canada. If you know the name of the statute

Figure 15.12   e-Laws "Browse Current Consolidated Law" Page for the Letter "D"

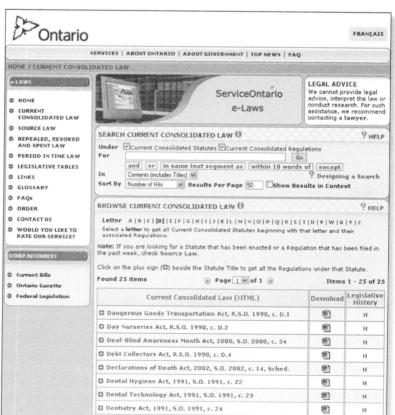

Figure 15.13   Text of the Dog Owners' Liability Act

Français

Dog Owners' Liability Act

R.S.O. 1990, CHAPTER D.16

Consolidation Period: From January 1, 2007 to the e-Laws currency date

Last amendment: 2006, c. 32, Sched. C, s. 13.

SKIP TABLE OF CONTENTS

CONTENTS

INTERPRETATION
1.   Definitions
CIVIL LIABILITY
2.   Liability of owner
3.   Application of Occupiers' Liability Act
PROCEEDINGS — PART IX OF THE PROVINCIAL OFFENCES ACT
4.   Proceedings against owner of dog
5.   Order to prohibit dog ownership
PRECAUTIONS BY DOG OWNERS
5.1   Owner to prevent dog from attacking
PIT BULLS — BAN AND RELATED CONTROLS
6.   Pit bull ban
7.   Ownership of restricted pit bulls
8.   Ownership of pit bull other than restricted
9.   Transfer of pit bulls
10.   Importation of restricted pit bulls
11.   Municipal by-laws
SEARCH AND SEIZURE
12.   Peace officers
13.   Warrant to seize dog
14.   Exigent circumstances
15.   Seizure in public place
16.   Necessary force
17.   Delivery of seized dog to pound
OFFENCES
18.   Offences
19.   Identification of pit bull
REGULATIONS
20.   Regulations

INTERPRETATION

Definitions

1. (1) In this Act,

"owner", when used in relation to a dog, includes a person who possesses or harbours the dog and, where the owner is a minor, the person responsible for the custody of the minor; ("propriétaire")

"pit bull" includes,

you are looking for, you can use the "Legislation" fields of the "Find/KeyCite a Document" template on the bottom of the LawSource home page.

Enter the name of the statute you are looking for under "Title," choose "Ontario" for jurisdiction, and click "Go." You can also include a section number to find a specific section of the statute. Click on the section of the Act that you want to look at. LawSource displays the text of statutes by sections only; you cannot view the text of the entire statute at once.

You can also find the text of Ontario statutes by browsing the table of contents. Select "Legislation" under the heading "Browse Tables of Contents" (on the left-hand side of the home page). Expand "Canada" (by clicking the + sign) and then expand "Ontario." Click on "Statutes" and then browse the alphabetical list of statutes to find the name of the statute you are looking for.

LexisNexis®Quicklaw™ ("Quicklaw")

The text of Ontario statutes is also available on the Internet as part of the Quicklaw subscription service. The easiest way to find the text of the current consolidation of Ontario statutes is to use the legislation search template. Click on the "Legislation" tab on the home page and choose "Search" under the heading "Current Consolidations." Select the appropriate source (for example, "Ontario Statutes") and enter the name of the statute you are looking for in the "Legislation Title" field. You can also include a section number to find a specific section of the statute. Results are displayed by sections of the statute—click on the section you want to see the text of.

To see the text of the entire statute, select "Show Document Options" from the View drop-down menu at the top of the section you are viewing. Click on the name of the statute in the "View More" box at the top right-hand side of the document.

You can also browse by title for Ontario statutes. Click on the "Legislation" tab on the home page and choose "Browse" under the heading "Current Consolidations." Select the appropriate source and then browse the alphabetical list of statutes to find the name of the statute you are looking for.

Canadian Legal Information Institute (CanLII): http://www.canlii.org

The Canadian Legal Information Institute (CanLII) website at www.canlii.org provides access to the text of Ontario statutes. Choose "Ontario" under the heading "Databases" and then enter the name of the statute in the "Statute Name" field. Or, choose "Ontario" and then click on "Statutes and Regulations" under the heading "Legislation." Select the letter that is the first letter of the name of the statute you are looking for (under the heading "Consolidated Statutes of Ontario") to link to the text of the statute. Figure 15.14 illustrates CanLII's "Statutes and Regulations of Ontario" page.

When you link to the text of the statute, you are given the option of noting-up the statute, linking to regulations, or comparing different versions of the statute side-by-side, as discussed above for federal statutes.

Figure 15.14   CanLII's "Statutes and Regulations of Ontario" Page

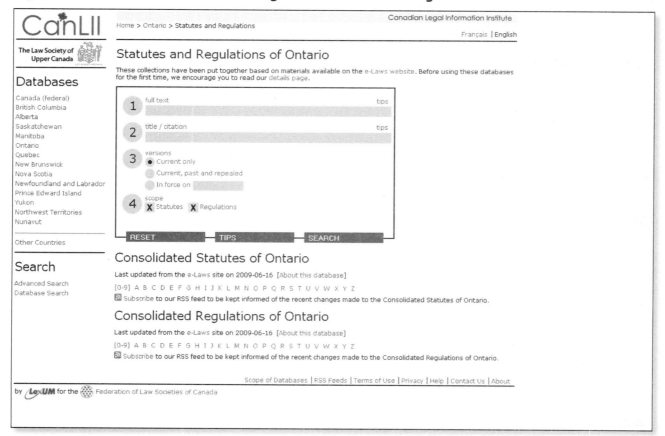

FINDING THE TEXT OF STATUTES OF PROVINCES OR TERRITORIES OTHER THAN ONTARIO

Here is how you can find the statutes and regulations of provinces other than Ontario:

- Most provinces and territories have a government website that provides access to provincial statutes. An easy place to start when you're looking for the website for any of the provinces or territories is the government of Canada link to all of them at http://canada.gc.ca/othergov-autregouv/prov-eng.html.

- LawSource provides a link to the statutes of all the provinces.

- Quicklaw provides a link to legislation databases for all provinces.

- The CanLII website provides a link to the statutes of all the provinces.

UPDATING STATUTES

Most computerized sources are quite current. However, to fully update a statute, you must make sure that there have been no legislative changes since your source was last updated, and you must check for the status of any bills that refer to that statute.

Federal Statutes

To find out whether there are any bills pending (a bill is a statute that has not yet been passed by Parliament) that might affect a statute you're interested in, check the LEGISinfo page of the Library of Parliament website at http://www2.parl.gc.ca/Sites/LOP/LEGISINFO/index.asp?Language=e. The status of bills section is updated daily. You can also check Quicklaw's federal Status of Bills database. This database is usually kept current to within one or two days.

In addition, you can update statutes using the Canada Statute Service on CD-ROM or Internet, the computerized equivalent of the *Canada Statute Citator*, available online by subscription from Canada Law Book.

Ontario Statutes

If you find the text of the statute on e-Laws, be sure to check the notice of currency (at the beginning of the statute) that states whether there are outstanding amendments to be consolidated into the statute or whether the consolidation is current. The notice also gives information about proclamations naming a day on which provisions of the statute come into force, if that information is not already reflected in the consolidated statute. Notices of currency are usually up to date to within two business days. For more current amendment information, the notices of currency direct you to the site's table of public statutes—legislative history overview.

To find out whether there are any bills pending that might affect a particular statute, check the website for the Legislative Assembly of Ontario at http://www

.ontla.on.ca. The status of bills section (bills before the House) is updated daily. You can also check Quicklaw's status of bills database for Ontario. This database is usually kept current to within one or two days.

In addition, you can update statutes using the Ontario Citator Service, the computerized equivalent of the *Ontario Statute Citator*, available online by subscription from Canada Law Book. However, this service is not as up to date as the Ontario e-Laws site.

CHAPTER 16

Finding and Updating Regulations

As we stated in Chapter 10, regulations are as important as statutes and sometimes may be more important. Once you learn that a statute is relevant to the area of law you are researching, you must find out whether any regulations have been made under that statute. If you determine that a regulation is relevant to your research, you must be able to locate the text of that regulation. Fortunately, once you know how to find the text of a statute using computerized sources, it is easy to find and update any regulations made under that statute.

In Chapter 10 we talked about how to find and update regulations using paper sources. In this chapter we tell you how to find and update regulations using computerized sources.

HOW REGULATIONS ARE PUBLISHED IN COMPUTERIZED FORMAT

As we mentioned in Chapter 10, regulations are published in paper format by both the federal and Ontario governments; the official text of the regulations is contained in the government revised regulations volumes and gazettes. The federal and Ontario (as well as other provincial) governments publish their regulations on the same statute websites discussed in Chapter 15. As with statutes, copies of regulations that are obtained from Ontario's government site are official copies of the law. As with statutes, copies of regulations that are obtained from both the Ontario and federal government's sites are official copies of the law.

Federal Regulations

Federal regulations are available at the federal Department of Justice website: http://laws.justice.gc.ca/. The site contains consolidated versions of the federal regulations ("consolidated" means that the version incorporates all amendments made to the text of the regulation up to the most recent update). Regulations are organized alphabetically under the title of the statute pursuant to which they were made.

See figure 15.1, Chapter 15, for the website's home page as of July 6, 2009.

Ontario Regulations

Ontario regulations are available at the Ontario government's e-Laws website: http://www.e-laws.gov.on.ca. This website contains current consolidated versions of most Ontario regulations. (Exceptions are listed in the site's table of unconsolidated and unrevoked regulations.)

Consolidated regulations are organized alphabetically by the name of the statute under which they were made. At the beginning of each consolidated regulation, there is a notice of currency, which provides the consolidation period for the regulation. The consolidation period for most regulations is up to date to the "e-Laws currency date." Click on the "e-Laws currency date" link in the notice of currency to see the e-Laws currency date for the regulation. The government's goal is to provide consolidated law that are up to date within three business days of enactment of a new law or amendment of an existing law. In addition to consolidated versions of the regulations, the website also contains:

- All regulations as they read when filed under the *Regulations Act*, dating back to January 1, 2000 (referred to as "source law"). These are organized first by the year in which the regulation was filed and then alphabetically by the name of the statute under which the regulation was made.

- Consolidated versions of a regulation as they read during different periods in time (referred to as "period in time" or "PIT" law).

- Historical versions (a consolidated version of a regulation as it read immediately before a change to the regulation) of regulations that have been amended since January 1, 2004.

- A list of all the regulations that were filed during a specified year (dating back to 2000).

- The text of some repealed, expired, or spent regulations.

FINDING FEDERAL REGULATIONS

Use any of the following sources to find out, first, if regulations have been made under a federal statute, and, next, the text of the regulations:

- the Department of Justice website,

- Westlaw Canada's LawSource,

- LexisNexis®Quicklaw™ ("Quicklaw"), or

- the Canadian Legal Information Institute (CanLII) website.

Generally, you will use the same source that you used to find the statute itself.

Department of Justice Website: http://laws.justice.gc.ca

When you use the Department of Justice website to find statute law by title (see Chapter 15), you do not have to conduct a separate search for regulations. When you find the statute you are looking for, you will also find a link to any regulations made pursuant to the statute.

When you retrieve the statute you are looking for, the search results page lists all related regulations below the table of contents. Figure 16.1 illustrates the results of a search for the *Canada Health Act*. It shows that there is one related regulation, dealing with extra-billing and user charges information.

Click on the text to link to the regulation. You will be sent to a page that provides the table of contents of the regulation (see figure 16.2). If you click on the title of the regulation, you will be taken to a page that sets out the full name, citation, and text of the regulation.

There is also a search template that lets you search directly for consolidated regulations. Figure 16.3 is a copy of the Search Consolidated Regulations template.

If you know the name of the regulation you are looking for, you can find the regulation by browsing the "Regulations by Title" link. Regulations are listed alphabetically by name of the regulation. Most people, however, usually know the name of the statute only, and not the name of the regulations made pursuant to it. It is, therefore, usually much easier to find regulations by first finding the statute to which they are related.

Figure 16.1   Search Results for the Canada Health Act

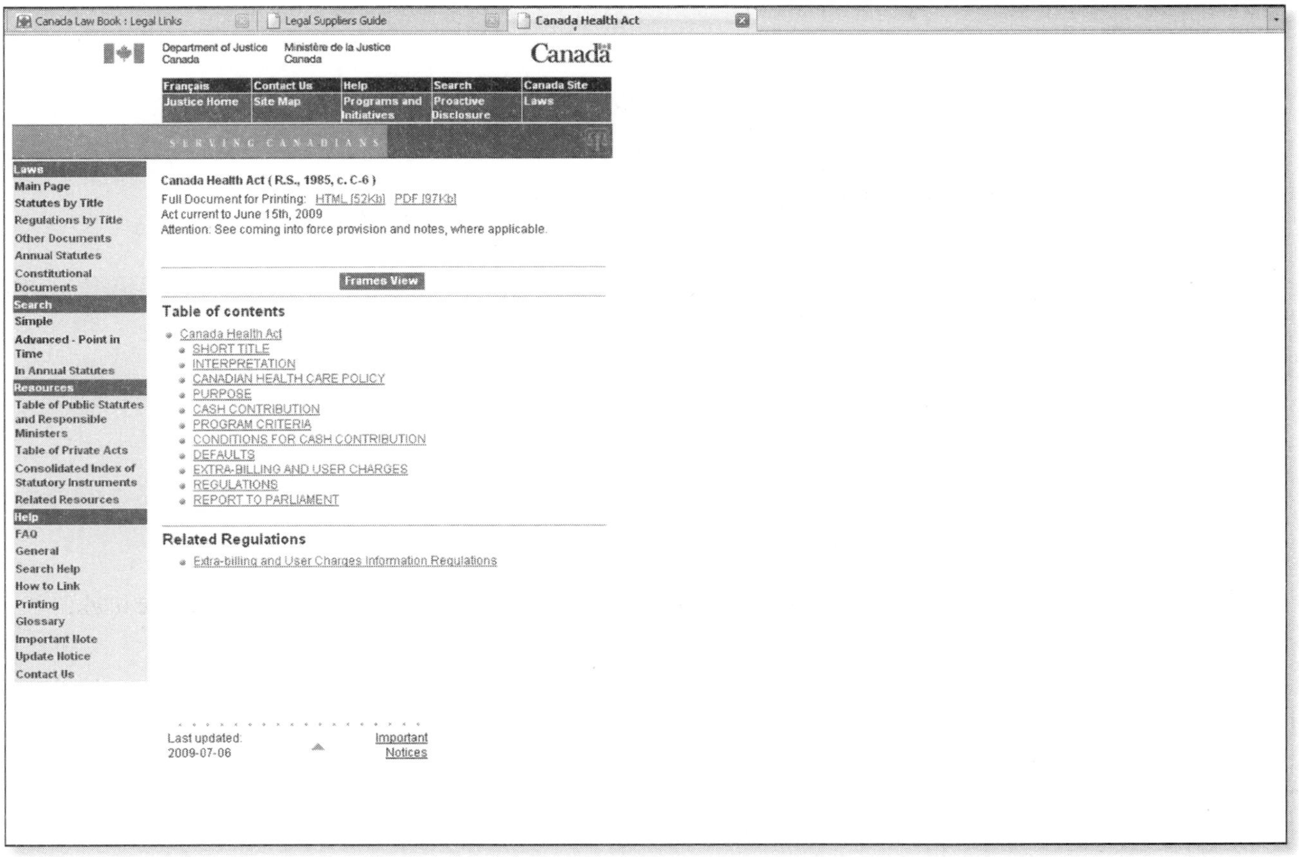

Figure 16.2   Table of Contents of Regulation Under the Canada Health Act

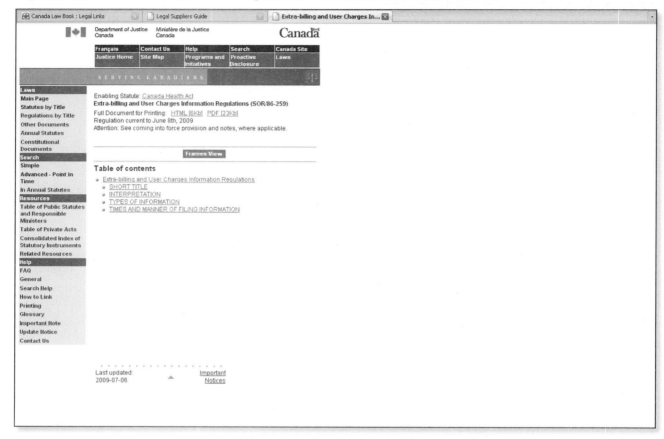

Figure 16.3   Simple Search Template (Completed to Find "Extra-Billing and User Charges Information Regulations"

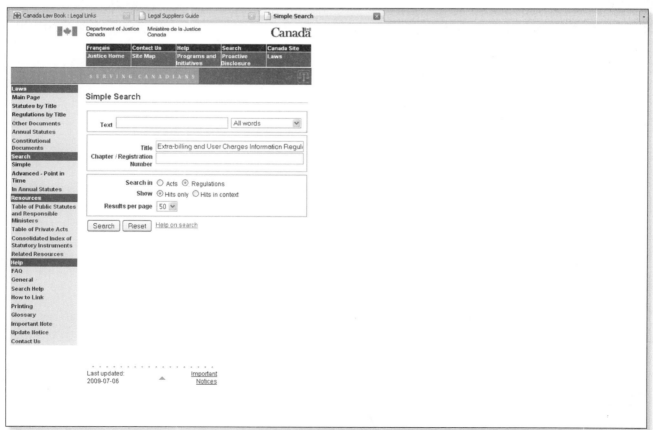

Westlaw Canada's LawSource

The text of federal regulations is available on Westlaw Canada's LawSource. To research federal regulations, click on the legislation link under "Browse Tables of Contents," on the left-hand side of the home page. Click on "Canada" and then expand the heading "Legislation." Choose "Federal" and then click on "Regulations." Figure 16.4 illustrates the table of contents.

An alphabetical list of statute names will appear. Click on the name of a statute to see a list of regulations made pursuant to that statute. Click on the name of the regulation to link directly to the text of the regulation. Figure 16.5 illustrates a list of regulations made under the *Divorce Act*.

If you know the name of the regulation you are looking for, you can use the "Legislation" fields of the "Find/KeyCite a Document" template on the bottom of the LawSource home page. Type in the name of the regulation, choose "Federal" under the jurisdiction drop-down menu, and click "Go." Your regulation will then appear in a result list.

LexisNexis®Quicklaw™ ("Quicklaw")

The text of federal regulations is available on the Internet as part of the Quicklaw subscription service. The easiest way to find the text of a federal regulation is to browse by title using the name of the statute that the regulation is made pursuant to. Click on the Legislation tab on the home page and choose "Browse" under the

Figure 16.4   LawSource Table of Contents (Canadian Federal Regulations)

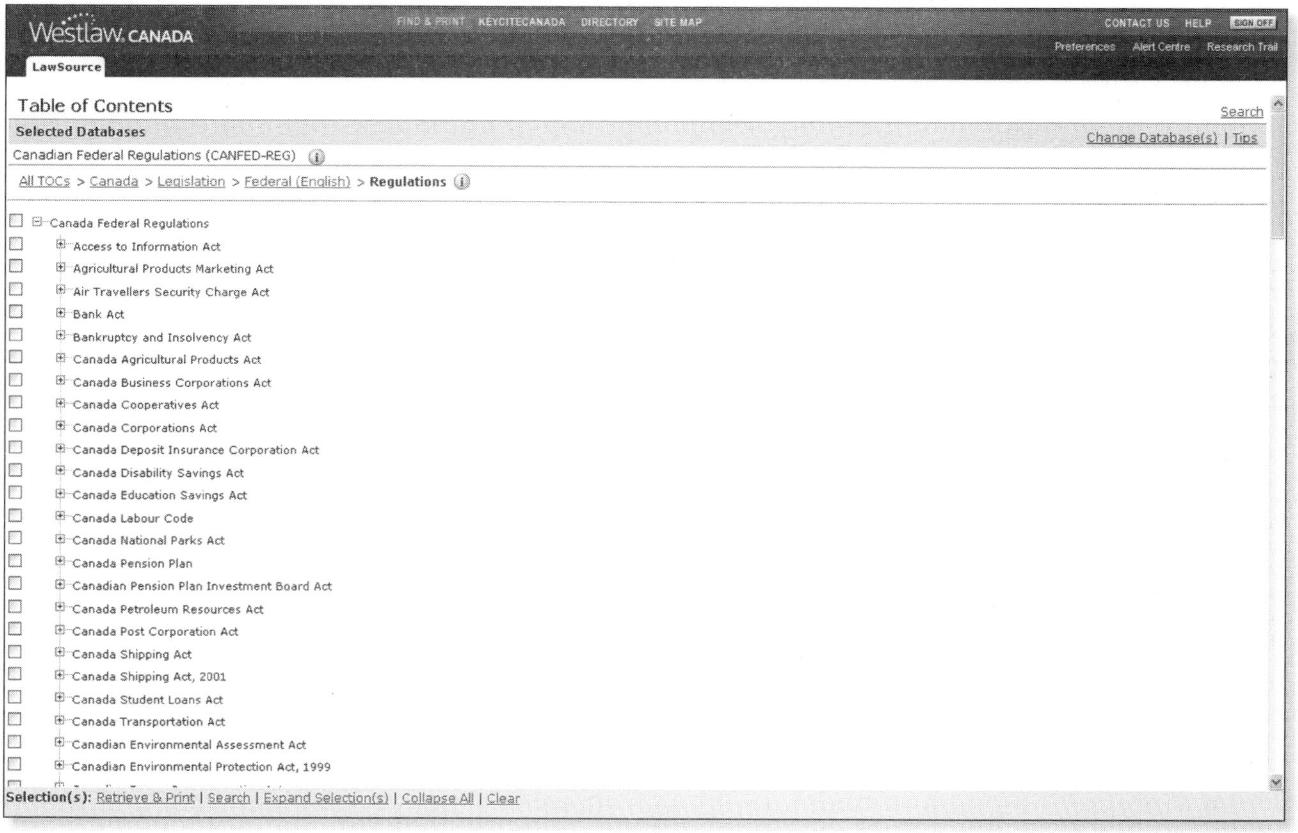

Figure 16.5   Regulations Under the Divorce Act

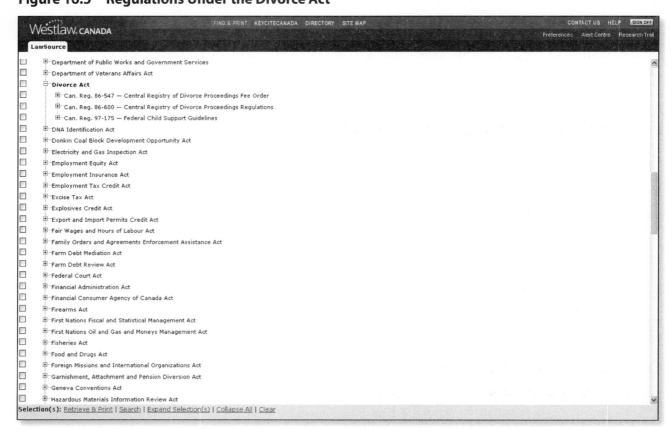

heading "Current Consolidations." Select the appropriate source ("Canada Regulations") and then browse the alphabetical list of statutes to find the name of the statute associated with the regulation you are looking for. Click on the + sign beside the name of the statute to see the regulations made pursuant to that statute.

If you know the name of the regulation you are looking for, you can use the legislation search template. Click on the Legislation tab on the home page and choose "Search" under the heading "Current Consolidations." Select the appropriate source (for example, "All Canadian Regulations") and enter the name of the regulation in the "Legislation Title" field.

Canadian Legal Information Institute (CanLII): http://www.canlii.org

The Canadian Legal Information Institute (CanLII) maintains a website at http://www.canlii.org. This website provides access to the text of federal statutes. Choose "Federal" under the heading "Databases" and then enter the name of the statute associated with the regulation you are looking for in the "statute name" field box. Related regulations will be displayed in the results list. Or, choose "Federal" and then click on "Statutes and Regulations" under the heading "Legislation." Select the letter that is the first letter of the name of the statute associated with the regulation you are looking for (under the heading "Consolidated Statutes of Canada"). A link to enabled regulations is provided. For example, to find regulations under the *Divorce Act*, select the letter "D" to see a list of all federal statutes starting with that letter. Figure 15.9 in Chapter 15 illustrates the list of Consolidated Federal Statutes beginning with the letter "D." When you find the *Divorce Act*, click on the "Enabled Regulations" link to view the seven regulations made under this statute. If you know the name of the regulation you are looking for, click on "Consolidated Regulations of Canada" and then select the letter that is the first letter of the name of that regulation.

FINDING ONTARIO REGULATIONS

Use any of the following sources to find out if regulations have been made under an Ontario statute and then to find the text of the regulations:

- the Ontario e-Laws website,
- Westlaw Canada's LawSource,
- LexisNexis®Quicklaw™ ("Quicklaw"), or
- the Canadian Legal Information Institute (CanLII) website.

Generally, you will use the same source that you used to find the statute itself.

Ontario e-Laws Website: http://www.e-laws.gov.on.ca

When you use the Ontario e-Laws website to find statute law (discussed in Chapter 15), you do not have to conduct a separate search for regulations. When you find the statute you are looking for, you will also find a link to any regulations made pursuant to that statute. When you find the name of the statute you are looking for, you will see that there is a + sign next to it. (See figure 15.12, Chapter 15, for an illustration.) By clicking on the + sign, you will generate a list of all regulations made pursuant to the statute. Figure 16.6 shows that there is one regulation under the *Dog Owners' Liability Act*, dealing with pit bulls. Click on the name of the regulation to retrieve the text of the regulation.

Westlaw Canada's LawSource

The text of Ontario regulations is available on LawSource. Under the heading "Browse Tables of Contents," select "Legislation." Expand "Canada" and then expand "Ontario." Click on "Regulations." An alphabetical list of Ontario statutes will be displayed. Expand the name of the statute to see a list of regulations. Expand the name of the regulation to link directly to the text of the regulation.

If you know the name of the regulation you are looking for, you can use the "Legislation" fields of the "Find/KeyCite a Document" template on the bottom of the LawSource home page. Type in the name of the regulation, choose "Ontario" under the jurisdiction drop-down menu, and click "Go." Your regulation will then appear in a result list.

Figure 16.6   Regulations Under the Dog Owners' Liability Act

⊕ Dentistry Act, 1991, S.O. 1991, c. 24		H
⊕ Denturism Act, 1991, S.O. 1991, c. 25		H
⊕ Development Charges Act, 1997, S.O. 1997, c. 27		H
⊕ Development Corporations Act, R.S.O. 1990, c. D.10		H
⊕ Developmental Services Act, R.S.O. 1990, c. D.11		H
⊕ Dietetics Act, 1991, S.O. 1991, c. 26		H
⊕ Discriminatory Business Practices Act, R.S.O. 1990, c. D.12		H
⊕ Disorderly Houses Act, R.S.O. 1990, c. D.13		H
⊕ Dissolution of Inactive Corporations Act, 2006, S.O. 2006, c. 19 , Sched. J		H
⊕ District Social Services Administration Boards Act, R.S.O. 1990, c. D.15		H
⊖ Dog Owners' Liability Act, R.S.O. 1990, c. D.16		H
O. Reg. 157/05 PIT BULL CONTROLS		H
⊕ Donation of Food Act, 1994, S.O. 1994, c. 19		H
⊕ Drainage Act, R.S.O. 1990, c. D.17		H
⊕ Drug and Pharmacies Regulation Act, R.S.O. 1990, c. H.4		H
⊕ Drug Interchangeability and Dispensing Fee Act, R.S.O. 1990, c. P.23		H
⊕ Drugless Practitioners Act, R.S.O. 1990, c. D.18		H
⊕ Duffins Rouge Agricultural Preserve Act, 2005, S.O. 2005, c. 30		H

⊛ Page 1 ⌄ of 1 ⊛

HOME | ONTARIO.CA | FRANÇAIS

▷Ontario
This site is maintained by the Government of Ontario, Canada.

PRIVACY | IMPORTANT NOTICES

Copyright information:© Queen's Printer for Ontario, 2007
Last Modified: July 25, 2007

LexisNexis®Quicklaw™ ("Quicklaw")

The text of Ontario regulations is also available on the Internet as part of the Quicklaw subscription service. The easiest way to find the text of an Ontario regulation is to browse by title using the name of the statute that the regulation is made pursuant to. Click on the Legislation tab on the home page and choose "Browse" under the heading "Current Consolidations." Select the appropriate source ("Ontario Regulations") and then browse the alphabetical list of statutes to find the name of the statute associated with the regulation that you are looking for. Click on the + sign beside the name of the statute to see the regulations made pursuant to that statute.

If you know the name of the regulation you are looking for, you can use the legislation search template. Click on the Legislation tab on the home page and choose "Search" under the heading "Current Consolidations." Select the appropriate source (for example, "Ontario Regulations") and enter the name of the regulation in the "Legislation Title" field.

Canadian Legal Information Institute (CanLII): http://www.canlii.org

The Canadian Legal Information Institute (CanLII) website at http://www.canlii.org provides access to the text of Ontario regulations. Choose "Ontario" under the heading "Databases" and then enter the name of the statute associated with the regulation you are looking for in the "statute name" field box. Link to the text of the statute by clicking on its name in the result list. CanLII will display the name and citation of regulations associated with the statute. Click on the name of the regulation you want to see the text of; or, choose "Ontario" and then click on "Statutes and Regulations" under the heading "Legislation." Select the letter that is the first letter of the name of the statute associated with the regulation you are looking for (under the heading "Consolidated Regulations of Ontario") and a link to associated regulations is provided. If you know the name of the regulation you are looking for, click on "Regulations of Ontario" and then select the letter that is the first letter of the name of that regulation.

FINDING REGULATIONS OF PROVINCES AND TERRITORIES OTHER THAN ONTARIO

Here is how you can find regulations of provinces other than Ontario:

- Most provinces and territories have a government website that provides access to regulations as well as provincial statutes. An easy place to start when you're looking for the website for any of the provinces or territories is the government of Canada link to all of them at http://canada.gc.ca/othergov-autregouv/prov-eng.html.

- LawSource provides a link to the regulations of all the provinces.

- Quicklaw provides a link to regulation databases for all provinces.

- The CanLII website provides a link to the statutes and regulations of all the provinces.

UPDATING REGULATIONS

Regulations are issued and amended on a regular basis. Even though computerized sources tend to be fairly current, it is important to find the most current version of a regulation. The best source for updating regulations is a gazette—the *Canada Gazette* for Canadian regulations and the *Ontario Gazette* for Ontario regulations (the other provinces and territories have gazettes as well).

Federal Regulations

Federal regulations are published in the *Canada Gazette Part II*, available online at http://www.gazette.gc.ca/rp-pr/p2/index-eng.html.

Ontario Regulations

Ontario regulations are published in the *Ontario Gazette*, available online at http://www.ontariogazette.gov.on.ca/.

CHAPTER 17

Finding and Updating Cases

Once you've determined whether there are any statutes or regulations relevant to the issue you are researching, then (as we said in Chapter 11) you must find out whether there is any relevant case law. You may be able to do this by looking in the *Canadian Encyclopedic Digest*, the computerized version of which we discussed in Chapter 14, but there are other computerized finding tools as well. If the finding tools tell you that there is case law relevant to your problem, you must be able to locate the text of the cases, and you can also use computerized sources to do this.

FINDING TOOLS: ARE THERE ANY RELEVANT CASES?

In Chapter 11 we discussed finding cases using paper legal research sources. We told you about a number of different secondary sources you can use to find case law on the issue you are researching; the source you use will depend on whether you are looking for

- cases dealing with a specific subject or legal issue,

- cases that have interpreted a statute or a section of a statute,

- cases considering a word or a phrase,

- cases when you've got only partial or incorrect citations (treasure hunting), or

- unreported cases.

When you're using computerized legal research sources, the two most comprehensive case-finding tools are the *Canadian Abridgment*'s *Canadian Case Digests* (CCD) and Quicklaw, both of which can be used in all the above situations. Both sources allow you to find relevant case law using keyword searches. Unlike Quicklaw, the CCD is an edited source, so it also allows you to browse through a table of contents related to your topic. This feature makes it easier to focus your search by looking for a specific issue within the relevant subject title.

You can also find case law using BestCase, an online research service provided by Canada Law Book, and CanLII (Canadian Legal Information Institute), a not-for-profit organization created by the Federation of Law Societies of Canada. Each of these sources contains a broad collection of Canadian case law.

Canadian Abridgment Case Digests

case digest
summary of how a legal
issue was decided in a
particular case

Canadian Abridgment Case Digests (CCD) contains **case digests**, or summaries of cases, from all Canadian courts and many tribunals, and organizes them by subject area. Each digest gives a brief summary of how a legal issue was decided in a particular case, together with a summary of all necessary background facts and the reasons for the decision. Each digest deals with only a single legal issue. If a case covers several legal issues, there is a separate digest for each issue.

The CCD is available in two computerized formats: CD-ROM and online. Both are organized in the same way as the print version. Topics or main areas of law are arranged alphabetically, by subject title. Each subject title is then broken down into increasingly more detailed subtopics, according to a multi-level classification system, called the **key classification system**. Each individual digest has a key classification number and a specific case digest number. The classification and digest numbers are the same as in the print version. See Chapter 11 for a complete discussion of the key classification system in the CCD.

key classification system
multi-level classification
system

Case Digests Online

The *Canadian Abridgment Case Digests* is available online via the Internet as part of LawSource, a subscription service offered by Westlaw Canada. *Case Digests* online acts as a finding tool, allowing you to learn the names and citations of relevant cases. It also gives you access to the text of the cases by linking directly to LawSource's large database of case decisions.

There are two main tools for finding relevant case law using the online version of the *Canadian Abridgment Case Digests*:

1. table of contents, and

2. custom search templates.

Table of Contents

The table of contents lists all the subject titles in alphabetical order. It is made up of several levels that you can reach by clicking on the + sign next to a heading. You can view the table of contents alone only. It is not possible to view it in a split screen side by side with the text. You can get access to the table of contents by clicking on the "Canadian Abridgment Digests" link under the heading "Browse Tables of Contents" on the left side of the home page. Figure 17.1 illustrates how the subject title "Torts" is broken down in the table of contents.

Once you have identified your research topic in the table of contents, click on the words to display the relevant case digests. The left-hand side of the screen will show the classification of your research topic and the total number of case digests. The text of the case digests dealing with the topic will be displayed on the right-hand side of the screen. Figure 17.2 illustrates the results of a table of contents search under the subject title "Torts" for the following topic: dog owners' liability for injuries caused by their dog (under bylaw or statute).

Figure 17.1 Online Case Digests Table of Contents for the Subject Title "Torts"

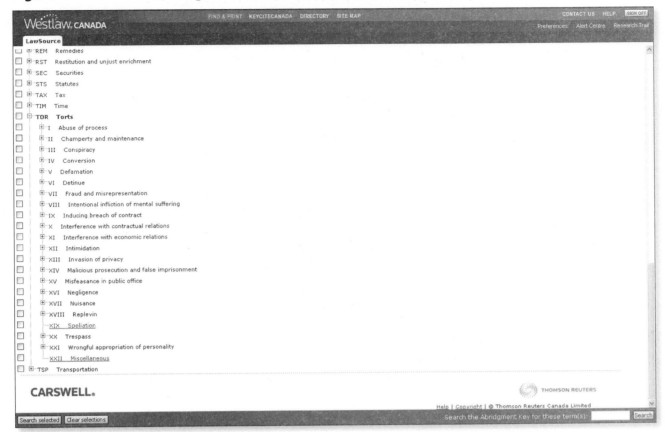

Custom Search Templates

There are three custom search templates available:

1. standard search,

2. terms and connectors search, and

3. natural language search.

The **standard search** template allows you to search for information using keywords associated with your research problem. You get access to this template by clicking on the "Canadian Abridgment Digests" link on the right side of the home page, under the heading "Custom Search Templates." Enter the relevant keywords and then select the desired connector from the drop-down menu within the template. You can choose to search for

- any keyword you entered,

- all the keywords you entered,

- the exact phrase you entered,

- all the keywords you entered within five words of each other,

- all the keywords you entered in the same sentence, or

- all the keywords you entered in the same paragraph.

standard search
allows you to search for information using keywords and a connector that is selected from the drop-down menu

Figure 17.2 Results of Table of Contents Search Under the Subject Title "Torts" (Dog Owners' Liability for Injuries Caused by Their Dog Under Bylaw or Statute)

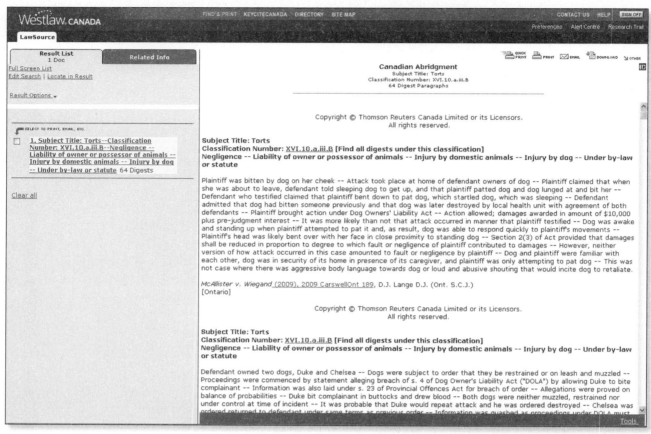

The template allows you to limit your keyword search to

- the subject title,

- a classification number or phrase,

- the name of the case,

- the citation of the case, or

- the year of the decision.

You can also limit your search to a specified jurisdiction and date range. Figure 17.3 illustrates the standard search template.

The **terms and connectors search** template allows you to construct a Boolean search using keywords and your own Boolean connectors and expanders. It is, therefore, not as limiting as the standard search template. You get access to this search tool by clicking on the "Terms and Connectors Search" link at the top right-hand side of the standard search template screen. You can use this tool to search all the *Case Digests* or you can limit your search to parts of the *Case Digests* by adding field and date restrictions to your search. Figure 17.4 illustrates the terms and connectors search template.

As we said in Chapter 13, each computerized source has its own search syntax, which will be explained by the source. The search syntax for the online version of the *Case Digests* is the same as the syntax used in the online version of the CED. It is set out below the terms and connectors search window, as illustrated in figure 17.4.

Figure 17.3 Online Case Digests Standard Search Template

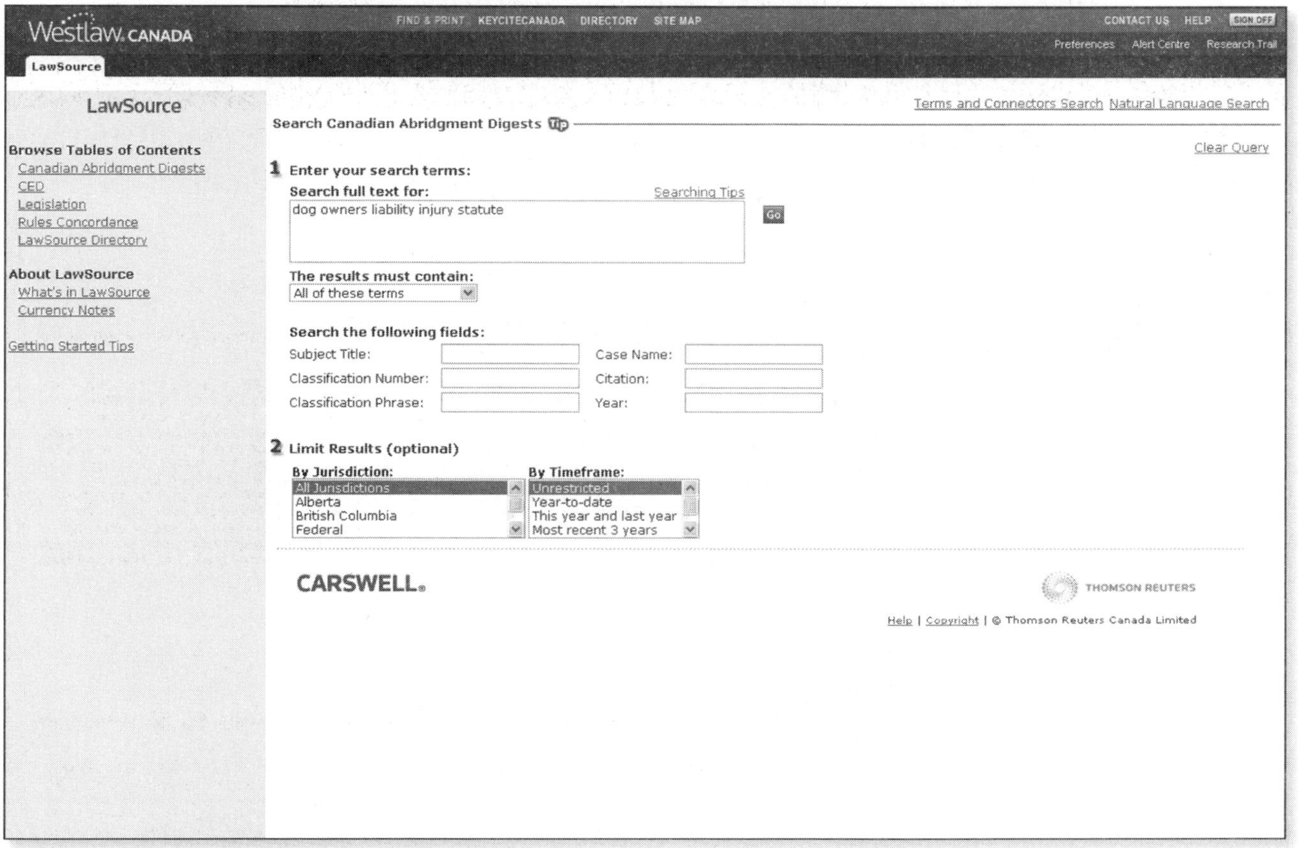

The terms and connectors search template contains a built-in thesaurus that provides related terms for all the keywords you enter. There is a link to this feature beside the terms and connectors search window.

The **natural language search** allows you to search for information by asking your legal question using plain language. You get access to this search tool by clicking on the "Natural Language Search" link at the top right side of the standard search template screen. You can also get a link to this search template by clicking on the Natural Language Tab while you are in the terms and connectors search template. You simply enter your question in the description box. You do not need to use any operators or connectors—Are dog owners in Ontario liable for an injury caused by their dog?—is an example of a natural language search, as illustrated in Figure 17.5

As discussed in Chapter 14, to get the best results, use the "Require/Exclude Terms" link (at the bottom of the natural language search template screen) to specify which terms you require to be present in your search and which terms (if any) may be excluded. In our example, the term "caused" may be excluded from the search.

The natural language search template, like the terms and connectors search template, contains a built-in thesaurus.

natural language search allows you to search for information by asking your question using plain language

Linking to the Text

Figure 17.6 illustrates the results of a natural language template search for the following research question: Are dog owners in Ontario liable for an injury caused by their dog?

Figure 17.4   Online Case Digests Terms and Connectors Search Template

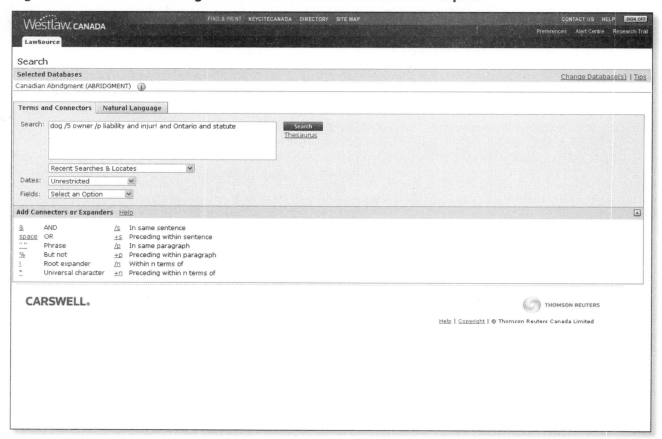

Figure 17.5   Online Case Digests Natural Language Search Template

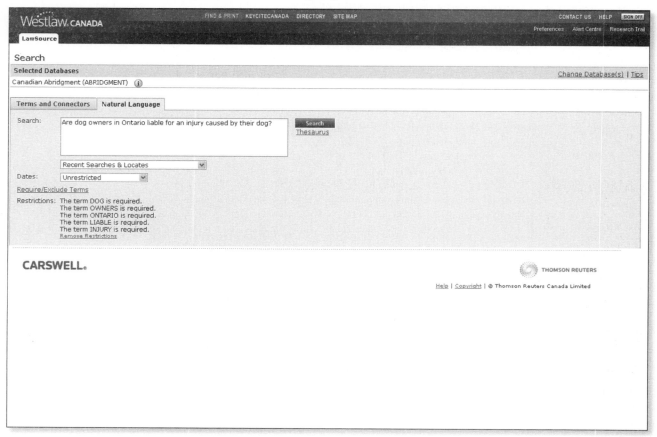

Figure 17.6   Results of a Natural Language Search

Each result number is a hyperlink to the text of the entire case digest. To view the text of a particular digest, simply click on the number in the result list that contains the digest you want to read. Figure 17.7 displays the first case digest in the results list. Each digest provides a summary of the point of law discussed in the case and includes the name, citation, and jurisdiction of the case being summarized. The citation provides a hyperlink to the text of the case. By clicking on the hyperlink, you can retrieve the full text of the case.

You will likely find many case digests that are relevant to your research topic. You will have to scan them all to determine which cases you should read in full.

LAWSOURCE'S CASE DATABASE FINDING TOOLS

LawSource, as we mentioned above, is a subscription service offered by Westlaw Canada that maintains a large database of case decisions. The CCD finding tools provide a direct link to the text of the cases in the LawSource database. The CCD is only one of the many finding tools available to search that database. Others are set out below.

Search Cases Custom Search Template

This tool allows you to conduct a keyword search of the LawSource database directly. It is particularly useful if you have a specific case in mind, have some information about it, but don't know the complete citation. Click on the "Cases" link under

Figure 17.7   Case Digest from the Results of a Natural Language Search

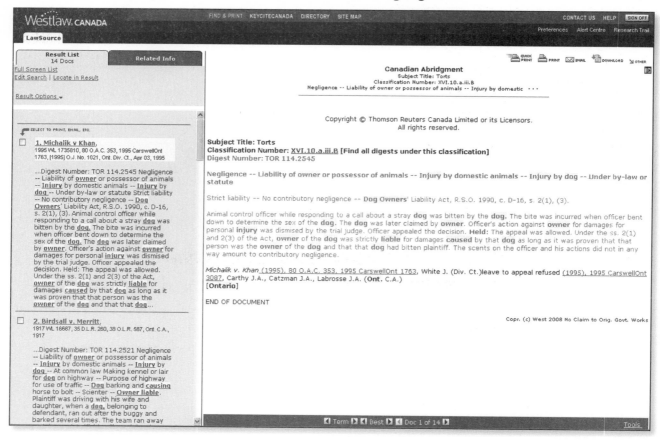

"Custom Search Templates" on the home page. Enter your keywords and choose the desired relationship between those keywords from the drop-down menu of choices. Enter any information you have about the name, court, jurisdiction, judge, counsel, or year of the case and LawSource will search for your keywords only in cases with the name, court, judge, or counsel you have specified.

For example, assume you are looking for an Ontario case about dog owners' liability and you know that one party's name is Strom. Enter the keywords "dog," "owner," and "liability" in the text box and choose "all of these terms" from the drop-down menu. Enter "Strom" in the "Case Name" field. Choose "Ontario" to limit your search to this jurisdiction only. Figure 17.8 illustrates this search template. Figure 17.9 illustrates the result of this search. Note how the full case report is displayed with the search keywords highlighted.

Find/KeyCite a Document

The KeyCite option allows you to search for case law that cites a statute generally or a specific section of a statute. Use the "Find/KeyCite a Document" templates located on the lower half of the home page. Choose "KeyCite" and enter the name, section number(s), and jurisdiction of the statute you are researching in the field boxes beside the heading "Legislation." Figure 17.10 illustrates the KeyCite search template completed to request cases citing s. 2(1) of the *Dog Owners' Liability Act*, R.S.O. 1990, c. D.16. Figure 17.11 illustrates the results of the search displaying the name and citation of cases citing this statute.

Figure 17.8   LawSource Search Cases Template

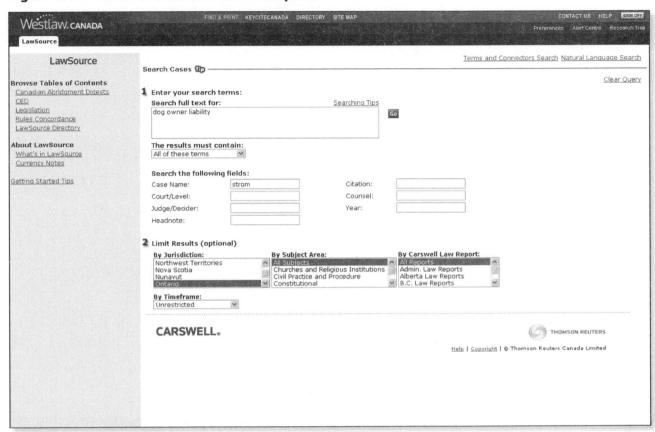

Figure 17.9   LawSource Search Cases Result

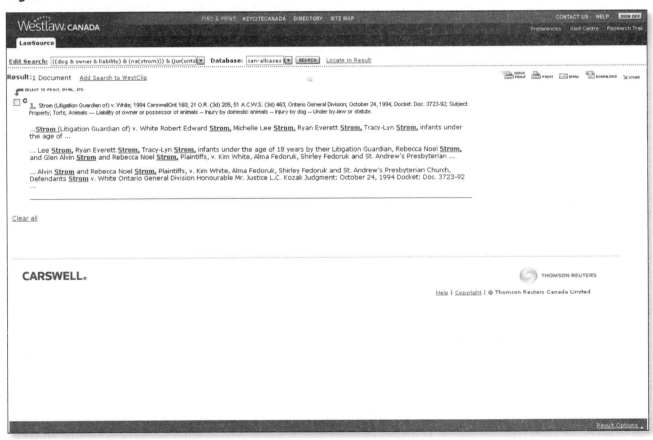

Figure 17.10   LawSource KeyCite Search Template

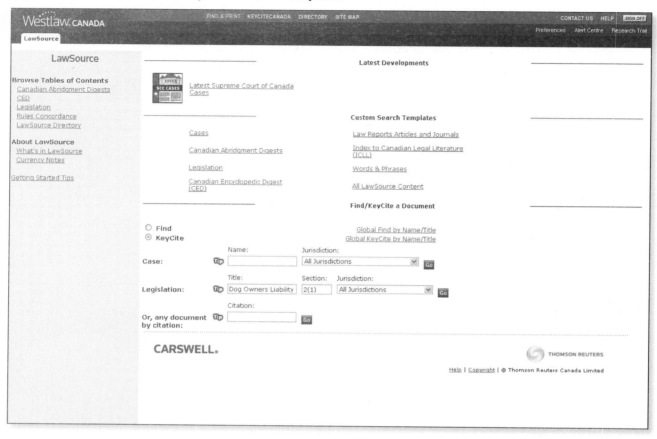

Figure 17.11   LawSource KeyCite Legislation Search Results

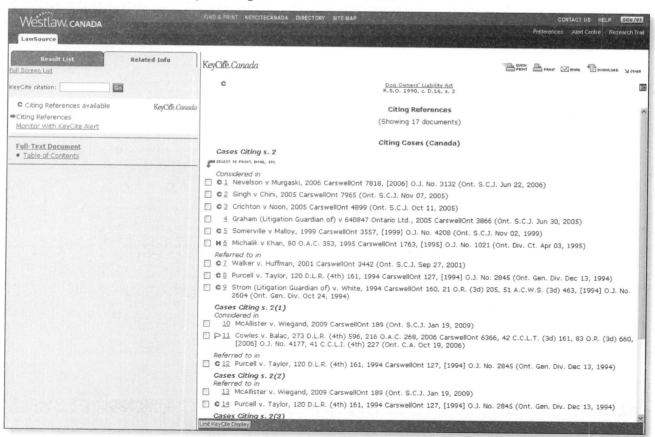

The "Find" option allows you to find a case when you know either part or all of the case name. Again, use the "Find/KeyCite a Document" templates on the home page. Choose "Find" and enter the information you have about the case name, including the jurisdiction, if you know it, in the field boxes beside the heading "Case." The results list displays all the cases that contain the name(s) you have entered in that jurisdiction, and provides a breakdown of the subject matter using the CCD's key classification system. (If you don't know the jurisdiction, you can search "All jurisdictions.") The results are numbered starting at 1, and each number is a hyperlink to the text of the case. Skim the list for a case that looks relevant to your research. Using the earlier example again, assume you are looking for an Ontario case dealing with dog owners' liability and you know that one of the parties is named Strom. Choose "Find" and enter "Strom" for the case name, choose "Ontario" under the jurisdiction drop-down menu, and click "Go." Figure 17.12 illustrates the results of that search. Note that case number 3 deals with the relevant subject—animals, in particular, dog owners' liability.

LEXISNEXIS®QUICKLAW™

LexisNexis®Quicklaw™ ("Quicklaw"), a subscription service, is also a popular case-finding tool. It provides access to a large number of cases collected in a number of databases. Each database contains cases from a particular report series, level of court, or jurisdiction. Quicklaw's databases are not edited, and so there is no table

Figure 17.12   LawSource Find Case Search Results

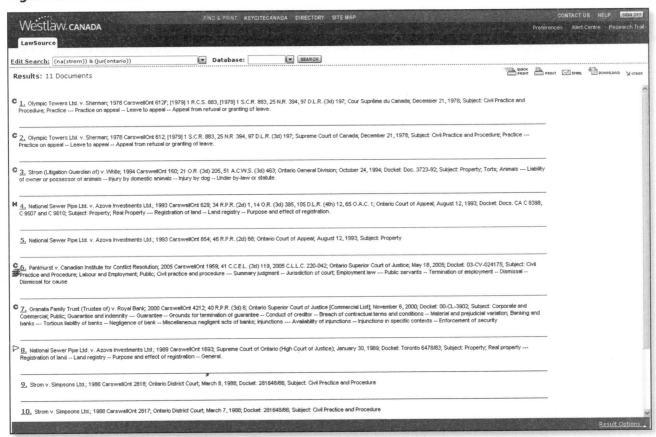

of contents to browse through. The only way to gain access to the contents of the database is by keyword searching. Quicklaw searches through the text of all cases in the database to find the keywords you enter. You must therefore search for keywords that are likely to appear in cases relevant to your research. Quicklaw matches the keywords you choose with the words contained in the database of cases. It will search for exact matches only. It will not automatically search for synonyms or alternate spellings of a word.

Searching for Case Law

Under the Search tab on the home page, choose a category for your search by selecting one of the following tabs:

- Home
- Case Law Search
- Tribunal Cases Search

The Home tab contains the Search Sources Form. You must select the source or database of cases you want to search. Quicklaw provides a drop-down menu of "Favourite Sources," but you can browse all sources in the source directory by clicking on the "Find More Sources" hyperlink or by choosing the Source Directory Tab on the home page. You can browse all available sources by publication type or area of law. If you know all or part of the name of the source you want to search, enter that information in the "Find a Source" field box. Each source provides a link to detailed information about the source, including its currency and coverage. To see this information, click on the "i" beside the name of the source.

After you select your desired source, enter a full Boolean search in the "Search Terms" field box. Quicklaw will look for documents containing your search terms only within the selected source.

The Case Law Search tab lets you "customize" your Boolean search by including information you may already have about a case you are looking for—for example, the case name, jurisdiction, date, court, judge, or counsel. Enter your Boolean search in the Search Terms field box and then choose your source. Then, restrict your search to a specific date, jurisdiction, name, court, judge, or counsel by adding any such information you may already have about the case. Quicklaw will look for documents containing your search terms only in cases with the date, jurisdiction, name, court, judge, or counsel you have specified.

Use the Tribunal Cases Search tab when you want to search for cases only within federal or provincial boards and tribunals. Enter your Boolean search and then choose to search in all boards and tribunals, or only selected boards and tribunals. You can restrict your search by date, jurisdiction, name, arbitrator, or counsel.

Remember, before entering a Boolean search, you must familiarize yourself with the search syntax used by Quicklaw. A detailed explanation of its search syntax is available on the Quicklaw site.

BESTCASE

BestCase, as mentioned above, is a web-based subscription case law research service containing Canada's leading law reports and case summary services. There are two main tools for finding relevant case law using BestCase:

- table of contents, and
- search templates.

Table of Contents

Click on the Table of Contents tab (from the home page) to look for relevant case law by browsing all the available content in BestCase. You can browse content by classification schemes, indices, full-text decisions, or case summaries. Expand desired folders by clicking the green + sign. To view your results, click on the yellow page icon that appears in the Table of Contents.

Search Templates

BestCase has four search templates to help you find relevant case law:

Case Law Search,

Index Search,

Advanced Custom Search, and

Boolean Search

Case Law Search

This search template lets you "customize" your search by case name, court, judge, counsel, date, catchline terms (terms that appear in the topical classification or headnote of a case), or keywords/phrases (in the text of the case). By default, it will search all of the content in BestCase. If you like, you can limit your search to specific content only.

Index Search

This search template lets you limit your search of words or phrases to specified indices. You can choose to search across all of the content of BestCase, or limit your search to specific indices only.

Advanced Custom Search

This search template requires you to enter your search terms in one or more of the text boxes provided. Each text box searches the terms within it in a specific predetermined way. For example, if you enter words in the "containing all of these words" text box, BestCase will search these words as an AND search. You can also exclude certain specified terms from your search (a NOT search), add synonyms to your search (an OR search), search an "exact phrase," and search words "near" each other (a proximity search). Enter your terms in the appropriate text boxes. You can also limit your search to specific content within BestCase.

The Advanced Custom Search will automatically search for alternate word forms, if this option (that is, "stemming") is selected.

Boolean Search

This template requires you to enter a full Boolean search using the BestCase query syntax (listed below the template).

Specify the desired content by using the "Select a Field (optional)" drop-down menu.

The search syntax used by BestCase is explained on its site.

CANADIAN LAW INFORMATION INSTITUTE (CANLII)

CanLII, as mentioned above, is a free Internet site containing a comprehensive collection of Canadian case law.

To search across the entire CanLII collection, use the default search template on the home page. Enter your search terms, using the CanLII search syntax, in the "full text" field box. Note that by default, words that are entered with a space between them will be searched as if there was an AND between them.

To search for cases from a specific jurisdiction, select the jurisdiction from the list under the heading "Databases" (on the left-hand side of the home page). You can restrict your search by date, and to specific courts and/or tribunals within that jurisdiction.

To search for cases from more than one jurisdiction, use the Advanced Search template or the Database Search template. The Advanced Search template lets you select multiple jurisdictions to search. It also lets you restrict your search by court level and, for board and tribunal decisions, by type of board or tribunal. The Database Search template lets you "customize" your search by jurisdiction and by specific courts and tribunals within that jurisdiction.

The search syntax used by CanLII is explained on its site.

You should note that a space defaults to AND and not OR in CanLII. In most other sources, a space defaults to OR.

FINDING THE TEXT OF A CASE

Once you know the name and citation of a case, it is easy to find the text of the case using any of several computerized sources:

- Quicklaw, LawSource, and CanLII all offer a "find by name or citation" feature that allows you to retrieve the text of a case simply by providing its name or its citation.

- BestCase also provides access to the text of many Canadian cases. If you know the citation of a case, you can browse Full-Text Decisions (by law report name) under the Table of Contents to find the text of the case.

Updating Cases

In Chapter 11 we told you that you have to update any relevant case you find to make sure that it is still useful to your research. By updating you will find out:

- Case history or appeal history—has the case been confirmed or overturned on appeal? What was the highest court that reviewed the decision?

- How has the case been treated by other judges—has it been followed, or not? Has it been distinguished?

See Chapter 11 for a complete discussion of the importance of updating cases.

Quicklaw, LawSource, BestCase, and CanLII all have comprehensive case citators that allow you to update cases easily. Each source has its own codes to indicate the judicial treatment of a case, so you will need to know the citator treatment codes used by the source you are using.

Quicklaw

Quicklaw's citator is called QuickCITE. You can get access to this tool in the following ways:

- by entering the name or citation of the case you want to update in the "Note up with QuickCITE" field, in the Find a Document form on the home page, or

- by clicking the "Note up with QuickCITE" link while viewing the text of a case.

LawSource

Update cases in LawSource by using the "Find/KeyCite a Document" templates located at the bottom of the home page. Choose "KeyCite" and then enter the name or citation of the case you want to update in the appropriate fields.

BestCase

Update cases by clicking the NoteUp tab that appears at the top of the screen, when viewing the text of a case.

CanLII

Update cases by clicking the "Noteup" link while viewing the text of a case. To see legislation and decisions cited in the case, click on "Reflex Record."

KEY TERMS

case digest

key classification system

natural language search

standard search

terms and connectors search

CHAPTER 18

Legal Research on the Internet

Our discussion of computerized legal research wouldn't be complete if we didn't add a few more words about Internet research. In the preceding chapters, we talked about sources available on the Internet through both subscription services and free-access websites. Our discussion has been structured according to the legal research functions that the sources serve—that is, as finding tools, primary sources, or updating tools. This chapter focuses on free-access websites, and the issues that arise when you use them, whatever function they serve.

TYPES OF FREE-ACCESS SITES

There are many types of free-access websites that you can use when conducting legal research. In addition to websites that provide access to primary sources—statutes (discussed in Chapter 15), regulations (discussed in Chapter 16), and cases (discussed in Chapter 17)—there are subject indexes and search engines, websites that contain law-related information, and bookmark lists.

Subject Indexes and Search Engines

Both subject indexes and search engines help a researcher locate Web documents or websites relevant to the topic being researched.

A **subject index**, also called a subject tree, is a website that categorizes or indexes Web documents or websites using subject classifications. Yahoo (at http://www.yahoo .com) is an example of a subject index. HierosGamos (at http://www.hg.org/index .html) is a legal subject index.

A **search engine** is an Internet site with a computer program that searches a database of Web documents or websites to match keywords that you supply. There are general search engines as well as specialized legal search engines.

The major general search engines are:

- AltaVista at http://www.altavista.com,

- Google at http://www.google.com,

- Lycos at http://www.lycos.com, and

- Yahoo at http://www.yahoo.com.

subject index
also called a subject tree, a website that categorizes or indexes Web documents or websites using subject classifications

search engine
website with a computer program that searches a database of Web documents or websites to match supplied keywords

Catherine P. Best, who developed and maintains the Best Guide to Canadian Legal Research website, recommends Google because it has the largest database of indexed pages; it also ranks its results so that higher quality sites appear first.

The main legal search engines are:

- FindLaw LawCrawler at http://lawcrawler.findlaw.com. This American site focuses primarily on U.S. law, but has a link that allows you to search legal websites from Canada.

- LawRunner at http://www.ilrg.com. This American site is run by the Internet Legal Research Group. It acts as an interface for Google to find law-related sites in 238 countries, including Canada, but with emphasis on the United States.

Websites Containing Law-Related Information

Many websites contain law-related information.

Government Sites

In addition to their statute sites, the federal and provincial governments maintain websites that contain useful information for lawyers and law clerks.

The main government of Canada site, at http://canada.gc.ca, provides information about government services for Canadians, non-Canadians, and Canadian businesses; it also provides information about the structure of the federal government and contains links to federal departments and agencies, provincial and territorial governments, and municipalities.

Other government of Canada websites that provide law-related information are:

- Statistics Canada at http://www.statcan.gc.ca—for statistics, including the consumer price index, population rates, and unemployment rates;

- Canada Revenue Agency at http://www.cra-arc.gc.ca—for income tax and GST information and forms;

- Industry Canada's business information site, Strategis, at http://www .strategis.ic.gc.ca—for information related to business.

Government of Ontario

The main government of Ontario site, at http://www.gov.on.ca, provides a complete services and offices directory, including all tribunals, boards, and agencies; a government of Ontario telephone directory; and links to specific ministries.

Other government of Ontario websites that provide law-related information are:

- Ministry of the Attorney General at http://www.attorneygeneral.jus.gov.on .ca—for information about, for example, going to court, getting a lawyer, family law matters, and Small Claims Court;

■ Guide to Ontario Courts at http://www.ontariocourts.on.ca—for links to the Court of Appeal, Superior Court of Justice, and Ontario Court of Justice.

Other Provincial Governments

Each province and territory has a website similar to the government of Ontario website. You can find them individually—for example, by doing a Google search for "[name of province] government"—or you can link to each one of them through the federal government's website at http://canada.gc.ca/othergov-autregouv/prov-eng.html.

Municipal Governments

All major Canadian cities have their own websites with information about matters like bylaws and contact information for city administrators. You can find a city's website by doing a Google search for "city of [name of city]."

Legal Research Sites

A number of sites contain information about legal research, including:

■ Best Guide to Canadian Legal Research at http://www.legalresearch.org. Run by Catherine Best, a research lawyer and adjunct professor with the University of British Columbia Faculty of Law, this site is an excellent source of information about legal research and contains links to legal sources.

■ Bora Laskin Law Library at http://www.law-lib.utoronto.ca. Run by the University of Toronto Faculty of Law, this site contains guides to legal research, community legal information, and links to legal resources.

■ William R. Lederman Law Library at http://library.queensu.ca/law/. Run by the Queen's University Faculty of Law, this site contains a comprehensive legal research manual. (However, you made the right decision by buying this book.)

General Legal Sites

Various law-related organizations maintain websites with access to information about the law, such as:

■ Access to Justice Network at http://www.acjnet.org. A project of the legal studies program of the University of Alberta, this site provides access to public legal education articles.

■ Canadian Legal FAQs at http://www.law-faqs.org. Also a project of the legal studies program of the University of Alberta, this site provides answers to commonly asked legal questions.

Most large law firms maintain websites that provide access to publications on legal topics written by members of their firms—for example:

■ Davies, Ward, Phillips & Vineberg at http://www.dwpv.com;

■ Gowling, Lafleur, Henderson at http://www.gowlings.com;

- McCarthy, Tetrault at http://www.mccarthy.ca; and

- Torys at http://www.torys.com.

You can get access to a comprehensive list of Canadian law firms, by practice area, by going to the Canadian Law List website at http://www.canadianlawlist.com.

Bookmark Lists

Bookmark lists are websites that provide a list of links to other sites. Canadian bookmark lists include:

- Best's Legal Bookmarks at http://legalresearch.org/docs/bookmark.html—part of the Best Guide to Canadian Legal Research site;

- Jurist Canada at http://jurist.law.utoronto.ca—hosted by the University of Toronto Faculty of Law, but, in fact, a project of a law professor at the University of Pittsburgh; and

- LexUM at http://www.lexum.umontreal.ca/index_en.php—maintained by the University of Montreal Law Faculty.

CONCERNS WHEN RESEARCHING ON THE INTERNET

Enormous amounts of information, legal and otherwise, are available on the Internet. This is the Internet's strength, but also its weakness as a research tool. The sheer volume of material can be overwhelming. The amount of information that comes back from a search request can be far too much to sift through and evaluate.

In addition, information on the Internet is not organized in any way. Add to that the fact that Internet sites change quickly, then, as the movie critic Roger Ebert said, "Doing research on the Web is like using a library assembled piecemeal by packrats and vandalized nightly." Or, as the Queen's University Law Library site says, "[Doing research on the Web is] like using a library in which all of the books have been dumped on the floor."

Internet research can be time-consuming. You must take the time to learn the search syntax used by search engines at different sites. If you use incorrect search syntax, you may miss relevant documents or retrieve many irrelevant documents. To add insult to injury, response times to searches can be slow if you are researching during times of heavy Internet traffic or if you are downloading large files.

Finally, as Catherine Best says, "There is no guarantee that information posted on the Internet for free access is comprehensive, current, or reliable." When you use free-access websites you must ask yourself:

- Who has written or edited the content for the website? Look for the author's or editor's name, credentials, and contact address.

- Is the site affiliated with a known, law-based organization?

- Is the site associated with an impartial organization, or with a political or advocacy group? Does the site show a bias?

- How current is the information on the site? How often is the site updated?

But, take heart. You can generally rely on information found on sites maintained by

- governments,

- universities,

- law schools, and

- courts.

KEY TERMS

search engine

subject index

CHAPTER 19

Computer Exercises

It's once more time to apply your knowledge and do some legal research using computerized sources.

You often have a choice of computerized sources to find the information you are looking for. Once you have chosen your source, there may be more than one way to look for information with it. While it is best to become familiar with all finding tools that a source has to offer, the choice of finding tool is up to you. However, whichever finding tool you use, you should find the same information.

The questions below require you to look for the same information you were looking for when using paper sources in Chapter 12.

SAMPLE QUESTIONS

Read the questions below. For each one,

- identify the kind of information you're being asked for—for example, is it a statute, a regulation, a case, an update, or something other?;

- decide what computerized source(s) you will need (given what you have access to, naturally);

- decide how you will look for the required information using your chosen computerized source(s); and

- answer the question, citing correctly any statute, regulation, or case you are asked to find.

1. Is there an Ontario statute that governs transplanting of human organs after death?

    a. What kind of information are you being asked for?

    b. Which research tools will you need?

    c. Which tools are available in your library?

    d. Your answer to the question.

2. Find the federal statute that deals with the sentencing of young offenders.

    a. What kind of information are you being asked for?

    b. Which research tools will you need?

    c. Which tools are available in your library?

    d. Your answer to the question.

3. The federal *Tobacco Products Control Act* is no longer in force. On what date was it repealed and by what statute?

   a. What kind of information are you being asked for?

   b. Which research tools will you need?

   c. Which tools are available in your library?

   d. Your answer to the question.

4. Find the *Criminal Code* section that deals with possession of prohibited weapons and update it to the present.

   a. What kind of information are you being asked for?

   b. Which research tools will you need?

   c. Which tools are available in your library?

   d. Your answer to the question.

5. Are there any cases in your province that followed the Supreme Court of Canada decision in *Crocker v. Sundance Northwest Resorts Ltd.*, [1988] 1 S.C.R. 1186?

   a. What kind of information are you being asked for?

   b. Which research tools will you need?

   c. Which tools are available in your library?

   d. Your answer to the question.

6. Was the 1992 Ontario case *Dunn v. Dunn Estate* appealed? If so, what happened on appeal?

   a. What kind of information are you being asked for?

   b. Which research tools will you need?

   c. Which tools are available in your library?

   d. Your answer to the question.

7. Find two recent texts on torts that are available in the library in which you are working. Give the author's name, book title, publisher, and date of publication.

   a. What kind of information are you being asked for?

   b. Which research tools will you need?

   c. Which tools are available in your library?

   d. Your answer to the question.

8. Are there any Manitoba Court of Appeal cases dealing with renewal of franchising contracts?

   a. What kind of information are you being asked for?

   b. Which research tools will you need?

   c. Which tools are available in your library?

   d. Your answer to the question.

9. Choose a specific provision of the Ontario *Limitations Act* and then find out if that provision has been cited in case law. Remember that you may have to concord the provision to trace the same section back through previous statute revisions.

   a. What kind of information are you being asked for?

   b. Which research tools will you need?

   c. Which tools are available in your library?

   d. Your answer to the question.

10. Are there any cases that have cited s. 181(2) of the 1985 federal *Bankruptcy and Insolvency Act*?

   a. What kind of information are you being asked for?

   b. Which research tools will you need?

   c. Which tools are available in your library?

   d. Your answer to the question.

11. Find the Ontario statute that provides information about who may adopt infants and children. Are there any regulations made under it?

    a. What kind of information are you being asked for?

    b. Which research tools will you need?

    c. Which tools are available in your library?

    d. Your answer to the question.

12. Your firm's client resides in British Columbia. She recently defaulted in her mortgage payments and the mortgagee is suing for a final order for foreclosure. Which B.C. statute provides information about the effect of a final order for foreclosure? Find the text of this statute.

    a. What kind of information are you being asked for?

    b. Which research tools will you need?

    c. Which tools are available in your library?

    d. Your answer to the question.

13. There is a 1982 Alberta Court of Appeal case involving Holt Renfrew and another corporation. Find the name and citation of this case. Locate the case report and provide the names of all the judges.

a. What kind of information are you being asked for?

b. Which research tools will you need?

c. Which tools are available in your library?

d. Your answer to the question.

PART VI

Putting It All Together

CHAPTER 20

The Best of Both Worlds

You now know about both paper and computerized legal research sources. You have learned (perhaps painfully) that there are usually several ways to find an answer when researching an issue using paper sources, and several more ways to find the same answer when using computerized sources.

In this chapter we look at how to choose between paper and computerized sources—how to have the best of both worlds.

ISN'T COMPUTER-ASSISTED RESEARCH ALWAYS BETTER?

In a word, no. There are advantages and disadvantages to working with computerized legal research sources, just as there are advantages and disadvantages to working with paper sources. When you use a computer in your research, or whether you use one at all, will depend on the particular research you are doing.

Advantages of Computerized Sources

Computerized sources have paper sources beaten hollow for some uses:

- Some computerized sources can give you immediate access to recently decided cases weeks or months before those cases are published in a report series. Several months pass from the time a case is decided until it is reported in a series.

- Some computerized sources can give you access to a digest or the full text of unreported decisions that will never be reported. Sometimes it is difficult or impossible to find unreported decisions any other way (this is particularly true of administrative tribunal decisions).

- Some computerized sources almost instantly provide information—for example, names of unreported cases, appeal history of a case, and judicial consideration of a case—that might take a researcher hours to find in paper sources.

- Computerized sources have the ability to search large amounts of data at one time—for example, to search a database for all cases containing certain words—or to search a statute database for specific words. Most paper statutes come with neither an index nor a table of contents.

Disadvantages of Computerized Sources

Computerized sources are not without their drawbacks:

- A particular computerized source may not always be available where you're doing your research—if you're working in a law library, do you go back to your office and use LawSource or Quicklaw, or do you use a paper resource that's available in the library and continue your work without interruption?

- Computerized sources can be frustrating to a researcher who is not experienced in online search techniques and, worse, an inexperienced researcher may miss important cases or statutes. For some research problems, if you do not know exactly what you're looking for, you will waste much time narrowing the vast amount of material that the database will provide.

- A computerized source may not cover all reported cases in a report series database; sometimes coverage extends back only into the 1980s, when publishing companies began computerizing. Check the starting date of the database. The incredibly important case relevant to your research may have been decided in 1953.

- Some computerized databases contain typographical errors. If you don't misspell your keyword in exactly the same way the database has misspelled the word you're looking for, you may miss an important case or statute. But if, for example, you're working with a paper source on a problem involving a surgeon's negligence and you see the word "malpratice," you carry on without missing a beat.

- Computerized subscription services can be expensive to use. Even though most law firms are on flat-rate accounts, usage will determine the renewal rate for the account, and each user is identifiable. If you're slow as molasses in January, there's no charge for reading paper sources.

Advantages of Paper Sources

Even though you may be itching to get your hands on a computer to do your research:

- Print sources are better at providing context and a sense of where a legal issue fits into an area of the law, because you can skim through surrounding material. If you're not really familiar with the area of law you're researching and you're doing more than updating a case, you're better off starting with the broad view that paper sources can give you.

- Print sources tend to be more comprehensive in coverage, especially for older cases and historical versions of statutes. In fact, as we pointed out above, for some cases and statutes paper sources are the only sources.

- There is no charge to use print sources that are already in a library.

Disadvantages of Paper Sources

On the other hand, paper sources aren't perfect:

- Print sources tend not to be as current as computerized sources.

- It often takes longer to find information using print sources because more volumes must be consulted and there are often more steps involved.

A COMBINED APPROACH

The best approach to legal research combines paper and computerized sources in a way that is efficient and cost-effective. The following approach assumes that you have access to all possible sources. In reality, your approach will likely be determined by the sources that are available to you at the time of your search.

Use Paper Sources To Find a General Statement of the Law

As we've stated several times—in fact, it's starting to seem like nagging even to us—it is usually wise to start your research with secondary sources, using them to gain an understanding of the law and as finding tools to direct you to the primary sources that actually create the law. If you don't know much about the area of law you're researching, you should start by reading a legal encyclopedia or a text or article on the subject. This will give you an overview of the law in addition to the name of any relevant statute and the names of leading cases in the area. While encyclopedias, texts, and articles come in both paper and computerized formats, it is best to do your preliminary reading using paper sources. A computerized source gives you only what you ask for. Looking at a book allows you to skim through surrounding material, which may be where you find the key to your problem's solution.

Use Computerized Sources To Find and Update Statutes and Regulations

Once you have the name of a relevant statute, it is far easier to find the up-to-date text of that statute and any associated regulations with computerized sources than with paper sources.

Use Both Paper and Computerized Sources To Find Additional Cases

If you are looking for the names of cases dealing with a subject generally, your best source is the *Canadian Abridgment Case Digests*, which is available in both paper and computerized format. You may find it easier to work with the paper version so that you can browse through surrounding material. However, computerized sources are better if you are looking for

- cases that have interpreted a statute or a section of a statute;

- cases considering a word or a phrase;

■ cases for which you've got only a partial or incorrect citation—that is, when you're treasure hunting; or

■ unreported cases.

Use Paper or Computerized Sources To Locate the Text of Cases

Once you have the names of the cases you're interested in, you will have to locate the text of those cases in order to review them. Depending on the sources available to you, you can use either print law reports or computerized versions of the case. If you are using computerized sources, use a free-access website such as CanLII rather than a subscription service.

Use Computerized Sources To Update Cases

It is far faster to work with computerized sources—LexisNexis®Quicklaw™, Law-Source, BestCase, or CanLII—than with paper sources to update cases.

If you use our combined approach to research and make use of both paper and computerized sources at appropriate times, you will find that you get through your work efficiently. You won't miss important ideas about the law because you're starting off with too much focus (on the computer), and you won't miss important recent developments in case or statute law because you couldn't find one of the little update brochures (in the paper sources).

CHAPTER 21

Legal Writing

When you complete your legal research, you will most likely have to communicate your research findings in writing. It is important that you be able to do this in a clear and concise manner. This chapter talks about the requirements of good legal writing and discusses two types of legal writing: case briefs and memos of law.

WHAT IS LEGAL WRITING?

The term "legal writing" is used to describe the drafting of any type of law-related document—for example,

- court pleadings such as a statement of claim, a statement of defence, or a third-party claim;
- affidavits;
- contracts;
- wills;
- letters, including opinion letters to clients;
- case briefs; and
- memos of law.

Case briefs and memos of law are discussed in more detail below.

WHAT IS GOOD LEGAL WRITING?

Good legal writing does not require complex language and a lot of "legalese"—in fact it avoids both. It simply requires writing that is well-organized, concise, understandable, accurate, and free of grammatical and spelling errors. In other words, good legal writing isn't very different from plain, ordinary, good writing.

To write well, you must pay attention to your

- audience,
- purpose,
- tone,
- constraints,
- grammar,

- spelling, and
- presentation.

You must also pay attention to the general rules of good writing.

Audience

The audience for your writing is the intended reader. Ask yourself who will be reading your document, and then write for that reader. Your audience may be a legal professional such as a law clerk, articling student, lawyer, or judge; or a layperson, such as a client. A legal professional will be more familiar and comfortable with legal terms and concepts than a layperson. Therefore, when you write for a legal professional, you can use legal terms and concepts without having to define, explain, or translate them as you would for a layperson. But, in either case, your writing should be as clear, simple, and straightforward as possible.

Whoever your intended reader is, you should always keep in mind that you are writing for a business purpose. You should therefore maintain a level of formality in your writing, avoiding slang and colloquial language (such as "cops" for "police officers") and contractions (such as "isn't" for "is not").

Purpose

The purpose of the document you are writing could be, for example, to record the results of your research in the form of a memo to file or to another legal professional; to write a letter to a client requesting information; or to use your research to give the correct structure to an affidavit or a will that your client will sign. Whatever your purpose, you have to make sure that the content and organization of the document achieves that purpose.

Tone

The choice of the appropriate tone of your document is largely determined by your purpose. For example, a letter requesting information from a client requires a cordial tone, while a demand letter requires a neutral or even a stern tone. The choice of tone may also be influenced by your audience. Your choice of words and sentence structure will help you establish the proper tone of your writing.

Constraints

Make sure you are clear about any constraints on your writing. Determine whether there is a limit on the length of the document, or whether there are any formatting or style requirements that you must follow, such as font type, font size, spacing, page numbering, etc. These constraints may be dictated, for example, by court rules or by your law firm's policies or standard operating procedures.

Don't forget that there may be a deadline for completing and/or sending off your document that you must make sure to meet. If your document must be written and sent within one hour, for example, adjust your writing plan accordingly.

Grammar

Grammar is the proper treatment of connected words in a sentence in order to express thoughts without confusion or error. Good writing requires good grammar—properly constructed sentences using proper punctuation. Grammatically incorrect writing not only annoys people who know something about grammar (count among them judges, lawyers, and, not infrequently, clients), but is often unclear. Clarity is very important in legal documents, so that means that good grammar is also very important.

We can't give you a grammar course in this book, but here are some tips to help you avoid a few of the most common and most glaring grammar mistakes.

1. Use Apostrophes Correctly

The apostrophe (')is used for two different purposes: to form a possessive and to create a contraction.

To form the possessive of a noun, add " 's" after the end of the noun, unless it is a plural noun ending in "s." In that case, add the apostrophe only. Examples: "the plaintiff's claim" (for a single plaintiff); the "plaintiffs' claim" (for more than one plaintiff).

To form a contraction, place an apostrophe where the missing letter(s) would go. Examples: "do not" becomes "don't"; "cannot" becomes "can't"; "you are" becomes "you're"; "it is" becomes "it's."

"It's" is a contraction for "it is" or "it has" and is NEVER a possessive. Examples: "It's time to go"; "It's been two weeks since the case began." "Its" is the possessive form of "it." Example: "The corporation? I've got its address here."

2. Use "I" and "Me" Correctly

"I" is a subject and "me" is a direct or indirect object. Writers get tangled up especially when there is more than one individual populating the sentence. "Please respond to John and I" is incorrect; "Please respond to John and me" is correct. An easy way to decide whether to use "I" or "me" is to remove the other individual. The correct choice is then usually clear.

- He ordered John and (I or me?) to pay costs.

"He ordered *I* to pay costs"?   ✗   "He ordered *me* to pay costs"?   ✓

- If Nancy and (I or me?) are sued, we will hire a lawyer.

"If *me* am sued"?   ✗   "If *I* am sued"?   ✓

Don't use "myself" as a way to get around deciding whether the correct answer is "I" or "me"!

3. Use "There," "Their," and "They're" Correctly

- "There" is an adverb indicating place ("The pleadings are over there on the table"). It can also introduce a sentence or clause ("There is a hearing scheduled for 10 a.m.").

- "Their" is a possessive pronoun ("Their briefcases are on the counsel table").

- "They're" is a contraction for "they are" ("They're meeting with the judge this afternoon").

4. *Make Sure the Verb Agrees with the Subject*

A singular subject requires a singular verb. If there is more than one subject in the sentence, the form of the verb must be plural.

Examples:

- "The court is in session."

- "The judge and the bailiff are conferring about the next case on the docket."

- "The lawyer for the defendant, accompanied by the lawyer for the plaintiff, is approaching the bench."

Collective nouns may take a singular or plural verb, depending on the sentence.

Example:

- The jury has reached its verdict. [One group working together]

- The jury are going home. [The group does not share a home. However, you can avoid the issue of whether "jury" is a collective noun by saying "The jurors are going home."]

The pronouns "everyone" and "each" also require a singular verb. Other frequently used words that require a singular verb are: anyone, neither, either.

5. *Try To Avoid Splitting Infinitives*

An infinitive is made up of "to" plus a verb. "To argue" and "to ignore" are both infinitives. When you put an adverb between "to" and the verb, you "split" the infinitive. Although some grammar experts think there's nothing wrong with splitting an infinitive ("to boldly go where no man has gone before" would sound strange now if the infinitive were *not* split), others are horrified by split infinitives. For safety, don't split an infinitive if you can avoid doing so. It is usually possible to find a reasonably graceful spot in the sentence for the adverb other than between "to" and the verb. For example, "It was difficult to ignore her argument completely" is both natural-sounding and grammatically unassailable.

6. *Put "Only" in Its Proper Place*

In most cases, the word "only" should be placed directly before the word or phrase you are emphasizing. The meaning of a sentence changes depending on the placement of the word "only." Consider the following sentences:

- "You only have to interview one witness." (This is the sole thing you have to do.)

- "You have to interview only one witness." (You do not have to interview more than one witness.)

- "Only you have to interview one witness." (You are the person who has to interview one witness—presumably others have to interview more than one.)

Think about what you mean, and then make sure you place the word "only" only where it belongs!

If you are not sure about where to place "only," consider omitting it. Most often, the easiest way to fix the problem with "only" is to remove it.

7. Use "Principal" and "Principle" Correctly

"Principal" can be used as an adjective or a noun. When used as an adjective, "principal" means "most important" or "highest in rank." When used as a noun, it refers to the head or director of a school ("The principal is leading the school assembly."), or to an amount of money that has been lent or borrowed ("The investor is earning 4% interest on the principal."), or, as a legal term, to an individual who gives authority to another to act on his or her behalf ("The principal gives authority to the agent.").

"Principle" is a noun and means "law," "rule," or "general truth."

8. Use "Lay" and "Lie" Correctly

Many people have trouble with "lay" and "lie" (including Bob Dylan). "Lay" is a transitive verb, which means that it has to have an object. "Lie" is an intransitive verb, which means that it must not have an object. Examples: "I'm going to lie down on the sand and get some sun"; "I'm going to lay a towel on the sand, lie down, and get some sun." So when Bob Dylan wrote "Lay, lady, lay, lay across my big brass bed," he was being ungrammatical (but he still wrote a best-selling song). For a more commercial example of "lay," consider this sentence: "Lay out the terms of the deal and we'll take a look at them."

In the past tense, the trouble continues. The past tense of the intransitive verb "lie" is "lay." Examples: "I'm going to lie down and get some sleep"; "I lay down last night and got some sleep." The past tense of the intransitive verb "lay" is "laid." Example: "The client laid down her money and laid out her expectations."

So, never use the transitive verb "to lay" (past tense "laid") unless you can put an object in the sentence. "He is laying on the floor" is always wrong. ("He is lying on the floor" is correct, although it's not good behaviour in a law office or courtroom.)

Spelling

Good writing also requires correct spelling. Improper spelling, just like incorrect grammar, not only makes the writer look unprofessional, but can change the meaning of what you have written, even if the grammar, content, and organization of your document are otherwise flawless. You probably noticed that several of the grammar tips above involve making sure you choose the correct spelling of certain words that sound alike but are spelled differently. You need to brush up on the spelling not only of your general vocabulary, but also of your legal vocabulary, which often includes words that nobody but legal professionals have ever heard of—for example, "waive" and "enure," which are *never* to be confused with "wave" and "ensure." Check your documents for spelling errors by proofreading them thoroughly. Use the spell-check feature of your word processing software, but do not rely on spell-check alone; it will not pick up words that are improperly spelled only in the context in which they are used and it will probably not tell you the correct spelling of unusual words like "enure."

Be aware of spelling variations of some Canadian and American words. Choose Canadian spelling—but keep in mind that your spell-checker may use American spelling. You may want to set your computer's language to English (Canada) rather than English (United States) when running a spell-check.

Presentation

Your writing must not only be well organized, but also be well presented. Consider what font style and size you want to use (or are required to use), as well as line spacing, headings, and paragraph numbering. Your formatting should be consistent throughout your document. For example, if you choose to italicize and underline your headings, make sure all the headings in your document are formatted this way. If your document is more than one page long, include page numbers.

When you have finished your writing, take the extra time to proofread and, if necessary, edit or revise. Make sure your writing

- achieves its purpose;

- is clear and easy to read;

- is well organized and in the correct format; and

- contains relevant and necessary information only.

Proofread slowly and check that all words are spelled correctly. You should also check for other typing errors such as extra spaces, or repeated words.

SOME RULES OF GOOD WRITING

Here are some basic rules to help you develop good writing skills.

- Use proper sentence structure—The simplest structure usually works best: subject–verb–object. For example: "The judge handed down her decision."

- Insert adjectives and adverbs to add information that describes the subject, verb, or object: "The procrastinating judge finally released a lengthy decision."

- Use the active voice and the passive voice appropriately—In the active voice, the subject performs the action ("The plaintiff delivered the statement of claim"). In the passive voice, the object of the verb in the active voice becomes the subject of the verb, and the subject receives the action ("The statement of claim was delivered by the plaintiff"). The active voice is usually clearer, simpler, and more direct, as the above examples show. However, you should use the passive voice when (1) you want to "hide" the actor who is performing the action, (2) the actor is unimportant, unknown, or obvious, or (3) you want to emphasize the receiver of the action. A good rule of thumb is to use the active voice unless you have a good reason not to.

- Omit needless words and phrases—Very often when it comes to good writing, "less is more." Revise wordy sentences by omitting extra words and phrases that do not add to the meaning of your writing. For example, instead of writing "because of the fact that," or "due to the fact that," write "because." Instead of writing "a sufficient number of," write "enough." Instead of writing "it is true and correct," write either "it is true" or "it is correct"; both words are not needed. Omit from your writing any needless phrases such as "what I want to say is" or "the point is that."

■ Use transitional phrases to help the reader follow your writing—"There are three issues. The first issue is . . ."; or "The relevant law is set out in . . ." tell the reader where you are heading.

■ Avoid turning verbs into nouns—Verbs that have been turned into nouns are "nominalizations." Nominalizations often make sentences too wordy and passive. Use their base verbs instead. For example, instead of "he will make a suggestion that," use the more direct "he will suggest."

■ Use paragraphs effectively—Each paragraph should focus on only one matter. The paragraph should start with a "topic sentence" that introduces the main point of the paragraph.

■ Use parallel construction—Present all similar elements (words, phrases, or clauses) of a sentence in the same form. For example, instead of writing "the witness took the stand, was testifying, and then he leaves the courtroom," write "the witness took the stand, testified, and then left the courtroom." Instead of writing "the lawyer needs to interview the client, the witness should be contacted, and there has to be some legal research done," write "the lawyer needs to interview the client, contact the witness, and research the law."

■ Use quotations and quotation marks correctly—Quotation marks are used to show borrowed words. If you quote a sentence from a case, as long as it's not a paragraph-length sentence, enclose it in quotation marks. However, if you want to quote a longer passage from a book or case, set it off from the main text and do not put quotation marks around it.

Examples:

As Lord Atkin asked in *Donoghue v. Stevenson*, "Who, then, in law is my neighbour?"

Lord Atkin wrote in *Donoghue v. Stevenson*:

Who, then, in law is my neighbour? The answer seems to be—persons who are so closely and directly affected by my act that I ought reasonably to have them in contemplation as being so affected when I am directing my mind to the acts or omissions which are called in question.

■ Avoid "legalese"—Even though you are doing "legal writing," it's best to avoid using little-known legal terms and expressions when you can. Use plain English instead. Using legalese will not make your writing sound more intelligent or more "legal."

Examples:

DON'T USE	USE
the party of the first part	the first party
endeavour	try
heretofore	before
inasmuch as	because
in the event that	if
execute the contract	sign the contract
per annum	a year

- Use positive forms to make your writing easier to understand—Instead of writing "he was not uncooperative," write "he was cooperative."

WRITING A CASE BRIEF

A case brief is a document that provides a clear and concise summary of a court decision by setting out the facts of the case, the legal issues involved, the court's decision, and the reasons for that decision. See Chapter 4 for a complete discussion of the elements that make up a court decision or case.

There is no standard format for a case brief, but it should contain all of the following:

1. the citation of the case (see Chapter 11 if you don't remember what a citation is);

2. a summary of the facts of the case;

3. a summary of the issues in the case (or, if there are many issues and some are clearly irrelevant to your research, the relevant issues);

4. the disposition or judgment of each (relevant) issue in the case; and

5. a summary of the judge's reasons for his or her decision with respect to each (relevant) issue.

WRITING A MEMO OF LAW

The results of legal research are often recorded in a memorandum or memo of law. In a memo of law, the writer sets out a question or a fact situation that he or she has been presented with and the law that relates to that question or fact situation; the writer may suggest possible courses of action and the legal consequences of each course of action.

Before you prepare a final memo of law in the format below, work your way through the memo according to the flow chart that appears below, under the heading "Flow Chart for a Memo of Law."

FORMAT OF A MEMO OF LAW

Most memos of law appear in the following format:

Memo

To:

From:

Re:

File No.:

Date:

Introduction

Briefly state what you have been asked to do and why. State the question(s) that the client or lawyer has asked or the fact situation that he or she has described. If the lawyer is familiar with the field, the question asked may turn out to be the issue as well. If the lawyer knows little about the field, the question may not be the same as the legal issue that actually had to be researched.

Facts

These are facts that are relevant to the issue(s), in chronological order.

Issue(s)

What is the issue of law that must be examined here—that is, what problem must be solved in order to reach a solution? Issues are usually introduced by the word "whether." There may be just one issue, or several.

Law

Set out the relevant statutory or regulatory provisions as they appear in the statute or regulation with a full citation of the statute or regulation and section; set out the relevant passages from cases, with a full citation of each case. If there is more than one issue, restate each issue exactly as it appeared in the issue section before setting out the law on that issue.

Do not set out diverging lines of authority that you find in a case. You are quoting the case for the law the judge followed and the decision that the judge reached, not for the law the judge decided not to follow. If you think the law the judge did *not* follow is useful to you, get the cases and quote from them directly.

Discussion

Discuss or analyze the statute, regulation, and/or case law in light of the given fact situation. This is the appropriate place to discuss

1. whether the facts in the cases you have found are sufficiently similar to your client's situation for the law in those cases to be applicable to your fact situation;

2. the state of the law if it is changing, or if there are conflicting cases or conflicting statutory or regulatory provisions;

3. whether existing statutes, regulations, and cases in fact address the problem in your fact situation. Is yours a new or unusual point of law? If so, can you use existing law to suggest a likely solution to the problem?; and

4. whether previously unforeseen problems for the client arise out of your study of the law.

Be objective. A client will not be helped by a memo that ignores problems that arise in the law, nor will a client be helped by a memo that ignores possible solutions when the law generally seems to go against the client.

Conclusion

Draw together the facts and the law. State what you have concluded from applying the law to the facts in your situation. There should be one paragraph or section in the conclusion for each issue. Also point out any further information that is required or problems that need further research.

References

Make sure to reference any law that you cite. Include the name and citation of the case or statute in the body of your memo. Or, provide only the name of the case or statute in the body of the memo, and then provide the citation in a footnote.

Attachments

Attach any cases and statutory and regulatory provisions that you refer to in your memo.

FLOW CHART FOR A MEMO OF LAW

1. Analyze the fact situation.

2. Research the law.

3. Prepare a draft memo of law. At this point, try to see the problem as a whole, which is necessary to prepare your memo. A draft memo of law gives you a chance to try out different ideas about what you think is going on from a legal point of view and settle on the true issues, the important facts, and the relevant law. You may have to rework your draft once or twice before you're satisfied that you've approached the problem from the correct angle.

   In your draft memo, you should NOT start with the *facts* and work down. Start with the *question* asked by the client or lawyer.

   Then set out the legal *issues* that arise out of the question, out of the facts, and out of the law you have found in your research.

Then set out the *law*.

When you have done all this, you will be able to look at the facts and decide which ones are relevant to the principles of law involved. Delete irrelevant facts. Emphasize essential facts.

Discuss the law as it relates to the facts in your particular case.

Finally, reach a conclusion. Suggest possible action and potential consequences of such action.

4. Prepare a final memo of law in the format above. Remember that a memo of law is not a 5,000-word term paper; keep it short and to the point. The lawyer reading the memo is also going to read the attached statute, regulatory provisions, and case law and draw his or her own conclusions.

Exercises

I. Prepare a memo of law from the information and materials provided below.

Memo

To: You

From: Lawyer

Re: *Giller and Keaton Estate*

Date: December 12, Year Zero

Elizabeth Giller is our 58-year-old client.

Elizabeth met Jack Keaton in Year Minus Six and they became involved with each other. Elizabeth had been separated from her husband for 12 years at that time (she is still not divorced from him). Jack was a widower and had two adult daughters from his marriage. For two years, she and Jack spent much time together, slept over at each other's residences, and went on vacations together, but did not live together. She decided to leave her apartment and move into his house in January, Year Minus Four, because his health was beginning to fail and they agreed that he shouldn't live alone. By early Year Minus Two, he was so ill that she quit her job to be with him full time. They were able to live fairly comfortably on his pension and investments, although Elizabeth ended up spending money looking after him and she now has debts. In August Year Zero, Jack died. In his will (which he never changed after meeting Elizabeth), he left everything to his two adult daughters.

Elizabeth was a senior secretary at an investment firm before she stopped working to look after Jack. She is starting to suffer from arthritis in her hands and finds it difficult to keyboard. She began looking for work after Jack's death but quickly realized that she would have a lot of trouble re-entering the work force at her age. She has saved a little money on which she is now living, and she will receive a pension, but not until she turns 65. Elizabeth believes that she would not be in financial trouble if she had not looked after Jack, of whom she was very fond. In addition, she was shocked and hurt that he left her nothing at all in his will.

Elizabeth wants to know if there is anything in law that can be done to help her. She would like an income, if possible—at least until she starts receiving pension benefits—and money to pay her debts that relate to looking after Jack.

Further information: The law of Ontario applies.

NOTE: Don't forget to consider in your memo

- whether the client has the legal status to make an application under the Act,

- what factors the court is likely to look at *in this case* to determine whether to order support, and

- whether the Act provides for what Elizabeth wants (an income and money to pay off debts).

Selected provisions of the *Succession Law Reform Act*, R.S.O. 1990, c. S.26:

PART V
SUPPORT OF DEPENDANTS

57. **Definitions**—In this Part,

"child" means a child as defined in subsection 1(1) and includes a grandchild and a person whom the deceased has demonstrated a settled intention to treat as a child of his or her family, except under an arrangement where the child is placed for valuable consideration in a foster home by a person having lawful custody;

"cohabit" means to live together in a conjugal relationship, whether within or outside marriage;

"court" means the Ontario Court (General Division);

"dependant" means,
    (a) the spouse of the deceased,
    (b) a parent of the deceased,
    (c) a child of the deceased, or
    (d) a brother or sister of the deceased,
to whom the deceased was providing support or was under a legal obligation to provide support immediately before his or her death;

"letters probate" and "letters of administration" include letters probate, letters of administration or other legal documents purporting to be of the same legal nature granted by a court in another jurisdiction and resealed in this province;

"parent" includes a grandparent and a person who has demonstrated a settled intention to treat the deceased as a child of his or her family, except under an arrangement where the deceased was placed for valuable consideration in a foster home by a person having lawful custody;

"spouse" means a spouse as defined in subsection 1(1) and in addition includes either of a man and woman who,
    (a) were married to each other by a marriage that was terminated or declared a nullity, or
    (b) are not married to each other and have cohabited,
        (i) continuously for a period of not less than three years, or
        (ii) in a relationship of some permanence, if they are the natural or adoptive parents of a child.

58.(1) **Order for support**—Where a deceased, whether testate or intestate, has not made adequate provision for the proper support of his dependants or any of them, the court, on application, may order that such provision as it considers adequate be made out of the estate of the deceased for the proper support of the dependants or any of them.

(2) **Applicants**—An application for an order for the support of a dependant may be made by the dependant or the dependant's parent.

(3) **Idem**—An application for an order for the support of a dependant may also be made by one of the following agencies:

(a) the Ministry of Community and Social Services in the name of the Minister;

(b) a municipal corporation, including a metropolitan, district or regional municipality, but not including an area municipality;

(c) a district welfare administration board under the *District Welfare Administration Boards Act*; or

(d) a band approved under section 15 of the *General Welfare Assistance Act*,

if the agency is providing or has provided a benefit under the *Family Benefits Act* or assistance under the *General Welfare Assistance Act* in respect of the dependant's support, or if an application for such a benefit or assistance has been made to the agency by or on behalf of the dependant.

(4) **Idem**—The adequacy of provision for support under subsection (1) shall be determined as of the date of the hearing of the application.

59. **Suspensory order**—On an application by or on behalf of the dependants or any of them, the court may make an order suspending in whole or in part the administration of the deceased's estate, for such time and to such extent as the court may decide.

60.(1) **Application**—An application under this Part may be made to the court by notice of application in accordance with the practice of the court.

(2) **Idem**—Where an application for an order under section 58 is made by or on behalf of any dependant,

(a) it may be dealt with by the court as; and

(b) in so far as the question of limitation is concerned, it shall be deemed to be,

an application on behalf of all persons who might apply.

61.(1) **Limitation period**—Subject to subsection (2), no application for an order under section 58 may be made after six months from the grant of letters probate of the will or of letters of administration.

(2) **Exception**—The court, if it considers it proper, may allow an application to be made at any time as to any portion of the estate remaining undistributed at the date of the application.

62.(1) **Determination of amount**—In determining the amount and duration, if any, of support, the court shall consider all the circumstances of the application, including,

(a) the dependant's current assets and means;

(b) the assets and means that the dependant is likely to have in the future;

(c) the dependant's capacity to contribute to his or her own support;

(d) the dependant's age and physical and mental health;

(e) the dependant's needs, in determining which the court shall have regard to the dependant's accustomed standard of living;

(f) the measures available for the dependant to become able to provide for his or her own support and the length of time and cost involved to enable the dependant to take those measures;

(g) the proximity and duration of the dependant's relationship with the deceased;

(h) the contributions made by the dependant to the deceased's welfare, including indirect and non-financial contributions;

(i) the contributions made by the dependant to the acquisition, maintenance and improvement of the deceased's property or business;

(j) a contribution by the dependant to the realization of the deceased's career potential;

(k) whether the dependant has a legal obligation to provide support for another person;

(l) the circumstances of the deceased at the time of death;

(m) any agreement between the deceased and the dependant;

(n) any previous distribution or division of property made by the deceased in favour of the dependant by gift or agreement or under court order;

(o) the claims that any other person may have as a dependant;

(p) if the dependant is a child,

(i) the child's aptitude for and reasonable prospects of obtaining an education, and

(ii) the child's need for a stable environment;

(q) if the dependant is a child of the age of sixteen years or more, whether the child has withdrawn from parental control;

(r) if the dependant is a spouse,

(i) a course of conduct by the spouse during the deceased's lifetime that is so unconscionable as to constitute an obvious and gross repudiation of the relationship,

(ii) the length of time the spouses cohabited,

(iii) the effect on the spouse's earning capacity of the responsibilities assumed during cohabitation,

(iv) whether the spouse has undertaken the care of a child who is of the age of eighteen years or over and unable by reason of illness, disability or other cause to withdraw from the charge of his or her parents,

(v) whether the spouse has undertaken to assist in the continuation of a program of education for a child eighteen years of age or over who is unable for that reason to withdraw from the charge of his or her parents,

(vi) any housekeeping, child care or other domestic service performed by the spouse for the family, as if the spouse had devoted the time spent in performing that service in remunerative employment and had contributed the earnings to the family's support,

(vii) the effect on the spouse's earnings and career development of the responsibility of caring for a child,

(viii) the desirability of the spouse remaining at home to care for a child; and

(s) any other legal right of the dependant to support, other than out of public money.

(2) **Evidence**—In addition to the evidence presented by the parties, the court may direct other evidence to be given as the court considers necessary or proper.

(3) **Idem**—The court may accept such evidence as it considers proper of the deceased's reasons, so far as ascertainable, for making the dispositions in his or her will, or for not making adequate provision for a dependant, as the case may be, including any statement in writing signed by the deceased.

(4) **Idem**—In estimating the weight to be given to a statement referred to in subsection (3), the court shall have regard to all the circumstances from which an inference can reasonably be drawn as to the accuracy of the statement.

63.(1) **Conditions and restrictions**—In any order making provision for support of a dependant, the court may impose such conditions and restrictions as the court considers appropriate.

(2) **Contents of order**—Provision may be made out of income or capital or both and an order may provide for one or more of the following, as the court considers appropriate,

(a) an amount payable annually or otherwise whether for an indefinite or limited period or until the happening of a specified event;

(b) a lump sum to be paid or held in trust;

(c) any specified property to be transferred or assigned to or in trust for the benefit of the dependant, whether absolutely, for life or for a term of years;

(d) the possession or use of any specified property by the dependant for life or such period as the court considers appropriate;

(e) a lump sum payment to supplement or replace periodic payments;

(f) the securing of payment under an order by a charge on property or otherwise;

(g) the payment of a lump sum or of increased periodic payments to enable a dependant spouse or child to meet debts reasonably incurred for his or her own support prior to an application under this Part;

(h) that all or any of the money payable under the order be paid to an appropriate person or agency for the benefit of the dependant;

(i) the payment to an agency referred to in subsection 58(3) of any amount in reimbursement for an allowance or benefit granted in respect of the support of the dependant, including an amount in reimbursement for an allowance paid or benefit provided before the date of the order.

(3) **Idem**—Where a transfer or assignment of property is ordered, the court may,

(a) give all necessary directions for the execution of the transfer or assignment by the executor or administrator or such other person as the court may direct; or

(b) grant a vesting order.

(4) **Agreement of waiver**—An order under this section may be made despite any agreement or waiver to the contrary.

(5) **Notice to parties before order**—The court shall not make any order under this section until it is satisfied upon oath that all persons who are

or may be interested in or affected by the order have been served with notice of the application as provided by the rules of court, and every such person is entitled to be present and to be heard in person or by counsel at the hearing.

(6) **Exception**—Despite subsection (5), where, in the opinion of the court,

(a) every reasonable effort has been made to serve those entitled to notice; or

(b) after every reasonable effort has been made, it is not possible to identify one or more of the persons entitled to notice,

the court may dispense with the requirement of notice in respect of any person who has not been served.

1. Prepare a draft memo of law.

   a. What are the questions being asked?

   b. What are the legal issues that you have identified? (Hint: Look at the note on page 234.)

   c. What are the sections in the statute that are relevant to the issues?

   d. What are the facts that are relevant to the law?

   e. Discuss the law as it relates to the facts in this case.

   f. What is your conclusion? What action can be taken for your client?

2. Prepare a formal memo of law.

II. Prepare a memo of law from the information and materials provided below.

Memo

To: You

From: Lawyer

Re: *Brown v. Litoff*

Date: December 23, Year Zero

As you know, this action for arrears of rent under a commercial lease has been dragging on for years, partly because of the client's unreasonable behaviour.

Mr. Brown came in to see me yesterday to instruct me to add a tort claim—an action for assault and false imprisonment—to the claim for arrears. He says he's been thinking about the last time he talked to the defendant, Litoff, in Year Minus Two, when he demanded that Litoff pay the rent. He says that Litoff threatened him with violence and prevented him from leaving a room. He says that since Litoff is making him go all the way to trial on this action, he wants to put some heat on Litoff.

See if you can find out whether we can amend or not.

Further information: The law of Ontario applies.

A. The pleadings in the *Brown v. Litoff* action:

Assault and false imprisonment were not specifically pleaded. One paragraph of the pleadings states:

> 8. On or about the 14th day of March, Year Minus Two, the plaintiff attended at the defendant's office to discuss with him the payment of outstanding rent. The plaintiff states that the defendant refused to discuss payment or settlement. The plaintiff further states that the defendant shook his fist at him and told him not to come asking for the outstanding rent again.

B. Discoveries in the *Brown v. Litoff* action:

Discoveries were held in Year Minus One. The following appears in the transcript of the discovery of the defendant:

197. Q. Did the plaintiff come to your office on March 14, Year Minus Two to ask you about paying the outstanding rent?
      A. Maybe. I think so.

198. Q. Can you tell me what happened at that meeting?
      A. I told him I had no money to pay the rent.

199. Q. Did the two of you argue?
      A. Yeah. He called me an S.O.B. and said he'd put me out of business.

200. Q. Did you say anything in reply?
      A. Yeah, I think I told him if he didn't leave me alone I'd give him a good punch in the nose. Or maybe I took a swing at him. I don't remember.

201. Q. Did you hit him?
      A. Nah, the pipsqueak. He took off as fast as he could.

202. Q. Did you try to prevent him from leaving?
      A. Why would I? I was glad to see the back of him.

C. Ontario *Rules of Civil Procedure*, R. 26.01

> 26.01 On motion at any stage of an action the court shall grant leave to amend a pleading on such terms as are just, unless prejudice would result that could not be compensated for by costs or an adjournment.

D. *Limitations Act, 2002*, S.O. 2002, c. 24, Sched. B, s. 4

> 4. **Basic limitation period**—Unless this Act provides otherwise, a proceeding shall not be commenced in respect of a claim after the second anniversary of the day on which the claim was discovered.

E. *Denton v. Jones et al. (No. 2)* (1976), 14 O.R. (2d) 382 (H.C.J.)

APPEAL from an order of the Senior Master refusing plaintiff's application to amend the statement of claim.

> R.E. Anka, for defendant, R.W. Marshall.
> J.S. McNeil, for plaintiff.

GRANGE, J.:—This is an appeal from the order of the Senior Master refusing the plaintiff's application to amend her statement of claim. The appeal has a sad history. When it originally came on before me a preliminary objection was taken that the order appealed from was a final order and the appeal therefore lay to the Divisional Court. I reserved judgment on the objection and heard the appeal on its merits. I then decided that the preliminary objection was well taken and adjourned the motion to the Divisional Court under Rule 225(3) [rep. and sub. O. Reg. 115/72, s. 5].

Unfortunately at the time of making the latter order I did not appreciate that the writ in the action had been issued prior to April 17, 1972, when the *Judicature Amendment Act, 1970 (No. 4)*, 1970 (Ont.), c. 97, which gave the Divisional Court jurisdiction, was proclaimed. Accordingly, *A.J. Freiman Ltd. v. M.W. Kosub Ltd. et al.*, [1973] 2 O.R. 608, applied and this appeal lay to a Judge in Chambers regardless of whether the order was final or interlocutory. It has therefore been referred back to me for disposition.

The action is one for dental malpractice and in the claim as originally delivered the plaintiff alleged negligence on the part of the defendant Marshall in that he was instructed to extract certain upper teeth and had, in fact, extracted not only those upper teeth but all of the lower teeth as well.

Upon the publication of *Schweizer v. Central Hospital et al.* (1974), 6 O.R. (2d) 606, 53 D.L.R. (3d) 494, the plaintiff brought application to amend the statement of claim to allege trespass to the person based upon the same facts. The application came on before the Senior Master in December, 1975, and was dismissed. From that decision this appeal, after its many vicissitudes comes on for determination.

The main reason advanced in opposition to the amendment is, of course, that the dental operation took place on October 7, 1969, and that in the interval the limitation period, be it for dental malpractice (six months under the *Dentistry Act*, R.S.O. 1970, c. 108, s. 28, or one year under the *Health Disciplines Act*, 1974 (Ont.), c. 47, s. 17), for assault (four years under the *Limitations Act*, R.S.O. 1970, c. 246, s. 45(1)(j)), or upon the case (six years, *Limitations Act*, s. 45(1)(g)), had expired.

The defendant relies upon the principle stemming from the dicta of Lord Esher, M.R., in *Weldon v. Neal* (1887), 19 Q.B.D. 394 at p. 395, as follows:

> We must act on the settled rule of practice, which is that amendments are not admissible when they prejudice the right of the opposite party

as existing at the date of such amendments. If an amendment were allowed setting up a cause of action, which, if the writ were issued in respect thereof at the date of the amendment, would be barred by the Statute of Limitations, it would be allowing the plaintiff to take advantage of her former writ to defeat the statute and taking away an existing right from the defendant, a proceeding which, as a general rule, would be, in my opinion, improper and unjust. Under very peculiar circumstances the Court might perhaps have power to allow such an amendment, but certainly as a general rule it will not do so.

This principle was acknowledged in *Radigan v. Canadian Indemnity Co. et al.*, [1953] O.W.N. 788, [1953] 3 D.L.R. 653, [1951-55] I.L.R. 488; where the Court of Appeal held it inapplicable to a situation where the insured sought to add an alternative claim under the same policy and was applied in *Pitt v. Bank of Nova Scotia et al.*, [1956] O.W.N. 872, where the Senior Master refused an amendment to claim recovery in nuisance against a municipality where the original claim was in negligence. Many other instances are given in Professor Garry Watson's learned discussion on the matter to be found in "Amendment of Proceedings After Limitation Periods." 53 *Can. Bar Rev.* 237 (1975), particularly at pp. 242-3.

I am not sure that the mere pleading of an alternative ground for relief arising out of the same facts constitutes the raising of a new cause of action—see *Canadian Industries Ltd. v. Canadian National R. Co.*, [1940] O.W.N. 452, [1940] 4 D.L.R. 629, 52 C.R.T.C. 31 [affirmed [1941] S.C.R. 591, [1941] 4 D.L.R. 561, 53 C.R.T.C. 162], where an amendment in a contract action was permitted to claim relief in negligence based upon the same facts upon the ground that such new claim did not create a new cause of action, but merely an alternative claim with respect to the same cause. We must always bear in mind the distinction between "forms of action" and "causes of action." . . .

But even if the amendment here asked does constitute a new cause of action, I consider that there are circumstances justifying a departure from the general rule. In *Basarsky v. Quinlan et al.*, [1972] S.C.R. 380, 24 D.L.R. (3d) 720, [1972] 1 W.W.R. 303, Hall, J., equated the word "peculiar" in Lord Esher, M.R.'s exception with "special" in current usage and found that circumstances existed to justify an amendment, after the expiration of the limitation period, setting up a claim under the *Fatal Accidents Act* of Alberta where the original claim had been under the *Trustee Act* of that province. Among those circumstances were many that apply equally here. There as here, all the facts upon which the later claim could be based were already pleaded. There as here, there was no need to reopen discoveries and most important there as here, there was no possibility of prejudice to the defendants other than the inevitable prejudice of what might turn out to be the successful plea. To me this amendment comes within the spirit and intent of our Rules, particularly Rule 185 which is as follows:

> 185. A proceeding shall not be defeated by any formal objection, but all necessary amendments shall be made, upon proper terms as to costs and otherwise, to secure the advancement of justice, the determining of the real matter in dispute, and the giving of judgment according to the very right and justice of the case.

Moreover, the amendment seems to me to be precisely in line with the decision of Reid, J., in *Royal v. Municipality of Metropolitan Toronto et al.*

(1975), 9 O.R. (2d) 522, which is almost the converse of the case at bar. There an amendment to include a claim for negligence was permitted after the limitation period had expired when the original claim was one for assault.

I would therefore allow the appeal and permit the amendment sought. Costs of the appeal should be in the cause.

Appeal allowed.

1. Prepare a draft memo of law.

    a. What are the questions being asked?

    b. What are the legal issues that you have identified?

    c. i.   What are the sections in the statute that are relevant to the issues?

        ii. What are the passages in the case law that are relevant to the issues?

    d. What are the facts that are relevant to the law?

    e. Discuss the law as it relates to the facts in this case.

    f. What is your conclusion? What action can be taken for your client?

2. Prepare a formal memo of law.

APPENDIX A

Standard Abbreviations for Commonly Used Report Series and Statutes

A

A.C. . . . . Law Reports, Appeal Cases (England)

A.C.W.S. . . . . All Canada Weekly Summaries

A.R. . . . . Alberta Reports

Admin. L.R. . . . . . . Administrative Law Reports

All E.R. . . . . All England Reports

Alta. L.R. . . . . Alberta Law Reports

App. Cas. . . . . Law Reports, Appeal Cases (England)

B

B.C.L.R. . . . . British Columbia Law Reports

B.L.R. . . . . Business Law Reports

C

C.B.R. . . . . Canadian Bankruptcy Reports

C.B.R. (N.S.) . . . . . Canadian Bankruptcy Reports (New Series)

C.C.C. . . . . Canadian Criminal Cases

C.C.E.L. . . . . Canadian Cases on Employment Law

C.C.L.I. . . . . Canadian Cases on the Law of Insurance

C.C.L.T. . . . . Canadian Cases on the Law of Torts

C.C.S.M. . . . . Continuing Consolidation of the Statutes of Manitoba

C.E.D. (Ont. 3rd) . . Canadian Encyclopedic Digest (Ontario Third Edition)

C.E.L.R. . . . . Canadian Environmental Law Reports

C.L.R. . . . . Construction Law Reports

C.P.R. . . . . Canadian Patent Reporter

C.P.R. (N.S.) . . . . . . Canadian Patent Reporter (New Series)

C.R. . . . . Criminal Reports

C.R.R. . . . . Canadian Rights Reporter

C.T.C. . . . . Canada Tax Cases

C.T.R. . . . . Canada Tax Reports

Can. Abr. (2d) . . . . Canadian Abridgment (Second Edition)

D

D.L.R. . . . . Dominion Law Reports

E

E.R. . . . . English Reports

E.T.R. . . . . Estates and Trust Reports

F-H

F.T.R. . . . . Federal Trial Reports

I-J

Imm. L.R. . . . . Immigration Law Reporter

K

K.B. . . . . Law Reports, King's Bench (England)

L

L.A.C. (3d) . . . . Labour Arbitration Cases (Third Series)

L.R. . . . . Law Reports (England)

L.R. Ch. .... Law Reports Chancery Cases (England)

L.R.C.P. .... Law Reports Common Pleas (England)

L.R. Eq. .... Law Reports Equity (England)

L.R. Ex. .... Law Reports Exchequer (England)

L.R.H.L. .... Law Reports House of Lords (England)

L.T.R. .... Law Times Reports (England)

M

M.P.L.R. .... Municipal and Planning Law Reports

M.V.R. .... Motor Vehicle Reports

Man. L.R. .... Manitoba Law Reports

Man. R. .... Manitoba Reports

N

N.B.R. .... New Brunswick Reports

N.R. .... National Reporter

N.S.R. .... Nova Scotia Reports

Nfld. & P.E.I.R. ... Newfoundland and Prince Edward Island Reports

O-P

O.A.C. .... Ontario Appeal Cases

O.M.B.R. .... Ontario Municipal Board Reports

O.R. .... Ontario Reports

O.W.N. .... Ontario Weekly Notes

Q

Q.A.C. .... Quebec Appeal Cases

R

R.F.L. .... Reports of Family Law

R.P.R. .... Real Property Reports

R.S.A. .... Revised Statutes of Alberta

R.S.B.C. .... Revised Statutes of British Columbia

R.S.C. .... Revised Statutes of Canada

R.S.M. .... Revised Statutes of Manitoba

R.S.N. .... Revised Statutes of Newfoundland

R.S.N.B. .... Revised Statutes of New Brunswick

R.S.N.W.T. .... Revised Statutes of Northwest Territories

R.S.O. .... Revised Statutes of Ontario

R.S.P.E.I. .... Revised Statutes of Prince Edward Island

R.S.Q. .... Revised Statutes of Quebec

R.S.S. .... Revised Statutes of Saskatchewan

R.S.Y.T. .... Revised Statutes of Yukon Territory

S

S.A. .... Statutes of Alberta

S.C.R. .... Supreme Court Reports

S.B.C. .... Statutes of British Columbia

S.C. .... Statutes of Canada

S.M. .... Statutes of Manitoba

S.N. .... Statutes of Newfoundland

S.N.B. .... Statutes of New Brunswick

S.N.W.T. .... Statutes of Northwest Territories

S.O. .... Statutes of Ontario

S.P.E.I. .... Statutes of Prince Edward Island

S.Q. .... Statutes of Quebec

S.S. .... Statutes of Saskatchewan

S.Y.T. .... Statutes of Yukon Territory

Sask. L.R. .... Saskatchewan Law Reports

T

T.L.R. .... Times Law Reports (England)

U-V

U.C.C.P. .... Upper Canada Common Pleas Reports

U.C.Q.B. .... Upper Canada Queen's Bench Reports

W-Z

W.C.B. .... Weekly Criminal Bulletin

W.D.C.P. .... Weekly Digest of Civil Procedure

W.L.R. .... Weekly Law Reports (England)

W.W.R. .... Western Weekly Reports

W.W.R. (N.S.) .... Western Weekly Reports (New Series)

Y.R. .... Yukon Reports

For abbreviations not found here, consult the front pages of any volume of *Canadian Case Citations* or *Canadian Statute Citations* or *Cardiff Index to Legal Abbreviations* at http://www.legalabbrevs.cardiff.ac.uk/.

APPENDIX B

Law-Related Internet Sites*

SITES THAT PROVIDE ACCESS TO PRIMARY SOURCES

Statutes

- Ontario statutes—http://www.e-laws.gov.on.ca
- Federal statutes—http://laws.justice.gc.ca

Cases

- Supreme Court of Canada—http://www.lexum.umontreal.ca/csc-scc/en/index.html (cases back to 1983)
- Federal Court—http://decisions.fct-cf.gc.ca/fct/index.html (cases back to 1990)
- Ontario Court of Appeal—http://www.ontariocourts.on.ca/coa/en (cases back to 1998)
- Ontario Superior Court of Justice—http://www.canlii.org/en/on/onsc (cases back to 1987)
- Links to statutes and cases of other jurisdictions are available through the Canadian Legal Information Institute website at www.canlii.org

Government Sites

- Government of Canada—http://canada.gc.ca
    - ◆ information about government services
    - ◆ links to
        - ◇ Departments and Agencies—alphabetical listing of government of Canada departments and agencies with links to their sites

---

* Sites may be moved, altered, or closed at any time.

◇ Structure of the government of Canada—including information on the Canadian ministries, members of the House of Commons, and Senate

◇ Provincial and territorial governments

◇ Municipalities by provinces and territories

■ Specific government of Canada sites:

◆ Statistics Canada—http://www.statcan.gc.ca (for statistics on things such as the consumer price index, population rates and unemployment rates)

◆ Canada Customs and Revenue—http://www.ccra-adrc.gc.ca (for information and forms regarding income tax, GST, customs)

◆ Strategis—Industry Canada's business information site— http://www.strategis.ic.gc.ca (includes information relating to business)

■ Government of Ontario—http://www.gov.on.ca

◆ government propaganda

◆ links to

◇ specific ministries

◇ a complete services and offices directory—included in the list are tribunals, boards, and agencies

◇ a government of Ontario telephone directory

◇ information about contacting MPPs

◇ Site map is very helpful for finding the location of information

■ Specific government of Ontario sites:

◆ Attorney General—http://www.attorneygeneral.jus.gov.on.ca for information about

◇ going to court

◇ getting a lawyer

◇ family law matters

◇ small claims court

◆ Guide to the Ontario Courts—http://www.ontariocourts.on.ca (with links to the Court of Appeal, Superior Court of Justice, and Ontario Court of Justice)

■ Law Society of Upper Canada—http://www.lsuc.on.ca for information about

◆ the legal profession

◆ finding a lawyer

◆ the legal profession's opionions of paralegals

General Legal Sites

- Access to Justice Network—http://www.acjnet.org

  - a project of the legal studies program of the University of Alberta

  - provides access to public legal education articles

- Canadian Legal FAQs—http://www.law-faqs.org (also a project of the legal studies program of the University of Alberta)

- Jurist Canada—http://jurist.law.utoronto.ca

  - hosted by University of Toronto faculty of law, but in fact a project of a law professor at University of Pittsburgh School of Law

  - information about law, studying law, and legal research

- Cardiff Index to Legal Abbreviations—http://www.legalabbrevs.cardiff .ac.uk

  - provides the meaning of abbreviations for legal publications

- CLEONet—http://www.cleonet.ca

  - provides resources on topics affecting low-income and disadvantaged communities

- Best Guide to Canadian Legal Research—http://www.legalresearch.org

  - site run by Catherine Best, professor at UBC Faculty of Law, and former director of legal research and writing

  - excellent source of information about legal research

  - also has links to legal sources

- Bora Laskin Law Library (U of T Faculty of Law)—http://www.law-lib .utoronto.ca

  - contains guides to legal research

  - provides community legal information

  - also has links to legal resources

Glossary

A

advanced query   function accessible through the search menu on the toolbar that allows you to search the full database using a Boolean search

appeal history   history of a case—for example, whether the case has been confirmed or overturned on appeal and the name of the highest court that reviewed the decision

B

bills   proposed statutes that are before Parliament or a provincial legislature but have not yet been passed

binding decision   existing decision that a judge must follow if the facts in that case and in the case before the court are sufficiently similar

binding law   law that must be followed by a court

Boolean search   method by which the computer hunts through thousands of documents to locate requested combinations of words or phrases; in a keyword search, used when you don't want to restrict your search by case name, court, judge, or counsel

C

case citation query template   allows you to search by case name or citation

case digest   summary of how a legal issue was decided in a particular case

concordance   a tool for finding corresponding sections in either an earlier or a later version of a statute

Contents Key   alphabetical list of all the subject titles in the CED

D-E

disposition   judge's orders set out at the end of a case

dissent   different decision by a minority of appeal judges

F

framework legislation   legislation for which the details are worked out in the regulations

G

general index   one of two finding tools to locate digested cases

H

headnote   editor's explanation of the case before the body

housekeeping provisions   sections that cover the details of statutes, such as the date of coming into force

I–J

index   alphabetical, detailed list of names, places, and subjects discussed in a source and the pages on which each entry appears

Index Key   separate binder combining the individual indexes from all titles and containing an alphabetical list of keywords, together with extensive cross-references within and among subject titles

issues   specific problems that the judge must solve to reach a decision

K

key and research guide   one of two finding tools to locate digested cases that uses the key classification system

key classification system   multi-level classification system

keyword and field query template   allows you to limit your keyword search to specific jurisdictions, specific years, and/or specific subject areas and/or classification phrases

keywords   words by which researchers search computerized sources for information stored randomly in databases

L

law of evidence   sets out the manner in which facts are proved in a trial or a proceeding

legislative history   given at the end of each provision in a statute

lines of authority   statement of existing law found in statutes, cases, and texts

long title   full, unabbreviated title of a statute

M

master   judge-like officer who decides certain procedural matters in the superior court of some provinces

N

natural language search   allows you to search for information by asking your question using plain language

O

obiter dicta   Latin for "words by the way"

P

persuasive law   law that a court is not required to follow, but may follow if it wishes (usually case law)

preamble   part of a statute that outlines its purpose and main principles

primary sources   the actual statutes, regulations, and case decisions that create the law

private law   governs the relationship between persons, and includes such areas as contracts, family law, property law, real estate, torts, and wills and estates

procedural law   sets out the procedure that a party must follow to enforce his or her rights in a court proceeding or to defend a proceeding

provision   section or subsection

public law   governs the relationship between persons (individuals and corporations) and the state, and includes such areas of law as municipal law, immigration and refugee law, environmental law, constitutional law, criminal law, and tax law

purpose   the nature of the proceedings

Q

query box   small box located on the toolbar that works like the advanced query, but with less space in which to craft your query and without access to the word wheel

query templates   accessible through the search menu on the toolbar; allows you to narrow your search to specific parts of the database

R

ratio decidendi   Latin for "reasons for deciding"—the pre-existing principle of law on which the judge based the decision on an issue applied to the facts of the particular case

reasons for decision   term for a case before it is included in a report series or legal database

regulations   rules made under the authority of a statute

reported case   judge's decision and reasons about a case published in a law report series

Rules and Regulations Key   alphabetical list of the rules of court and regulations referred to in the CED's subject titles

S

search engine   website with a computer program that searches a database of Web documents or websites to match supplied keywords

search operators   keywords and Boolean connectors and expanders

secondary sources   sources that summarize, discuss, or explain primary sources, and include legal encyclopedias, digests of cases, indexes to statutes, textbooks, and articles

short title   abbreviated title of a statute

standard search   allows you to search for information using keywords and a connector that is selected from the drop-down menu

stare decisis   Latin for "to stand by those things that have been decided"

statute   law created by Parliament or a provincial legislature

Statutes Key   alphabetical list of all current federal and provincial statutes referred to in the various subject titles in the CED

statutory instrument   general term that includes federal regulations

style of cause   names of the parties in an action

subject index   also called a subject tree, a website that categorizes or indexes Web documents or websites using subject classifications

substantive law   defines legal rights and obligations; legal rights may be enforced by way of legal proceedings, to which substantive law sets out the defences

substitution symbol   symbol used in a computerized search that replaces a single letter to find keywords spelled in more than one way

T

table of contents chronological listing of chapters or article titles in a source together with the page numbers where each chapter or article starts

template search in a keyword search, used when you have some information about a case you are looking for—for example, case name, court, judge, or counsel

terms and connectors search not as limiting as the standard search template; allows you to construct a Boolean search using keywords and your own Boolean connectors and expanders

theory of the case the cause of action or the defence, and the evidence that supports that cause of action or defence—also known as "the theory"

truncation symbol symbol used in a computerized search to find all possible endings of a root word

U-Z

unreported case case not published in a law report series

user's guide information in a research source about how to use that source

Index